THE CORNUCOPIA

THE
CORNUCOPIA

BEING A KITCHEN ENTERTAINMENT
AND COOKBOOK

CONTAINING

*Good Reading and Good Cookery from more
than 500 years of Recipes, Food Lore &c.*

AS CONCEIVED AND EXPOUNDED BY

*the Great Chefs & Gourmets of the Old and New Worlds
between the years 1390 and 1899*

NOW COMPILED AND PRESENTED TO THE PUBLIC
IN A SINGLE HANDSOME AND CONVENIENT VOLUME

Copiously Illustrated

Judith Herman and *Marguerite Shalett Herman*

HUNTINGTON LIBRARY
San Marino, California

The quotation on page 58 is from *The Star Chamber Dinner Accounts*, 1959, by André L. Simon. Reprinted by permission of Mrs. W. Rouet Guillet.

The quotations on pages 35 and 217 are from *The Oxford Dictionary of Nursery Rhymes* edited by Iona and Peter Opie, copyright 1951 by Oxford University Press. Reprinted by permission of The Clarendon Press, Oxford.

SECOND PRINTING

Book design by Lydia Link
Cover design by Doug Davis

Library of Congress Cataloging-in-Publication Data

The cornucopia : being a kitchen entertainment and cookbook containing good reading and good cookery from more than 500 years of recipes, food lore, etc. as conceived and expounded by the great chefs & gourmets of the old and new worlds between the years 1390 and 1899 / now compiled and presented to the public in a single handsome and convenient volume Copiously illustrated, Judith Herman and Marguerite Shalett Herman.
    p. cm.
 Reprint. Originally published: New York : Harper & Row, 1973.
 Includes bibliographical references and index.
 ISBN 0-87328-213-2 (hardcover : alk. paper)
 1. Cookery, American. 2. Cookery, European. 3. Food. I. Herman, Judith, 1943– II. Herman, Marguerite Shalett.
 TX715.H556 2005
 641.59--dc22

2005020867

In memory of

LEWIS HERMAN

CONTENTS

PREFACE

The Cornucopia offers a taste of other times and other places. It is made up of folklore, recipes and commentary selected from books or manuscripts written or published in the English language between 1390 and 1899. Each selection is followed by a short reference to its source, with a more complete citation in the bibliography.

For the reader who wants to experience the full flavor as we did, by testing and tasting, we have deliberately included only recipes that actually work, and have rejected those that were incomplete or misleading. At times we have tightened a selection or made grammatical or spelling changes for easier understanding, but we have not tampered with the integrity of the commentary or the recipes, for that would have been a betrayal of both the times and the tastes.

With food and drink as the contents of this cornucopia, the folklore and commentary provide a partial view of our world in earlier times and offer some insight into our world of today—for there is much in today's world that is comparable to the past.

We have enjoyed researching this book, and we have tried to share the experience with you—by letting the people speak for themselves about their foods, about their folklore, and about the time in which they lived.

Judith Herman
Marguerite Shalett Herman

Tujunga, California

After 32 years, I am delighted to find that our original preface holds true: the concerns and hopes of the people are thoughtful and compelling, the illustrations remain elegant, and the recipes can still be made—and they are delicious! However, one dramatic change has occurred since we researched and wrote *The Cornucopia:* the impact of technology.

The Forme of Cury was written c. 1390 on vellum with a quill. My mother and I conducted research in the Huntington Library's rare book room using electric typewriters with automatic carriage returns and carbon paper. Now, I write at a computer. Through the Internet, any person, at any time, can buy an ingredient, define a phrase or measurement, and even read some of the original manuscripts and books.

Nonetheless, a crucial element of our book endures: the Huntington Library, a gracious and timeless institution that assists its readers while they turn through the pages of the Huntington's collections of rare books and conduct hands-on research into subjects that offer insight into our history—because much in our past still speaks to today's world.

Judith Herman

Altadena, California

ACKNOWLEDGMENTS

We are deeply appreciative of the help given to us by various institutions and individuals. Miss Mary Isabel Fry and the staff of the Huntington Library, San Marino, California, were most generous and gracious in their patience and assistance to us, as were Mrs. Tutelman and the staff of the Sunland-Tujunga branch of the Los Angeles Public Library. Other libraries and organizations that must be acknowledged include Bath Municipal Libraries, England; British Museum, Rare Book Room, London, England; Budleigh Library, England; Corporation of Dundee, Scotland; Library of Congress, Washington, D.C.; Los Angeles County Museum of Natural History; Los Angeles Public Library.

We are also happy to acknowledge those who shared their books with us, as well as those who eagerly tasted or tested recipes, and certainly those who, at all times, gave us their moral support and encouragement. We cannot list them all, but we must include Nettie and Chet Baker, Evelyn and Dan Berman, Mr. and Mrs. Philip Cadish, Mr. and Mrs. John L. Cobb, Eleanor E. Cracraft,

Dr. and Mrs. Kaan Edis, Mrs. Dorothy Verharst Fields, Lydia Goranin, Marian L. Gore, Hershel Gruenberg, Mr. and Mrs. Dale L. Harvey, Mr. and Mrs. J. C. Henry, Michael Patrick Henry, Dr. Alfred H. Herman, Dorothy and Henry Herman, Marsha B. and Helmar B. Herman, Roma and Larry Herman, Margaret Hodgen, Ira Katz, Lydia Link, Dr. and Mrs. Robert A. Masumura, Mr. and Mrs. Dan Moore, Leslie Moore, Vikki and Jerry Nelson, Vera and Jürgen Pahl, Una Patterson, LeRae and Ron Phillips, Renée and Barney Polesky, Judy and Ray Schaefer, Hodi Shalett, Dolores Simon, Victor Sirelson, Mr. and Mrs. Tom Tackett, Gregory J. Verharst, Jeffrey L. Verharst, Stephanie H. and David M. Verharst, Sherna S. Vinograd, and Nahum J. Waxman.

HINTS AND EQUIVALENTS

The first recipe we tried was Thomas Gray's
Oxford Pudding, page 196. We used the sweet
butter substitution for suet (see below), and the
rind of one large lemon, and we boiled it in a
large pot for one hour, checking to be sure it
never stuck to the bottom. We served it on an
old-fashioned dish, sat down to taste it, ate it all
up—and made it again—and ate it all up again,
but this time we shared it with friends—and we
made it again—etc., etc. The following hints and
equivalents will be found helpful in preparing the
recipes in this book.

Fontaine à mains
pour cuisine

Always use fresh ingredients.

Recipes can be divided in halves, quarters, etc., to suit
your own needs, or for a first taste. Also, for first
tasting of Daryoles, etc., toast can be substituted for
pastry crust.

Although measurements have differed through the centuries for English pints, Scottish pints, American
pints, and so on, we used the standard American measure of 8 ounces to a cup and 2 cups to a pint. We

CUTLET
BAT

PASTE JAGGER

Bottle Jack and Screen, for roasting
without a spit and wooden screen

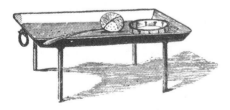

Dripping-pan and Ladle

experienced no problems in testing the breads, cakes, cookies, puddings, pastries, curds—all were successful.

"Two hours' beating" indicates a mixture well beaten, but the time reduces to a matter of minutes with an electric beater.

Seville orange is a bitter Spanish orange.

Salad oil is usually olive oil.

To "beard an oyster" is to cut off the frill or ruffle.

When the size of the spoonful is not indicated, the spoon size varies according to your taste.

The time indicated for cooking is relative and always was—but modern ovens usually require less time.

Letting bread rise "till your oven be hot" took about two hours in the 1600s.

Chopping, pounding, mashing, and so on can be done with an electric blender whether the food is nuts, curds, or lobster shells, and meat can be put through a grinder.

If the recipe calls for pounds or ounces, weigh the ingredients; if it calls for cups or spoons, measure them.

Boil usually means a gentle boil or simmer except for boiling puddings, when the water must be kept at a rolling boil.

Be sure the pudding cloth is free of soap.

Fresh, unsalted, sweet butter should always be used unless otherwise indicated.

A dish of butter is approximately one cup.

Butter all pans for cakes, rising of dough, biscuit or cookie sheets.

Use narrow loaf pans or a cake pan with a center tube, except for such cakes as the Banbury Cake.

If suet is not available, or not liked, one-half the amount of sweet butter may be substituted for it, or one-quarter the amount of both sweet butter and marrow.

If rose water, orange-flower water, musk, ambergris, etc., are not available, or not liked, any other flavoring can be used.

Fruit juices can be substituted for alcoholic ingredients.

A sieve lined with damp white paper toweling can be used to drain the whey from the curds.

Bladders are not generally available, but the Compound Egg (page 135) can be boiled in a piece of clean sheeting or pudding cloth.

Moist sugar is brown sugar; XXXX sugar is today's confectioners' or powdered sugar; and all other sugars (whether "powdered," "pounded," "loaf," or "caster") are today's granulated white sugar.

Gelatine, which should not be prewashed, may be substituted for isinglass—ounce for ounce.

Leftover yolks can be used to make Daryoles, a made dish of Curds; Gimblettes; Marmalade of Eggs, the Jews' Way; Mon Amy, or Puffs.

Leftover whites can be frozen for later use in French Bread or White Perfection Cake.

New milk is milk from a cow, i.e., milk with cream.

A grater may be used to remove burnt edges from cakes.

Some yeast (such as ale yeast or German yeast) is no longer available, but all yeast recipes proved themselves successful by our gauging the amount of liquid used (rather than the amount of yeast used) and adding one package of yeast to each cup of warm liquid; thus, a pint of warm ale and two packages of yeast were used for "one pint of Ale yeast" (see French Bread or Banbury Cake).

Toaster and Trivet

Read the recipe carefully. Set out all your ingredients before beginning. Be resourceful. Be brave. And have fun!

WEIGHTS AND MEASURES

Sixty drops of any thin liquid are equal to 1 teaspoonful, or 1 drachm.

Two teaspoonfuls to 1 dessertspoonful.

Four teaspoonfuls of liquid equal 1 tablespoonful.

Four tablespoonfuls of liquid equal one-half gill.

Four tablespoonfuls of liquid equal 1 wineglassful.

One tablespoonful of liquid equals one-half ounce.

Four even teaspoonfuls liquid equal 1 even tablespoonful.

A medium-sized teaspoon contains about a drachm.

Sixteen tablespoonfuls liquid equal 1 cupful.

One pint of liquid equals 1 pound.

Two gills of liquid equal one-half pint.

One kitchen cupful equals one-half pint.

Three even teaspoonfuls dry material equal 1 even tablespoonful.

Twelve tablespoonfuls dry material equal 1 cupful.

Two cupfuls equal 1 pint.

Four cupfuls equal 1 quart.

Four cupfuls flour equal 1 quart or 1 pound.

Two cupfuls solid butter equal 1 pound.

Two cupfuls granulated sugar equal 1 pound.

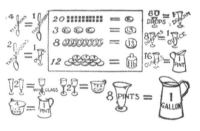

Liquid Measure

Graduated Measure

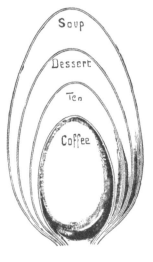

Two and a half cupfuls powdered sugar equal 1 pound.

One pint milk or water equals 1 pound.

One dozen eggs should weigh 1½ pounds.

One quart of sifted flour equals 1 pound.

Four cupfuls of flour equal 1 pound.

One tablespoonful of flour equals one-half ounce.

Three cupfuls of cornmeal equal 1 pound.

One and one-half pints of cornmeal equal one pound.

One cupful of butter equals one-half pound.

One tablespoonful of butter equals 1 ounce.

One pint of butter equals 1 pound.

One pint of chopped suet equals 1 pound.

Ten eggs equal 1 pound.

One pint of granulated sugar equals 1 pound.

One pint of brown sugar equals 13 ounces.

Two and one-half cupfuls of powdered sugar equal 1 pound.

Sixteen drams equal 1 ounce.

Sixteen ounces equal 1 pound.

Butter size of an egg, 2 ounces.

One kitchen cup, half pint.

One pound loaf sugar (broken) to 1 quart.

Twelve small eggs without the shells weigh 1 pound.

Ten medium eggs without the shells weigh 1 pound.

Nine large eggs without the shells weigh 1 pound.

An ordinary egg weighs from 1¼ to 2 ounces.

A duck's egg weighs from 2 to 3 ounces.

A turkey's egg weighs from three to four ounces.

A goose egg weighs from 4 to 6 ounces.

Two ounces unmelted butter equal in size an ordinary egg.

Two tablespoons liquid weigh 1 ounce.

Two heaping tablespoons powdered sugar weigh 1 ounce.

Two heaping tablespoons granulated sugar weigh 1 ounce.

Two rounded tablespoons of flour weigh 1 ounce.

Sugar, flour, butter, lard, drippings, currants, raisins, rice and cornstarch are measured by the rounding spoonful.

Salt, pepper and spices by the level spoonful.

Measuring Glass

Skim milk is heavier than whole milk and cream is lighter than either, while pure milk is 3 per cent heavier than water.

Spices.—Two saltspoonfuls make 1 after-dinner coffeespoon; 2 coffeespoonfuls make 1 teaspoonful; a dash of pepper equals quarter saltspoonful.

MAUD C. COOKE, *Twentieth Century Cook Book*, 1897

The most utterly lost of all days is
that on which we have not once laughed.

—SÉBASTIEN ROCH NICOLAS CHAMFORT (1741–1794),
French philosopher and son of a grocer

A riddle, a riddle,
As I suppose;
A hundred eyes,
And never a nose.

History of the Potato

The introduction of the potato as an article of diet forms a very interesting chapter in the history of the human race. It was brought into England by the colonists who were, in 1584, sent out by Queen Elizabeth, to "discover and plant new countries not possessed by Christians." Thomas Heriot, the mathematician, was one of these adventurers; he returned with the rest, after an expedition of two years, and it has been supposed that to him we are indebted for the potato. Sir Walter Raleigh, who headed the expedition of discovery to North America, introduced the potato into Ireland on his return from Virginia; but so little did he understand or care about this valuable root, that having planted and

THE USUAL answer to this nineteenth-century riddle is a sieve, which, as a matter of fact, is itself sometimes known as a riddle.

However, an equally correct answer is the potato.

The Potato

A strange objection to potatoes was urged by the Puritans, who denied the lawfulness of eating them, because they are not mentioned in the Bible; but whether we view this vegetable with reference to its adaptation to every soil and to almost every climate, or as a great source of food and nutritive properties, it must be ranked among the best gifts of Providence. *Cassell's Household Guide,* vol. III [c. 1885]

QUEEN ELIZABETH

reared the plant on his estate at Youghal, in the county of Cork, Raleigh ordered them to be rooted out. The gardener obeyed, and in so doing found a large quantity of tubers, which saved the plants from destruction.

For some time after its introduction the potato was planted in the gardens of the nobility as a curious exotic; in the reign of James I it was considered a delicacy, being provided in small quantities for the queen's household. Books upon gardening published about the end of the seventeenth century, a hundred years after their introduction, speak rather slightingly of them. Even the famous Evelyn regarded them with no favour. In *The Complete Gardener,* published in 1719, the well-known nurserymen, Loudon and Wise, completely ignore the potato; and in another work of the same period it is mentioned as inferior to radishes.

Gradually, however, the excellent qualities of the potato became recognized, and the use of the tuber spread. But it was not till the middle of the eighteenth century that potatoes were generally known over the country.

In Scotland the cultivation of potatoes in gardens was very little understood till about 1740. About the same time the potato was introduced into Saxony and some parts of Germany; and in the latter part of the century it made its way into France. There it owed much to the exertions of Parmentier. In some German districts, Government took an interest in the plant, and aided its culture by compulsory enactments.

In 1846 and 1847 terrible famine resulted in Ireland and elsewhere through the failure of the potato-crop. The potato disease was first noticed in Germany, and assumed a serious character at Liège in 1842. Two years later it invaded Canada, and at once proved very destructive there. In

1845 it was observed in the British Isles, and during that year its ravages were very considerable. They reached their height in 1846, when the Irish famine was the consequence. Since 1847 the potato-disease has gradually diminished, but it still breaks out in particular localities.

Cassell's Dictionary of Cookery [c. 1877]

SIR WALTER RALEIGH

Potatoes and Apples

Wash and peel the potatoes, cut them in pieces; peel, core and cut in quarters the same quantity of sour apples; parboil the potatoes in water, with some salt, strain them, add the apples, a good piece of butter and a little water, stir them often, and let them cook till quite tender. Potatoes are also often cooked with pears and plums in the same way; the only difference being that the pears or plums must be partly cooked by themselves with water, butter, and a little vinegar before they are added to the potatoes.

Lady Harriet St. Clair (Late Countess Münster), *Dainty Dishes* [1884]

English Potato Balls

Boil some floury potatoes very dry, mash them as smoothly as possible, season them well with salt and white pepper; warm them with about an ounce of butter to the pound, or rather more if it will not render them too moist; a few spoonfuls of good cream may be added, but they must be boiled very dry after it is stirred to them. Let the mixture cool a little, roll it into balls, sprinkle

BONELESS POTATOES

According to Tabitha Tickletooth in *The Dinner Question* (1860), a potato with a "bone" or moonlike disk in it is called "Au ghealeach."

To prevent the "bone," when the potatoes have boiled five minutes, pour off the *hot* water and replace it with *cold*. Salt is added and the potatoes are now boiled gently for one-half to three-quarters of an hour. Tickletooth adds: "By chilling its exterior with cold water, the heat of the first boiling strikes to the centre of the vegetable, and as its force gradually increases when the water boils again, by the time the outside has recovered from its chilling, the equilibrium is restored, and the whole potato is evenly done."

3

over them vermicelli crushed slightly with the hand, and fry them a fine light brown. They may be dished round a shape of plain mashed potatoes, or piled on a napkin by themselves. They may likewise be rolled in egg and fine breadcrumbs instead of in the vermicelli, or in rice flour, which answers very well for them.

ELIZA ACTON, *Modern Cookery,* 1852

Irish Way of Boiling Potatoes

In Ireland, where this root has been for so long a period the chief nourishment of the people, and where it takes the place of bread and other more substantial food, it is cooked so that it may have, as they call it, a bone in it; that is, that the middle of it should not be quite cooked. They are done thus:—Put a gallon of water with two ounces of salt, in a large iron pot, boil for about ten minutes, or until the skin is loose, pour the water out of the pot, put a dry cloth on the top of the potatoes, and place it on the side of the fire without water for about twenty minutes, and serve. In Ireland turf is the principal article of fuel, which is burnt on the flat hearth; a little of it is generally scraped up round the pot, so as to keep a gradual heat; by this plan the potato is both boiled and baked. Even in those families where such a common art of civilized life as cooking ought to have made some progress, the only improvement they have upon this plan is, that they leave the potatoes in the dry pot longer, by which they lose the *bone.* They are always served up with the skins on, and a small plate is placed by the side of each guest.

ALEXIS SOYER, *The Modern Housewife,* 1851

New Potatoes

The best way to clean New Potatoes, is to rub them with a coarse cloth or a flannel, or scrubbing brush.

N.B. NEW POTATOES are poor, watery, and insipid, till they are full two inches diameter—they are hardly worth the trouble of boiling *before Midsummer Day.*

Obs. Some Cooks prepare Sauces to pour over Potatoes, made with butter, salt, and pepper—or gravy, or melted butter and catsup—or stew the Potatoes in ale, or water seasoned with pepper and salt—or bake them with herrings, or sprats, mixed with layers of potatoes, seasoned with pepper, salt, sweet herbs, vinegar, and water—or cut mutton or beef into slices, and lay them in a stewpan, and on them potatoes and spices, then another layer of the meat alternately, pouring in a little water, covering it up very close, and stewing slowly.

[DR. WILLIAM KITCHINER], *The Cook's Oracle,* 1823

Potato Slicer

Potato Cheese

The following method, practiced in Saxony, makes a more healthful article of cheese than that with which our tables are usually furnished in this country: "Boil large white potatoes until cooked; let them cool; then peel, and mash them in a mortar. To five pounds of potatoes add one pound of sour milk, and a little salt; knead the whole; cover it, and let it remain undisturbed for three or four days, according to the season. At the end of this time, knead it again, and place

POTATO

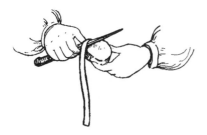

Cutting Potato Ribbons

the cheeses in small baskets where the superfluous moisture will evaporate. Then place them in the shade to dry, and put them in layers in large pots, or any other vessels, wherein they must remain fifteen days."

In my judgment this article is more wholesome when fresh made than after standing fifteen days. I recommend, therefore, the omission of the last clause of the recipe.

R. T. TRALL, M.D., *The New Hydropathic Cook-Book,* 1869

Potato Masher.

* Anne Bowman (*The New Cookery Book,* 1869) omits the cream, adds the yolks of four and the whites of two eggs, and bakes for twenty minutes.

† Pattipans = small tart pans.

Potato, or Lemon Cheesecakes

Take six ounces of Potatoes, four ounces of lemon-peel, four ounces of sugar, four ounces of butter; boil the Lemon-peel till tender, pare and scrape the Potatoes, and boil them tender and mash them; beat the Lemon-peel with the sugar, then beat all together very well, and melt the butter in a little thick cream,* and mix all together very well, and let it lie till cold: Put crust in your pattipans,† and fill them little more than half full: Bake them in a quick oven half an hour, sift some double-refined sugar on them as they go into the oven; this quantity will make a dozen small pattipans.

E. SMITH, *The Compleat Housewife,* 1739

To make paste of Potatoes

Boil your Potatoes very tender, pare them and pick out all the blacks of them. Put to every pound of them a grain of Muske, and beat them in a stone morter very fine. Then take as much refined Sugar as the pulp doth weigh, and boil it to a candy height with as much Rose-water as will dissolve it, then put in the pulp into the boiling Sugar. Let it boil always stirring it till it comes from the bottom of the pot, then lay it on a sheet of glass in round cakes or in what fashion you please, and set it in a warm Oven or Stove. And when it is candied on the top, then turn it on the other side, and let it candy, and in ten or twelve days it will be dry, then box it for your use.*

JOHN MURRELL, *A Delightfull Daily Exercise,* 1621

POTATO PASTY PAN

* According to Mrs. De Salis (*National Viands À La Mode,* 1895), the Cuban dish called Moniatillo is made in a similar way with sweet potatoes, sugar and plain water. The cakes are left to get cold and then covered with sugar.

A Good Potatoe Pudding, ye best

Take a pound of potatoes, boyl'd, peel'd & cold, mash them thro a strainer. Then add one pound of fresh butter melted, 10 Eggs, ½ pound of suggar, ½ a Nutmeg: mix these together & put it in a quick Oven. One hour will bake it.

The Receipt Book of Mrs. Ann Blencowe, 1694

SWEET POTATO

ARCHDRUID AND DRUIDS

A soul-cake, a soul-cake,
Please good mistress a soul-cake;
One for Peter and one for Paul
And one for the Lord who made us all;
An apple, a pear, a plum or a cherry,
Any good thing to make us merry.

THE SEED CAKE is a form of soul cake associated with the old Druid and early Christian rites that took place between Halloween and All Souls' Day (October 31 and November 2), when the spirits or souls of the dead were thought to rise up from their graves. Both children and

Seed Cake without Butter

Dry and warm 13 ozs. of flour and 1 lb. of loaf sugar pounded finely, 4 spoonsful of warm water, 4 of brandy, 1 of orange-flower water, and 2 ozs of carraway-seed; mix all together, then beat up 12 eggs with half the whites, add them to the cake, beat the whole well, and bake it 2 hours.

SARAH JOSEPHA HALE, *The Ladies' New Book of Cookery,* 1852

To make a rich Seed Cake

Take a pound of flour well dried, a pound of butter, a pound of loaf sugar beat and sifted, eight eggs, two ounces of carraway seeds, one nutmeg grated, and its weight of cinnamon; first beat your butter to a cream, then put in your sugar, beat the whites of your eggs half an hour, mix them with your sugar and butter, then beat the yolks half an hour, put it to the whites, beat in flour, spices, and seeds. A little before it goes to the oven, put it in the hoop,* and bake it two hours in a quick oven, and let it stand two hours. It will take two hours beating.

ELIZABETH RAFFALD, *The Experienced English House-Keeper,* 1778

adults would chant this rhyme, just as today children call out "trick or treat!" And this was also the time when the Heathens (i.e., those who lived on the heath) celebrated the last sowing of their wheat crop with these seed or soul cakes.

* Hoop = a deep, round cake pan of various diameters, usually with a removable bottom; sometimes called a spring-form.

Scottish Seed Cake

(Dundee)

12 eggs, 1¼ lbs. best flour, 1¼ lbs. best loaf sugar, 1 lb. butter, ¼ lb. orange peel, ¼ lb. lemon peel, ¼ lb. citron candied (these quantities will do for 2 cakes).

Cream the butter, then add the sugar and flour, then the eggs, which must be well beaten up one at a time, and added very gradually till all are in.

Lastly add the peel cut in small pieces and 1 oz. of carraway seeds. Bake in a buttered tin in a slow oven.

Do not cut this cake too fresh.

The Cookery Book of Lady Clark of Tillypronie [c. 1897]

FRENCH DEATH-CRIER—"PRAY FOR THE SOUL JUST DEPARTED."

Cinnamon is about the oldest known spice in the world, and comes from the bark of a species of laurel. In America and on the continent of Europe it is often confounded with cassia, which goes by the name of Chinese cinnamon. The true cinnamon is the cinnamon of Ceylon; but it also comes from Madras, Bombay, and Java, though of inferior quality. When the Dutch held possession of Ceylon, they were known at times to burn the cinnamon, in order to limit the supply and to keep up the price. But the supply is limited in any case, for though the bark grows again upon the cinnamon trees, it takes three years to do so; and a crop which comes but once in three years cannot be considered abundant. ([E. S. DALLAS], *Kettner's Book Of The Table,* 1877)

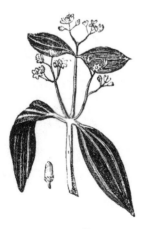

Cinnamon Tree

"Any good thing to make us Merry"

PRINTS ON APPLES AND PEARS.—A correspondent of the Charleston *Courier* gives the following: "I have just seen a very pretty and fanciful idea developed on pears and apples, in the orchard of a friend at West Roxbury, Mass. As you ramble among the trees, you are ever and anon saluted by an inscription on the fruit, done, as it were, by the hand of Nature herself. Here you meet with the familiar name of Mary or Alice, or a date, (1868,) in brief, everything that may suggest itself to your taste or fancy; and all done in the skin of the fruit, without abrasion or any foreign impression. The discovery was made by Hon. Arthur W. Austin, of West Roxbury, in 1851–2. He observed, during the former year, that apples did not redden in that part of the fruit where a leaf happened to lie upon it. In 1852, he cut letters from newspapers, and when the apples were yet green, he pasted them upon the fruit with gum tragacanth. The apples would redden to perfection, the letters were removed, and they would appear permanently outlined in green. So, again, when he pasted on the apple a paper in which the letters were cut out, the parts covered by the paper would be green, and the letters would appear distinctly turned in red, the green surrounding them. The experiment is a very pretty one, and produces a happy effect. Let our fruit growers try it."

J. S. BUELL, *The Cider Makers' Manual,* 1879

London Bridge, about 1616.

As I was going o'er London Bridge,
I heard something crack;
Not a man in all England
Can mend that!

A Witness to the Ceremony of Laying the FIRST STONE OF THE NEW LONDON-BRIDGE, on Wednesday, the 15th of June, 1825

By admission to the entire ceremony of laying the first stone of the new London-bridge, the editor of the *Every-Day Book* is enabled to give an authentic account of the proceedings from his own close observation.

At an early hour of the morning the vicinity of the new and old bridges presented an appearance of activity, bustle, and preparation; and every spot that could command even a bird's-eye

THE ANSWER is ice.

Ice has not only been a means of amusement for skaters in winter but for centuries it has also been stored for summer use, to chill beverages and freeze desserts.

PEAR ICE

11

TRAITORS' GATE, OLD LONDON BRIDGE.

SOME HISTORY OF THE LONDON BRIDGE

It is supposed that the first bridge of London was built between the years 993 and 1016; it was of wood. There is a vulgar tradition, that the foundation of the old stone bridge was laid upon wool-packs; this report is imagined to have arisen from a tax laid upon wool toward its construction. The first stone-bridge began in 1176, and was finished in 1209, was much injured by a fire in the Borough, in 1212, and three thousand people perished. On St. George's day, 1395, there was a great jousting upon it, between David, earl of Crawford, of Scotland, and lord Wells of England. It had a drawbridge for the passage of ships with provisions to Queenhithe, with houses upon it, mostly tenanted by pin and needle-makers: there was a chapel on the bridge, and a tower, whereon the heads of un-

view of the scene, was eagerly and early occupied.

So early as twelve o'clock, the avenues leading to the old bridge were filled with individuals, and shortly afterwards the various houses, which form the streets through which the procession was to pass, had their windows graced with numerous parties of well-dressed people. The buildings, public or private, that at all overlooked the scene, were literally roofed and walled with human figures, clinging to them in all sorts of possible and improbable attitudes.

The wharfs on the banks of the river, between London-bridge and Southwark-bridge, were occupied by an immense multitude. All the vessels hoisted their flags top-mast-high, in honour of the occasion, and many of them sent out their boats manned, to increase the bustle and interest of the scene.

The procession moved up Cornhill and down Grace-church-street, to London-bridge. While awaiting the arrival of the procession, wishes were wafted from many a fair lip, that the lord mayor of the day, as well as of the city, would make his appearance. Small-talk had been exhausted, and the merits of each particular timber canvassed for the hundredth time, when, at about a quarter to three, the lady mayoress made her appearance, and renovated the hopes of the company. They argued that his lordship as a family man, would not be long absent from his lady. The clock tolled three, and no lord mayor had made his appearance.

A sweeping train of aldermen were seen. Next in order entered a strong body of the common-councilmen. After these entered the recorder, the common sergeant, the city solicitor, the city clerk, the city chamberlain, and a thousand other city officers, "all gracious in the city's eyes." These were followed by the duke of York and the lord mayor.

The lord mayor took his station by the side of the stone, attended by four gentlemen of the committee, bearing, one, the glass-cut bottle to contain the coins of the present reign, another, an English inscription incrusted in glass, another, the mallet, and another, the level.

The ceremony commenced by the children belonging to the wards' schools singing "God save the King." They were stationed in the highest eastern gallery for that purpose; the effect produced by their voices, stealing through the windings caused by the intervening timbers to the depth below, was very striking and peculiar.

The lord mayor's address was received with cheers. His lordship then spread the mortar, and the stone was gradually lowered by two men at a windlass. When finally adjusted, the city sword and mace were placed on it crossways; the foundation of the new London-bridge was declared to be laid. Three cheers were afterwards given for the duke of York; three for Old England; and three for the architect, Mr. Rennie.

We delight to attend spectacles like the present, where the first germ of a stupendous work is to be prepared. We bethink ourselves of the stream of human life, which, some five years hence, will flow over the new London-bridge as thickly, and almost with as little cessation, as the waters of the Thames below: and then we reflect upon the tide of hopes and fears which that human stream will carry in its bosom. Trade, and science, and learning, and war, (Providence long avert it!) will at various periods pass across it. Will it fall before the wrath or willfulness of man, or is it to be displaced by new improvements and discoveries, in like manner as its old and many-arched neighbour makes way for it— and as *that* once superseded its narrower and shop-covered predecessor?

WILLIAM HONE, *The Every-Day Book*, vol. I, 1826

fortunate partisans were placed: in 1598 Hentzner, the German traveller, counted above thirty poles with heads. Upon this bridge was placed the head of the great chancellor, sir Thomas More, which was blown off the pole into the Thames and found by a waterman, who gave it to his [More's] daughter; she kept it during life as a relic, and directed at her death it should be placed in her arms and buried with her. (WILLIAM HONE, *The Every-Day Book*, vol. I, 1826)

Ice is one of the greatest of summer luxuries, and indeed is almost a necessity. It is so easily put up, even in the country, and so cheaply protected, that there is no reason why any one who is able to own or rent a house may not have it in liberal supply. A cheap ice-house may be made by partitioning off a space about twelve feet square in the wood-shed, or even in the barn. The roof must be tight over it, but there is no necessity for matched or fine lumber for the walls. They should, however, be coated with coal-tar inside, as the long-continued moisture puts them to a severe test and brings on decay. Ice should be taken from still places in running streams, or from clear ponds. It may be cut with half an old cross-cut saw, but there are saws and ice-plows made for the purpose to be had in almost every village. In cutting ice, as soon as it is of sufficient thickness and before much warm weather, select a still day, with the thermometer as near zero as may be. Ice handles much more comfortably and easily when it is so cold that it immediately freezes dry, thus preventing the wet clothes and mittens, which are the sole cause of any suffering in handling it; and ice put up in sharp, cold weather, before it has been subjected to any thaw, will keep much better

Apple Ice (very fine)

Take finely-flavored apples, grate them fine, and then make them *very* sweet, and freeze them. It is very delicious.

Pears, peaches, or quinces also are nice, either grated fine or stewed and run through a sieve, then sweetened *very* sweet, and frozen. The flavor is much better preserved when grated than when cooked.

CATHERINE E. BEECHER AND HARRIET BEECHER STOWE, *The New Housekeeper's Manual*, 1873

To make Apricot Ice Cream

Pare, stone, and scald twelve ripe apricots, beat them fine in a marble mortar. Put to them six ounces of double refined sugar, a pint of scalding cream, work it through a hair sieve, put it into a tin that has a close cover, set it in a tub of ice broken small, and a large quantity of salt put amongst it. When you see your cream grow thick round the edges of your tin, stir it, and set it in again till all grows quite thick. When your cream is all frozen up, take it out of your tin, and put it into the mould you intend it to be turned out of, then put on the lid, and have ready another tub with ice and salt in it as before. Put your mould in the middle, and lay your ice under and over it, let it stand four or five hours. Dip your tin in warm water when you turn it out; if it be summer, you must not turn it out till the moment you want it; you may use any sort of fruit if you have not apricots, only observe to work it fine.

ELIZABETH RAFFALD, *The Experienced English House-Keeper*, 1778

Plain Ice Cream

Whip a pint of fresh double cream, quite strong; when whipped, add to it six ounces of pounded sugar; put it into the freezing-pot, and work it well.

W. A. JARRIN, *The Italian Confectioner*, 1861

Buttermilk Cream

(Mrs. D. R.)

One gallon buttermilk, yolks of eight eggs, and whites of four, well beaten; three pints sweet milk. Boil the sweet milk and pour on the eggs; then thicken, stirring all the time. When cool stir in the buttermilk slowly, season and sweeten to taste, then freeze.

MARION CABELL TYREE, ed., *Housekeeping in Old Virginia*, 1879

Frozen Cream Cheese

Take 1 pint of cream cheese or curd, mash until perfectly smooth. It is best to mash it through a fine sieve. Add 1 quart rich cream, sweeten quite sweet with sifted powdered sugar, flavor with vanilla. Put in a freezer and freeze like any other ice cream.

Brown Bread Ice

Grate as fine as possible stale brown bread,* soak a small proportion in cream two or three hours, sweeten and ice it.

[MARIA ELIZA RUNDELL], *A New System of Domestic Cookery*, 1807

and be much more useful in the hot days of summer than if its packing had been delayed until later winter or early spring, and then the ice put up half melted and wet. (*Buckeye Cookery*, 1883)

STRENGTH OF ICE

Ice 2 ins. thick will bear men on foot.

Ice 4 ins. thick will bear men on horseback.

Ice 6 ins. thick will bear cattle and teams with light loads.

Ice 8 ins. thick will bear teams with heavy loads.

Ice 10 ins. thick will sustain a pressure of 1,000 lbs. per square ft.

This supposes the ice to be sound through its whole thickness, without "snow ice."

(OLD DOCTOR WILLIAM CARLIN, BEDFORD, ENGLAND, *Old Doctor Carlin's Recipes*, 1881)

* Some cooks use stale Boston brown bread.

15

Mint Sherbet

Soak a handful of mint in a cupful of good whiskey for one hour. Strain this and add 3 pints of strong lemonade; put in an ice cream freezer, and when half frozen, add the whites of two eggs beaten stiff, then freeze again. Requires longer to freeze than ice cream.

MRS. C. F. MORITZ AND MISS ADÈLE KAHN, *The Twentieth Century Cook Book,* 1898

London Sherbet

2 cupfuls of water,	½ lemon, the juice only,
2 cupfuls of sugar,	
1 cupful of fruit syrup,	½ cupful of chopped raisins,
½ cupful of orange juice,	1 teaspoonful of grated nutmeg,
½ cupful of port wine,	3 whites of eggs.

Boil the water and sugar together ten minutes. Remove from the fire, and pour over the raisins. When cold, add the orange and lemon juice, the fruit syrup, and the nutmeg. Turn into the freezing can. When partly frozen, add the wine, and the whites of the eggs, beaten stiff.

Any fruit syrup left from canned goods, such as strawberries, peaches, pears, etc., are nice and useful in preparing sherbets and ices.

Mrs. Gillette's Cook Book, 1899

ICEBOX

A RIDDLE:

As I was walking in a field of wheat,
I picked up something good to eat;
Neither fish, flesh, fowl, nor bone,
I kept it till it ran alone.

Space for Fowls

We are no advocates for converting the domestic fowl into a cage-bird. We have known amateur fowl-keepers—worthy souls, who would butter the very barley they gave their pets, if they thought they would the more enjoy it—coop up a male bird and three or four hens in an ordinary egg-chest placed on its side, and with the front closely barred with iron hooping! This system will not do. Every animal, from man himself to the guinea-pig, *must* have what is vulgarly, but truly, known as "elbow-room"; and it must be self-evident how emphatically this rule applies to winged animals. It may be urged, in the case of domestic fowls, that from constant disuse, and from clipping and plucking, and other

THIS RHYME, which has been dated to 1792, is one of several riddles to which the answer is "an egg." But when the egg was kept "till it ran alone," it became some form of fowl—a chicken, duck, goose, or turkey.

SAFFRON

It is the elegiac muse that ought to write the account of saffron, for its glory is departed. The stigmas of this autumnal crocus (*Crocus sativus*) were once all important in European cookery, and were supposed to possess the rarest virtues and attractions. There was a time when England was known as merry England; and Lord Bacon in his *History of Life and Death* says: "The English are rendered sprightly by a liberal use of saffron in sweetmeats and broth." Saffron is now but little used anywhere in human food to please the eye, to tickle the palate, or to strengthen the stomach; and in England it has been so completely ousted by curry that what once rejoiced the heart of man is now only sprinkled in water to cheer the melancholy of canaries.

Compare the saffron with the bean. At one time it was worse than parricide to eat beans; and beans are now in great repute. At one time it was a superstition to flavour and colour food with saffron; and now it is a farce. So the wheel goes round, and high becomes low and low becomes high. Let us be thankful that one thing will last while man lasts—the saffron-coloured morn. ([E. S. DALLAS], *Kettner's Book Of The Table*, 1877)

sorts of maltreatment, their wings can hardly be regarded as instruments of flight; we maintain, however, that you may pluck a fowl's wing-joints as bare as a pumpkin, but you will not erase from his memory that he *is* a fowl, and that his proper sphere is the open air. If he likewise reflects that he is an ill-used fowl—a prison bird—he will then come to the conclusion, that there is not the least use, under such circumstances, for his existence; and you must admit that the decision is only logical and natural.

MRS. ISABELLA BEETON, *The Book of Household Management,* 1861

Chickens in a thickened broth

Take and boil Chickens, & cut them to pieces. Then take Pepper, Ginger, and Bread crumbs, & mix it up with the same broth, and with Ale; and color it with Saffron, and boil it and serve it forth.

HARLEIAN MS. 279 [c. 1430]

Fowls forced

Cut a large fowl down the back, take the skin off whole, cut the flesh from the bones, and chop it with half a pint of oysters and an ounce of beef marrow, pepper, and salt. Mix it with cream, lay the meat on the bones, draw the skin over, and sew up the back. Lay thin slices of bacon on the breast, tie them on in diamonds, and roast it an hour by a moderate fire. Pour a brown gravy sauce into the dish, take the bacon off, and lay in the fowl. Garnish with pickles, mushrooms, or oysters, and serve it hot.

MRS. MARY HOLLAND, *The Complete Economical Cook*, 1837

Cock-A-Leekie

Put four pounds of lean beef into an iron pot with three quarts of water; simmer for four hours, skimming frequently. Take out the beef; strain the stock; wash and trim eight leeks; cut the white part into inch lengths, and put them into cold water. Boil the green part of the leeks in the beef stock till quite in a pulp, then rub it through a tammy* sieve. Have a fine young fowl trussed for boiling, put it into a stewpan, with the white pieces of leeks and the stock. Add two teaspoonfuls of salt and a saltspoonful of white pepper. Boil up quickly, then simmer very gently for an hour. Serve in a tureen; or the fowl may be sent to table separately, if preferred: in that case, reserve a cupful of soup to pour over it.†

* Tammy = a fine cloth of good quality.

† Cock-a-Leekie was sometimes thickened with rice, barley, or prunes. When thickened with toasted bread, it was called Welsh Leek Porridge.

Stock Meat

The stock meat may be made into a very savoury dish as follows:—Pound the meat to paste, season every pound with two saltspoonfuls of salt, one saltspoonful of black pepper, a grain‡ of cayenne, the sixth part of a nutmeg grated, the peel of half a lemon grated, a small onion finely chopped, a teaspoonful of chopped parsley, half a saltspoonful of mixed herbs, two ounces of good dripping or butter, and the white of an egg. Mix it well, and form it into cakes half an inch thick; dip them into the beaten yolk of egg, then dredge them with baked flour,§ and fry in plenty of good drippings for eight or ten minutes. It is also very good chopped, and mixed with salad.

Cre-Fydd's Family Fare, 1871

‡ By a *grain* is meant the sixtieth part of a drachm; and of most things a cayenne-spoonful will be equal to a grain. A drachm is the eighth part of an ounce; and of many things a teaspoonful is equal to a drachm. (*Cre-Fydd's Family Fare,* 1871)

§ Baked flour = flour dried in a slow oven.

19

Improved Roaster and Baker.

* The cook of Napoleon I is said to have invented this dish on June 14, 1800, following two strenuous battles between the French and the Austrians. According to Mrs. Isabella Beeton, in her *Book of Household Management*: "On the evening of the battle the first consul was very hungry after the agitation of the day, and a fowl was ordered with all expedition. The fowl was procured, but there was no butter at hand, and unluckily none could be found in the neighbourhood. There was oil in abundance, however; and the cook having poured a certain quantity into his skillet, put in the fowl, with a clove of garlic and other seasoning, with a little white wine, the best the country afforded; he then garnished it with mushrooms, and served it up hot. This dish proved the second conquest of the day, as the first consul found it most agreeable to his palate, and expressed his satisfaction. Ever since, a fowl à la Marengo is a favourite dish with all lovers of good cheer."

To marinade a Fowl

(*Glasse*, page 78. *Farley*, page 123.)

Raise the skin from the breast-bone of a large fowl with your finger, then take a veal sweetbread and cut it small, a few oysters, a few mushrooms, an anchovy, some pepper, a little nutmeg, some lemon-peel, and a little thyme; chop all together small, and mix it with the yolk of an egg, stuff it in between the skin and the flesh, but take great care that you do not break the skin; and then stuff what oysters you please into the body of the fowl. You may lard the breast of the fowl with bacon, if you chuse it. Paper the breast, and roast it. Make good gravy, and garnish with lemon. You may add a few mushrooms to the sauce.

Mrs. Mary Cole, *The Lady's Complete Guide*, 1791

Fowl, Sauté Marengo, Parisian*

Cut a fowl into pieces, seven or eight, as you like, which put into a stewpan, with three tablespoonfuls of salad-oil, over a moderate fire, shaking the stewpan round occasionally, until the pieces of fowl are rather browned, when mix in a tablespoonful of flour, which moisten with a pint of stock or water, let it simmer at the corner of the fire twenty minutes, skimming off the oil as it rises to the surface; add a few blanched mushrooms in slices, season with a little salt, pepper, sugar, and a piece of scraped garlic the size of a pea; take out the fowl, which pile upon your dish, laying the worst pieces at the bottom; reduce the sauce over the fire, keeping it stirred until sufficiently thick to adhere to the back of the spoon, then pour over the fowl and serve. Use brown sauce, if handy.

Alexis Soyer, *The Modern Housewife,* 1851

Several Sauces for roast Hens

§ Take beer, salt, the yolks of three hard eggs minced small, grated bread, three or four spoonfuls of gravy; and being almost boiled, put in the juice of two or three oranges, slices of a lemon and orange, with lemon-peel shred small.

§ Beaten butter with juice of lemon or orange, white or claret wine.

§ Gravy and claret wine boiled with a piece of onion, nutmeg, and salt, serve it with slices of oranges or lemons, or the juice in the sauce.

§ Or with oyster-liquor, an anchovy or two, nutmeg, and gravy, and rub the dish with a clove of garlic.

§ Take the yolks of hard eggs and lemon peel, mince them very small, and stew them in white-wine, salt and the gravy of the fowl.

Robert May, *The Accomplisht Cook,* 1678

Sauerkraut, "that excellent preparation" of the Germans, and of which they are so immoderately fond, is merely fermented cabbage. To prepare this, close-headed white cabbages are cut in shreds, and placed in a four-inch layer in a cask; this is strewed with salt, unground pepper, and a small quantity of salad oil: a man with clean wooden shoes then gets into the cask, and treads the whole together till it is well mixed and compact. Another layer is then added, which is again trod down, and so on until the cask is en- subjected to heavy pressure, and allowed to ferment; when the fermentation has subsided, the barrels in which it is prepared are closed up, and it is preserved for use. The preparing of sauer- kraut is considered of so much importance as to form a separate profession, which is principally engrossed by the Tyrolese. The operation of shredding the cab- bage is now performed by a ma- chine, which the men carry on their backs from house to house; this means for the abridgement of labour has not been invented more than ten or twelve years. Every German family stores up, according to its size, one or more large casks of this vegetable preparation. October and No- vember are the busy months for

Ducks

It is to be regretted that domestication has seri- ously deteriorated the moral character of the duck. In a wild state, he is a faithful husband, desiring but one wife, and devoting himself to her; but no sooner is he domesticated than he becomes polygamous, and makes nothing of own- ing ten or a dozen wives at a time. As regards the females, they are much more solicitous for the welfare of their progeny in a wild state than a tame. Should a tame duck's duckling get into mortal trouble, its mother will just signify her sorrow by an extra "quack," or so, and a flap- ping of her wings; but touch a wild duck's little one if you dare! she will buffet you with her broad wings, and dash boldly at your face with her stout beak. If you search for her next amongst the long grass, she will try no end of manoeuvres to lure you from it, her favourite *ruse* being to pretend lameness, to delude you into the notion that you have only to pursue her vigorously, and her capture is certain; so you persevere for half a mile or so, and then she is up and away, leaving you to find your way back to the nest if you can.

Mrs. Isabella Beeton, *The Book of Household Management,* 1861

Duck, with Sour-Crout

Sour-crout is sold ready pickled. Drain some, and put it into a braizing-pan with a piece of breast of bacon, a bunch of parsley and green onions, spices, bay-leaves, thyme, and mace; put also a little whole pepper. Next place the duck in the middle of the sour-crout, cover the whole with layers of bacon, and moisten with some liquor of braize, or top-pot (the fat which rises over the broth), strained through a silk sieve. If you happen to have a knuckle of ham, you may put it in after having blanched it. You may add a German sausage, together with some English sausages, observing that the small sausages must not be added till half an hour before serving up, otherwise they would be too much done. Three hours are required for the above to be done over a slow fire. When the sour-crout is done, put it into a large hair sieve to drain; then dish it in a deep dish with the duck in the middle, the sausages and bacon, &c., being put round it. The duck will be better if cut into four, as it is difficult to carve anything that has so many other things with it.

LOUIS EUSTACHE UDE, *The French Cook,* 1829

To pot Ducks, or any Fowls, or small Birds

Break all the bones of your Duck with a rolling-pin, take out the thigh-bones and as many others as you can, keeping the Duck whole, season it with pepper, salt, nutmeg and cloves; lay them close in a pot with their breasts down, put in a little red wine, a good deal of butter, and lay a small weight upon them. When they are baked, let them stand in the pot till they are near cold to suck up the seasoning the better; then put them in another pot, and pour clarified butter on them; if they are to keep long put away the gravy, if to spend soon put it in: take care to season them well.

E[LIZA] SMITH, *The Compleat Housewife,* 1739

the work, and huge white pyramids of cabbage are seen crowding the markets; while in every court and yard into which an accidental peep is obtained, all is bustle and activity in the concocting of this national food, and the baskets piled with shredded cabbage resemble "mountains of green-tinged froth or syllabub." (WILLIAM RHIND, *A History of The Vegetable Kingdom* [c. 1842])

ROAST DUCK

DUCKS' EGGS

Ducks and Peas

Stuff a fine plump pair of ducks with potato stuffing, made of boiled potatoes mashed very smooth with fresh butter; or, if for company, make a fine forcemeat stuffing, as for a turkey. Bake the ducks in an iron oven or bake-pan, and when nearly done, put in with them a quart of very young peas, and a few bits of fresh butter, seasoning slightly with black pepper. When the peas and ducks are all quite done, serve them all up on one large dish.

Miss Leslie's New Cookery Book, 1857

TENDING GEESE.—From a Painting by E. Meyerheim.——Engraved for the American Agriculturist.

Goose à la façon de Mecklenburg (German)

After the goose has been drawn and cleansed, stuff it with the following mixture. Cut up eight apples in quarters, removing peel and core. Mix in with them fourteen ounces of sultanas and currants, and season with a little cinnamon. Then add three handfuls of fine breadcrumbs, and two eggs. After stuffing the goose with this, truss it, and put it on a baking dish with a glass of water. Spread good dripping or butter all over it, cover with foolscap paper, and bake in a moderate oven for two hours, well basting it constantly. Whilst the goose is cooking chop a good-sized red cabbage and cook it gently in a little thin stock, and when nearly done add to it six sausages slightly fried in goose fat, and when the cabbage is quite done pour in three spoonfuls of vinegar. When the goose is cooked dish it with the red cabbage and sausages. Pour over a little broth to the cooking stock, let it boil up, strain it, and send up in sauce tureen.

Mrs. De Salis, *National Viands À La Mode,* 1895

Choose a young goose. This is more easily said than done, as geese are frequently offered for sale when they are much too old to be eaten. The breast should be plump, the skin white, and the feet pliable and yellow. If the last are red or stiff, the bird is old or stale. Although Michaelmas is *the* time for geese, they are in perfection about June; after Christmas the flesh is tough. A goose ought not to be eaten after it is a year old. It is said that Queen Elizabeth was the originator of the Michaelmas goose. She had one on the table before her, when the news arrived of the defeat of the Spanish Armada, and she commanded the same dish to be served every succeeding Michaelmas. Green or young geese come into season in March. (*Cassell's Dictionary of Cookery* [c. 1877])

A Goose in Hogepotte*

Take a Goose, and make her clean, and cut her in pieces, and put in a pot, and add Water, and boil together. Then take Pepper and Toasted bread, or Blood boiled, and grind together Ginger and Galingale† and Cumin and temper up with Ale and mix all together; and mince Onions, and fry them in fresh grease, and add thereto a portion of Wine.

Harleian MS. 279 [c. 1430]

* Hogepotte = hodge podge.

† Galingale, says the *Oxford English Dictionary,* is derived from "Chinese *Ko-liang-kiang,* lit. 'mild ginger from Ko,' a prefecture in the province of Canton."

25

Minced Goose

Take the entire breast of a goose, chop up fine in a chopping bowl; grate in part of an onion, and season with salt, pepper and a tiny piece of garlic. Add some grated stale bread and work in a few eggs. Press this chopped meat back on to the breast bone and roast, basting very often with goose fat. This is "Hungarian," and is very nice for a change.

"Aunt Babette's" Cook Book, 1891

The Old Way

The New Way

Stuffed Goose Neck

Remove the fat skin from the neck of a fat goose, being careful not to put any holes in it. Clean carefully and sew up the smaller end and stuff through larger end with the following:

Grind fine some pieces of raw goose meat (taken from the breast or legs), grind also some soft or "linda fat," a tiny piece of garlic, a small piece onion, when fine add 1 egg, and a little soaked bread, season with salt, pepper, and ginger. When neck is stuffed, sew up larger end, lay it in a pudding pan, pour a little cold water over it, set in stove and baste from time to time. Let brown until crisp. Eat hot.

Mrs. C. F. Moritz and Miss Adèle Kahn, *The Twentieth Century Cook Book*, 1898

Swan or Goose-pudding

Take the blood of either and strain it, and put therein Oatmeal to steep, or grated Bread in Milk or Cream, with Nutmeg, Pepper, sweet Herbs, minced, Beef-suet, Rosewater, minced Lemon-peel, with a small quantity of Coriander-seed: This is a very good Pudding for a Swan or Gooses Neck.

T. P. J. P. R. C. N. B. AND SEVERAL OTHER APPROVED COOKS OF *London* AND *Westminster, The Compleat Cook,* 1694

TOULOUSE GOOSE

Sauce for a Goose

Take parsley, grapes, cloves of garlic, and salt and put it in the goose, and let it roast. And when the goose is done, shake out that which is within it, and put it all in a mortar, and add 3 hard yolks of eggs; and grind all together and mix it up with verjuice* and cast it upon the goose thickly, and so serve it forth.

ASHMOLE MS. 1429 [c. 1430]

* Verjuice = the juice of unripe fruit, especially grapes and crab apples.

ROAST GOOSE

Where Turkeys and Geese are kept, handsome feather Fans may as well be made by the younger Members of the Family as to be bought. Never throw away Wings of fowls, they are most useful. Even the left-hand wings are useful to Ambidexters or left-handed People. (MARGARET HUNTINGTON HOOKER, *Yᵉ Gentlewoman's Housewifery*, 1896)

CARVING A TURKEY—THE WRONG WAY

The Turkey

The turkey, for which fine bird we are indebted to America, is certainly one of the most glorious presents made by the New World to the Old. Some, indeed, assert that this bird was known to the ancients, and that it was served at the wedding-feast of Charlemagne. This opinion, however, has been controverted by first-rate authorities, who declare that the French name of the bird, *dindon,* proves its origin; that the form of the bird is altogether foreign, and that it is found in America alone in a wild state. There is but little doubt, from the information which has been gained at considerable trouble, that it appeared, generally, in Europe about the end of the 17th century; that it was first imported into France by Jesuits, who had been sent out as missionaries to the West; and that from France it spread over Europe. To this day, in many localities in France, a turkey is called a jesuit. On the farms of N. America, where turkeys are very common, they are raised either from eggs which have been found, or from young ones caught in the woods: they thus preserve almost entirely their original plumage. The turkey only became gradually acclimated, both on the continent and in England: in the middle of the 18th century, scarcely 10 out of 20 young turkeys lived; now, generally speaking, 15 out of the same number arrive at maturity.

MRS. ISABELLA BEETON, *The Book of Household Management,* 1861

To dress a Turkey in the French mode, to eat cold, called a la doode

Take a turkey and bone it, or not bone it, but boning is the best way, and lard it with good big lard as big as your little finger, and season it with pepper, cloves and mace, nutmegs, and put a piece of interlarded bacon in the belly, with some rosemary and bay leaves, whole pepper, cloves and mace, and sew it up in a clean cloth, and lay it to steep all night in white-wine. Next morning close it up with a sheet of coarse paste in a pan or pipkin, and bake it with the same liquor it was steeped in; it will ask four hours baking, or you may boil the liquor; then being baked and cold, serve it on a pie-plate, and stick it with rosemary and bay leaves, and serve it up with mustard and sugar in saucers, and lay the fowl on a napkin folded square, and the turkey laid corner-ways.

Thus any large fowl or other meat, as a leg of mutton, and the like.

ROBERT MAY, *The Accomplisht Cook,* 1678

Nutmeg

Deviled Turkey

In old Virginia life the carver was always the gentleman of the house, until the oldest son took his place, both for the sake of his own education in what was esteemed a gentlemanly accomplishment, and to relieve his parent of an onerous duty. In many families it was the invariable custom, when a roast turkey was served, to cut off the legs, or one leg, when the fowl was first

CARVING A TURKEY—THE RIGHT WAY

carved, and send it into the kitchen with the gizzard and liver to be deviled, and brought in as an *entremet* later on in the meal. The deviling consisted in merely gashing the said parts of the fowl deeply, strewing them thickly with black pepper and butter, slightly with salt, and then broiling, sending in to table hot, when each person who wished it was helped to a small piece.

MARY STUART SMITH, *Virginia Cookery-Book,* 1885

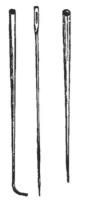

Larding and Trussing Needles

Turkey Legs

Take a sweetbread, clean and scald it, cut it in square pieces the size of dice, cut some mushrooms as nearly as possible the same shape; put them into a saucepan, with some grated bacon, parsley, small onions, shallot, and sweet basil, minced fine, some coarse pepper, and the yolks of two eggs; shake them well together. Take two raw turkey legs, remove the bones, leaving just a little bit at the end for show. Stuff the legs with the sweetbread, etc.; sew them up, so that nothing can come out. Put them to stew in a glass of good broth, one of white wine; add a bunch of parsley and small onions, and a little salt. Cover with slices of bacon, and stew over a gentle fire. When done, and but little sauce remains, skim it, take off the bacon and the bunch of parsley, add two spoonfuls of cullis,* and thicken with yolk of an egg, and serve. Just before sending to table, squeeze over the legs a little orange-juice.

LADY HARRIET ST. CLAIR (LATE COUNTESS MÜNSTER), *Dainty Dishes* [1884]

* Cullis = a strong, thickened stock, usually of meat.

Cranberry and Apple Sauce

To stew cranberries till soft, is all that is necessary to make cranberry sauce. When soft, stir in sugar and molasses to sweeten it. Scald the sugar in the sauce a few minutes. Strain if you please—'tis good without.

Apples should be pared and quartered. If tart, you may stew them in water; if not, in cider. After stewed soft, add a small piece of butter, and sweeten to the taste.

Another very good way is, to boil the apples without paring, with a few quinces and molasses, in new cider, till reduced one half. Strain the sauce when cool. Made thus, the sauce will keep good for months.

MRS. A. L. WEBSTER, *The Improved Housewife*, 1854

Stuffing for Ducks, Chickens, or Other Fowls—Spanish

(Mrs. J. G. Downey)

Take the gizzards, livers, and a piece of lean beef, and boil them; afterwards, when cold, chop them up fine. Take a small onion, two green Chilis, and a medium-sized tomato; cut them up fine. Then take a tablespoonful of lard or fresh butter and put in a frying-pan; fry for a few seconds, and then add the above ingredients; stir for a little while; then add a half teacupful of vinegar and a half cupful of pure water; add a little sugar and browned flour, a dozen olives, half cupful of raisins, and two hard-boiled eggs, chopped fine. Stir up together, and cover until the mass obtains consistency, when it is ready for use.

LADIES' AID SOCIETY, *Los Angeles Cookery*, 1881

CRANBERRIES

"Well, I have never seen turnips except mashed!" exclaimed the schoolgirl, to excuse herself when she failed to arrange that useful root in its right botanical order. We may be amused at her ignorance and shake our heads over the girl who is not allowed to enter the kitchen, yet how many useful and common articles of diet there are which we accept without inquiry as they are presented to us, knowing very little what they are, how they grow, or what are their special qualities. The cranberry now in season, is one, on the whole, so little known and so often passed over by the housewife in her catering that perhaps a brief description of it may not be unwelcome or useless.

The cranberries we see for sale at our grocer's, fruiterer's, and foreign importer's are, as we can readily see, of at least two kinds: the small, very deep red, and the large, which are lighter, brighter, and more mottled. The former we can be fairly sure are Russian cranberries, the largest American; but if we see a medium berry of which we are not quite sure, then we may conclude that it is most likely a German cranberry. In quality they are all much alike, except that the smaller they are the more full of flavour are they. (*The Housewife*, vol. X, 1895)

Saxon Emblems of the month of August.

As I went over the water,
The water went over me,
I heard an old man crying,
Will you buy me some furmity?

Firmity or Frumenty

This preparation of the grains of wheat is still a common Christmas-eve supper-dish in some of the provinces. Boil a quarter of a pint of wheat in milk for three or four hours, till swelled, but not broken. Then add another quart of new milk or cream, three ounces each of sugar and currants, a stick of cinnamon, or half a grated nutmeg, and boil up a quarter of an hour; then stir in a glass of brandy, and serve in cups.

ANNE BOWMAN, *The New Cookery Book,* 1869

REAPING

MILLING

Furmenty with venison

Take good wheat, and crack it in a mortar, and fan away the husks, and wash the wheat in clean water and let it boil until it breaks apart; then pour away the water and add sweet milk, and set it over the fire. Let it boil until it be thick enough. Add a good quantity of raw yolks of egg, and add Saffron, sugar and salt; but let it boil no more then, but set it on a few coals lest the mixture become cold. Then take fresh venison, and water. Boil it and cut it into thin slices. If it is salted venison, add fresh water, boil it, cut it as it shall be served forth, and then put it into a pot with fresh water and boil it again. And as it boils, blow away the grease. And serve it with the furmenty. Add a little of the broth in the dish all hot with the meat.

HARLEIAN MS. 4016 [c. 1450]

FURMITY, or fermenty, or frumenty was a greatly favored food in England for centuries. Basically it is made from hulled wheat, or sometimes barley, boiled and seasoned to taste. It was served at everyday meals as well as during festive occasions and held an honored place at the feast of the sheepshearers, where, in the words of an old sheepshearer's song, a high bowl was, at breakfast time, "filled full of furmety, where dainty swum the streaking sugar and the spotting plum."

THE NUTMEG

The nutmeg is a native of the Moluccas, and after the possession of these islands by the Dutch, was, like the clove, jealously made an object of strict monopoly. Actuated by this narrow-minded policy, the Dutch endeavoured to extirpate the nutmeg-tree from all the islands except Banda; but it is said that the wood-pigeon has often been the unintentional means of thwarting this monopolizing spirit, by conveying and dropping the fruit beyond these limits; thus disseminated, the plant has been always more widely diffused than the clove. (WILLIAM RHIND, *A History of The Vegetable Kingdom* [c. 1842])

Bobby Shafto's gone to sea,
Silver buckles on his knee;
He'll come back and marry me,
Bonny Bobby Shafto!

Traveller's Bread

Take Graham flour (unsifted); and currants, figs, dates or raisins may be used by chopping them; stir quite stiffly with the coldest water as briskly as possible, so as to incorporate air with it; then knead in all the unbolted wheat flour* you can; cut in cakes or rolls one-half inch thick, and bake in a quick oven.

The Home Cook Book, 1889

Concentrated Coffee

Procure one-half pound of the choicest roasted coffee berries you can command, let the same be ground under your own immediate eye, to prevent the opportunity of chicory or any other spurious drug being introduced among the genuine material. Submit the coffee to a clean saucepan, containing one quart of boiling water, stir it round twice or thrice with a suitably-sized spoon, adding, at the same time, two pieces of fresh white ginger. Place the saucepan over a slow fire, and let it simmer until the quantity of liquor is reduced to one pint; then strain the latter off into a smaller saucepan, and allow the liquor to simmer gently, adding to it at intervals as much white sugar as will qualify the character of a thick consistent syrup, when it may be taken up, and when thoroughly cold poured into jars or bottles, stopped closely down for use. It will keep for any length of time in any climate. An individual, possessing the above confection, may command a cup of strong, genuine coffee at a minute's notice; it is necessary only to introduce two or three teaspoonfuls of the essence into a coffeecup, and fill with boiling water.

S. Annie Frost, *Our New Cook Book,* 1883

Bobby Shafto was a real person who lived in the eighteenth century, and, as a matter of fact, there were actually two men by that name. According to Iona and Peter Opie (*Oxford Book of Nursery Rhymes,* 1951), the original Shafto of the song lived at Hollybrook, County Wicklow, and died in 1737. They note, however, that still more stories connect the song with the election of 1761, when it was used by supporters of one Robert Shafto of Whitworth, candidate for Parliament. Both men were reported bonny, blond, and fair of face.

But other men have gone to sea, and for them there was always the problem of food. Because they could not rely on ship's provisions, the hospitality of strangers, or on the availability of fresh supplies at ports of call, portable foods were a ready answer.

* Unbolted wheat flour = unsifted wheat flour or, in other words, whole wheat flour, also called graham flour.

GRAHAM'S FLOUR

They who would have the very best bread should certainly wash their wheat, and cleanse it thoroughly from all impurities, before they take it to the mill; and

35

when it is properly dried, it should be ground by sharp stones which will cut rather than mash it: and particular care should be taken that it is not ground too fine. Coarsely ground wheat meal, even when the bran is retained, makes decidedly sweeter and more wholesome bread than very finely ground meal. When the meal is ground, it should immediately be spread out to cool before it is put into sacks or casks: — for if it is packed or enclosed in a heated state, it will be far more likely to become sour and musty. And I say again, where families are in circumstances to do wholly as they choose in the matter, it is best to have but little ground at a time; as the freshly ground meal is always the liveliest and sweetest, and makes the most delicious bread. (SYLVESTER GRAHAM, *A Treatise on Bread*, 1837)

* Corn = grain.

Hollow Pipes

[*Macaroni*]

There is a certain victual in the form of hollow pipes, or wafers, with which (as also with oil for his armour, pieces, and other weapons) I furnished Sir *Frances Drake* on his last voyage. This food I am bold to commend in this place because I know that if the masters, owners or Mariners of ships, would advisedly look into it, they should find it one of the most necessary, and cheap provisions that they could possibly make, or carry with them. The particular commendation whereof, rests upon the following:

1. First, it is very durable, for I have kept the same both sweet and sound, for the space of 3 years, and it agrees best with heat, which is the principal destroyer of Sea victuals.

2. It is exceedingly light: for which quality Sir *Frances Drake* did highly esteem it; one man may carry, upon any occasion of land service, enough to feed two hundred men a day.

3. It is speedily prepared, for in one half hour it is sufficiently boiled, and this property saves much fuel which occupies room on a ship.

4. It is fresh, and thereby very pleasing to the Mariner in the midst of his salt meats.

5. It is cheap, for with the dearness of corn,* I dare undertake to feed one man sufficiently for 2 pence a meal.

6. It serves both instead of bread and meat, whereby it performs a double service.

7. Not being all used up it may be laid in store for a second voyage.

8. It may be made as delicate as you please, by the addition of oil, butter, sugar, and such like.

9. There is sufficient material to be had all the year long, for its composition.

10. And if I might once find any good encour-

agement, I would not hesitate but to deliver the same prepared in such manner as that without any further dressing of it, it should be both pleasing, and of good nourishment to a hungry stomach.

All those who are willing to stock their ships with it, if they come to me, I will upon reasonable warning, furnish them therewith to their good contentment.

[HUGH PLATT], *Sundrie new and Artificiall remedies against Famine*, 1596

Drake

Spice Box

To make a Catchup to keep seven Years

Take two quarts of the oldest strong beer you can get, put to it one quart of red wine, three quarters of a pound of anchovies, three ounces of shalots peeled, half an ounce of mace, the same of nutmegs, a quarter of an ounce of cloves, three large races* of ginger cut in slices. Boil all together over a moderate fire, till one third is wasted, the next day bottle it for use; it may be carried to the East-Indies.

ELIZABETH RAFFALD, *The Experienced English House-Keeper*, 1778

KETCHUP

No need to say much about this, which we owe, as we do soy, to the Japanese. It is a godsend to Englishmen, being not only full of flavour in itself, but the foundation of some of the best store-sauces—Harvey and Worcester —to which they fly when their cooks fail. It is the refuge from bad cookery. Pity that nobody seems to know how to spell it. Some write ketchup, others catsup, and I am told that the true Japanese word is kitjap. Here is indeed a puzzle for the spelling bees! ([E. S. DALLAS], *Kettner's Book Of The Table*, 1877)

* Races of ginger = roots or "fingers" of raw ginger.

CHERRY

* "Pemmican" comes from the Cree word "pimikkān," meaning "the least food with the most nourishment."

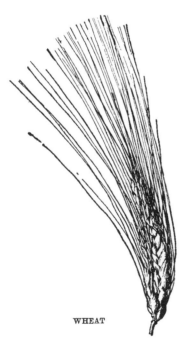

WHEAT

* Blades of green corn = kernels of ripe grain.

Pemmican

Venison, buffalo and beef, are the meats most in favor for the manufacture of pemmican.* Carefully separate the lean from the fat and dry the lean in the sun. This is called "jerked beef." It is cut in thin slices before drying. When dry it is pounded or minced and mixed with melted fat and sometimes dried fruit and compressed into bags. It contains much nutriment and is much in use by travelers on the plains. Explorers around Hudson Bay prepare pemmican by adding sugar to the melted fat and by stirring in with the meat a goodly quantity of wild berries or cherries. This serves instead of jelly. It can be pressed in jars also. It is eaten uncooked, or it may be served like sausage, or prepared in the form of a stew. It is very palatable and nutritious.

MAUD C. COOKE, *Three Meals A Day*, 189—

To make dry Vinegar

To make dry Vinegar which you may carry in your pocket, you shall take the blades of green corn* either Wheat or Rye, and beat it in a morter with the strongest Vinegar you can get till it comes to a paste; then roll it into little balls, and dry it in the sun till it be very hard, then when you have any occasion to use it, cut a little piece thereof and dissolve it in wine, and it will make a strong Vinegar.

[GERVASE MARKHAM], *Countrey Contentments*, 1623

A Travelling Sauce

*(always ready to be used with every kind of **Flesh**, **Fowl**, or **Fish** that require rich Sauces, and will keep good twelve Months; from Mr. Rozelli at the Hague.)*

Take two Quarts of Claret, a quarter of a Pint of Vinegar, and as much Verjuice; put these together in a new Stone-Jar that will admit of being stopp'd close: Put to this a quarter of a Pound of Salt that has been well dry'd over the Fire, an Ounce of Black-Pepper, a Drachm† of Nutmeg beaten fine, and as much Cloves, a Scruple* of Ginger, two or three little Bits of dry'd Orange-Peel, half an Ounce of Mustard-Seed bruised, half a dozen Shallots bruised a little, five or six Bay-Leaves, a little Sprig of Sweet Basil, or Sweet Marjoram, a Sprig of Thyme, and a little Cinnamon; then stop your Jar close, and let the Mixture infuse for twenty-four Hours upon hot Embers: when this is done, strain your Composition through a Linen Cloth, till you have express'd as much Liquor as possible, and put it in a dry Stone Bottle or Jar, and stop it close as soon as 'tis cold. You must keep this in a dry Place, and it will remain good twelve Months. This is a good Companion for Travellers, who more frequently find good Meat than good Cooks. My Author adds, that those who are Admirers of the Taste of Garlick, may add it to this Sauce, or diminish, or leave out any particular Ingredient they do not approve of. It may also be made of Water only, or of Verjuice, or of Wine, or of Orange or Lemon-Juice; but if it is made of Water, it will keep but a Month good: if it be made of Verjuice, it will last good three Months; if we make it of Vinegar, it will last a Year; or of Wine, it will last as long. Use a little of this at a time, stirring it well when you use it.

Professor R. Bradley, *The Country Housewife and Lady's Director,* 1732

CLOVE

There is little to be said of the clove which is not perfectly well known. Suffice it to say that, belonging to the order of myrtles, and best cultivated in the Moluccas, the clove tree is singular in its thirstiness. It so absorbs moisture that nothing will grow under it; and the cloves themselves —that is, the unexpanded flowers of the clove tree, which look drier than the driest teetotaler— will, if water is placed near them, miraculously increase their weight in a few hours. Hence a good amount of cheating on the part of growers and dealers.

It is a pity that the meaning of this word is lost in English. It conveys the most vivid description of the spice to which it refers, for the word is no other than the French *clou de girofle* —that is, a *nail* of the caryophyllum. One of the charms of gastronomy is in its names and the interesting associations which they awaken. It is always to be regretted, therefore, when on the one hand, as too often happens, names are multiplied without reason, and when on the other hand happy names are forgotten or lost in corruption. ([E. S. Dallas], *Kettner's Book Of The Table,* 1877)

† Drachm = three scruples.
* Scruple = the smallest division of weight—$\frac{1}{24}$ ounce.

Come, butter, come,
Come, butter, come;
Peter stands at the gate
Waiting for a butter cake,
Come, butter, come.

THIS OLD CHARM used to be chanted by dairy maids to keep away pixies, and other unseen creatures, who were thought to prevent the butter from "coming" as the milk or cream was churned. The effectiveness of this chant was testified to as long ago as 1656, and Hazlitt quotes from a report of an old woman who went into a house where a maid was churning butter. She had labored a long time, but when she "could not make her butter come, the old woman told the maid what was wont to be done when she was a maid, and also in her mother's young time, that

Butter

Was used by the Hebrews as a food in the Biblical times; but by the early Greeks and Romans only as an ointment; and even at the present day, it is rarely used in the countries along the Mediterranean, being sold chiefly by the apothecaries. The factory system of cheese-making—and its immediate outgrowth, the creamery system of butter-making—have very greatly improved the quality of the butter made in the United States. It is a very sensitive article, and absorbs any odor or flavor with which it comes in contact, and must, therefore, be kept in a cool, dry chamber, where it will be free from all such damage.

Butter is the fatty substance extracted from milk; the milk used in this country being solely that of the cow. The composition of the milk and cream, and consequently the quality and flavor of the butter, depends upon and varies with the breed, age and feed of the cow—all of which circumstances must be taken into consideration in the making of butter. When milk is allowed to stand, the globules of fat rise to the surface and form a layer of cream.

The process of churning consists in the violent agitation of the cream by the action of a dasher, which causes the fat globules to unite, and finally to entirely separate from the watery residue, which is called butter-milk. No other form of churn has yet been invented superior to the old-fashioned dasher-churn. The operation of churning occupies from forty-five minutes to one hour. If the butter comes sooner, it is apt to be frothy; and if much longer, it acquires a very disagreeable flavor.

Butter made from the milk of cows fed on rich pasture is of a deep yellow color; consequently poor and inferior butters are frequently colored with annatto, tumeric or carrot juice. The ordinary way of adulterating butter is by adding a large quantity of salt, so that it may absorb an excessive amount of water, and also increase the weight.

The Grocer's Companion, 1883

if it happened their butter would not come readily, they used a charm to be said over it whilst yet it was in beating, and it would come straightways. This, said the old woman, being said three times, will make your butter come, for it was taught my mother by a learned churchman in Queen Marie's [Mary's] days; whenas churchmen had more cunning, and could teach people many a trick, that our Ministers now a days know not.''

And this rhyme has continued on through the years. Peter and Iona Opie (*Oxford Dictionary of Nursery Rhymes,* 1951) noted that as recently as 1936 it was reported to have been heard to the splash of the churn in southern Indiana, and in the early forties Marjorie Kinnan Rawlings (*Cross Creek Cookery,* 1942) reported a similar version of this chant in Florida.

Almond Butter

Blanch about forty sweet Almonds in warm Water, and put them into cold water, then into a clean Morter, and beat them a little. Then put to them about half a pound of excellent good Sweet Butter, a quantity of Sugar in Powder, but the whitest you can get, and a little Orange-flowerwater: beat all this very well together,

BUTTER SYRINGE

41

and pass it through a Syringe or Squirt with an Iron Pin, forcing it out at the same hole, and then dress it up upon a Plate, and so serve it at discretion.

The Butter of Pistaches is made in the same manner, only you may colour it either red or green.

GILES ROSE, *The Officers of the Mouth,* 1682

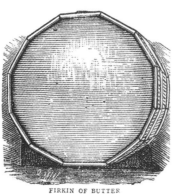

FIRKIN OF BUTTER

To make Fairy Butter

Take the yolks of four eggs boiled hard, a quarter of a pound of Butter; beat two ounces of sugar in a large spoonful of orange flower water, beat them all together to a fine paste. Let it stand two or three hours, then rub it through a colander upon a plate; it looks very pretty.*

ELIZABETH RAFFALD, *The Experienced English House-Keeper,* 1778

* E. Smith (*The Compleat Housewife,* 1739) uses half a pound each of sugar and sweet butter and calls this "French Butter." It is used as are other butters.

Chocolate Butter

Stir quarter of a pound of butter over the fire until quite soft and creamy; put two cakes of good vanilla-flavored chocolate on a tin plate, and add cream until they are soft enough to mix with the butter.† Stir all well together. Serve cold, to use like butter with bread or biscuit.

S. ANNIE FROST, *Our New Cook Book,* 1883

† The butter and chocolate should be only warm enough to be creamed together.

Lobster Butter

Take the spawn and coral of a hen lobster and pound them in a mortar with a little salt and cayenne pepper, and twice their weight in fresh butter. Rub them through a sieve, and put them in a cool place until wanted for use. This butter will keep a long time, and as lobsters with spawn cannot always be obtained, the cook should endeavour to keep some always on hand, as it is needed for sauce, and many dishes made with lobster. It should be of a beautiful red colour. When the spawn cannot be had, pound the shell of the lobster very finely with a quarter of a pound of fresh butter. Put it in a jar, and place this jar in a saucepan of boiling water. Let it boil gently for an hour, then press the butter through a cloth into a basin of cold water. When it has stiffened, lift it from the water, drain it, pass it through a sieve, and mix with it an equal quantity of fresh butter.

Cassell's Dictionary of Cookery [c. 1877]

MAHOGANY DINNER TRAY AND STAND

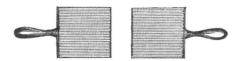

Butter-roller

43

BUTTER PAN

TAMIS

* Tamis = a sieve, strainer or bolting cloth.

Melted Butter—The English Way

I will now describe how to make a small quantity of melted butter, supposing only a quarter of a pound of butter used. First take the butter, and divide it into six equal portions—great accuracy not being essential—take one of these sixth parts and place it in a small enamelled stewpan to melt over the fire, and add to it not quite an equal quantity of flour, a small pinch of pepper, and a *suspicion* of nutmeg. When this little piece of butter is melted, and the flour, &c., well mixed with it, have ready half a tumbler of cold water, and pour the best part of it into the stewpan, and stir it up over the fire till the whole becomes about the same consistency as cream. When this is the case, gradually dissolve in it the remainder of the quarter of a pound of butter, taking care to stir it carefully, and not to apply too great a heat. It will sometimes be found that the melted butter thus made has a tendency to what cooks call "curdle," or to run oily. The moment any symptoms of this appear, add a spoonful of *cold* water, slacken the heat, and stir quickly. When all the butter thus made is dissolved, the whole may be poured into and sent through a tamis,* which causes it to present a much smoother appearance than it otherwise would.

Unfortunately, really good melted butter ought properly to be made from fresh butter; when, therefore, the circumstances of the house allow of fresh butter being used, a little salt must be added. However, very good melted butter can be made from salt or tub butter. We, however, are bound to admit that we live in an age of adulteration; and should it be your fate, therefore, to attempt to make melted butter from butter adulterated with fat, the blame of failure will not be yours, but the widespread dishonesty of the age in which we live. I firmly believe that before long, unless some more stringent laws are passed, successful trade will be incompatible with honesty. Tens of thousands of children die annually in this country from the slow but deadly poison of adulteration.

Cassell's Dictionary of Cookery [c. 1877]

ROLLER BUTTER-PRINT

Rum Butter

Mix with 1 lb. of brown sugar a small grated nutmeg and about 6 oz. of warmed butter, add 1 wineglassful of Rum, and beat the whole up well. Pour the butter on to a dish, and when cold, sift caster sugar over it. Serve with oatmeal biscuits. This is used in the counties of Westmoreland and Cumberland when a child is born; it is given for good luck to the mother and visitors who come to see her.

THEODORE FRANCIS GARRETT, ED., *The Encyclopædia of Practical Cookery* [1892-4]

Butterküchen

(Westphalian Recipe)

Sift three pounds of flour into a basin which has been slightly warmed; make a well in the middle, and put in two cupfuls of caster sugar, seven eggs, the peel of one lemon, and half a pint of milk in which two ounces of yeast have been dissolved. Warm a pound and a half of butter, and add it gradually to the other ingredients; then beat all together briskly. Butter thinly a baking sheet, spread the paste on it to the thickness of three-quarters of an inch, and set it in a warm place to rise. Butter the upper surface of the cake; sprinkle it with coarsely pounded sugar, and bake quickly. It can be varied after the dough has risen, by sprinkling it with a mixture of half a pound of coarsely pounded sugar, three ounces of chopped almonds, and some powdered cinnamon; and put small lumps of butter all over at regular intervals. Prick it well to avoid blisters rising. When taken from the oven, sprinkle it with half a cupful of rose water. It should be eaten fresh, and is generally cut into pieces two inches broad and five long.*

MRS. DE SALIS, *The Housewife's Referee*, 1898

* Brown sugar may also be sprinkled over the top, and the Late Countess Münster (*Dainty Dishes* [1884]) said that instead of the rose-water, either sugar-water or white wine could be used. She also noted: "This is a favourite German cake, made on all great occasions, such as weddings, christenings, etc. At Christmas and Easter, not the poorest peasant is without one, and the very servants in your house would revolt if at these times it was not given to them. It is a curious sight then to see a village baker's—everybody bringing their cake to be baked."

Come up, my horse, to Budleigh Fair;
What shall we have when we get there?
Sugar and figs and elecampane;
Home again, home again, master and dame.

The Fig

(ficus carica)

The traditions of the Greeks carried the origin of the fig back to the remotest antiquity. It was probably known to the people of the East before the *cerealia*; and stood in the same relation to men living in the primitive condition of society, as the banana does to the Indian tribes of South America, at the present day. With little trouble of cultivation, it supplied their principal necessities; and offered, not an article of occasional

THIS RHYME refers to a fair which seems to have been held in an English village that does not exist, and, indeed, may never have existed. There is an *East* Budleigh which was once a market town and may have had a fair. There is Budleigh-*Salterton*, formerly a fishing hamlet and now a fashionable resort. But there seems to have been no *plain* Budleigh.

47

The Fig

BACCHUS

luxury, but of constant food, whether in a fresh or a dried state. As we proceed to a more advanced period of the history of the species, we still find the fig an object of general attention. The want of blossom on the fig-tree was considered as one of the most grievous calamities by the Jews. Cakes of figs were included in the presents of provisions by which the widow of Nabal appeased the wrath of David. In Greece, when Lycurgus decreed that the Spartan men should dine in a common hall, flour, wine, cheese, and figs were the principal contributions of each individual to the general stock. The Athenians considered figs an article of such necessity that their exportation from Attica was prohibited. Either the temptation to evade this law must have been great, or it must have been disliked; for the name which distinguished those who informed against the violators of the law, compounded from συχον, a fig, and φαινω, to shew, became a name of reproach, from which we obtain our word, sycophant. As used by our older writers, sycophant means a *tale-bearer*; and the French employ the word to designate a liar and impostor generally, not a flatterer merely. At Rome the fig was carried next to the vine, in the processions in honour of Bacchus, as the patron of plenty and joy; and Bacchus was supposed to have derived his corpulency and vigour, not from the vine, but from the fig. All these circumstances indicate that the fig contributed very largely to the support of man; and we may reasonably account for this from the facility with which it is cultivated in climates of moderate temperature.

The double, and, in some climates, the treble, crop of the fig tree, is one of the most curious circumstances belonging to its natural history, and further illustrates the value attached to it in the countries of the East. It offers the people fruit through a considerable portion of the year.

But it would seem, from our old writers, and indeed from a common expression even of the present day, that, from some association of ideas, the fig was an object of contempt. "*Figo* for thy friendship," says Pistol. Stevens, the commentator on Shakspear, thinks that the "fig of Spain," mentioned in many of our old poets, alluded "to the custom of giving poisoned figs to those who were the objects of Spanish or Italian revenge;" and hence, probably, a vulgar prejudice against the fruit.

WILLIAM RHIND, *A History of The Vegetable Kingdom* [c. 1842]

To make a Composition of Figs, very cordial

First prepare your Figs ready in a clean vessel, which are to be conserved. Then boil the Honey and skim it well, and being hot put it on the Figs, and let them stand in it till it be cold. This you shall do four or five times, the last time you shall take new Honey and boil it well, and put to it Ginger, Cinnamon and Cloves, then put the Figs in the pot wherein they shall remain, being conserved. These Spices must be beaten small, and set the Figs in a vessel in the sun, and now and then put Honey mixed with the Spices aforesaid, and so the Figs will be conserved.

Epulario, Or, The Italian Banquet, 1598

HONEY

From the most remote antiquity, and in unrefined periods of almost all nations, we find honey to have been used, either as a dish of itself, or an ingredient in others. This would be the case, of course, in those countries, where the industry of the bee, supplied, without trouble, this agreeable article. Its use continued to be general, till the introduction of sugar afforded a sweetener more agreeable to the palate. We meet with it frequently in the bible, as a luxury well known at the patriarchal table. The Greeks also were fond of honey in their dishes. And the Roman cook was continually making use of it. The Danes were very partial to it also, and their favorite beverage, metheglin, was composed chiefly of it. The English possessed the same predilection for it, a predilection which on a particular occasion, proved fatal to a great many of them. For we are told, that the soldiers of Edward I, in marching through Palestine, ate so freely of honey, that vast numbers of them died in consequence of it. (REV. RICHARD WARNER, *Antiquitates Culinariae,* 1791)

The Fig-Tree

DISH OF FIGS

They say that the Fig-tree, as well as the Bay-tree, is never hurt by lightning; and also if you tie a bull, be he ever so mad, to a Fig-tree, he will quickly become tame and gentle. As for such figs that come from beyond the sea, I have little to say, because I write not of exotics; yet some authors say, the eating of them makes people lousy.

NICH. CULPEPPER, GENT., *The English Physician Enlarged,* 1653

Spiced Figs

(Mrs. John Foy, San Bernardino)

One quart of the best vinegar, three pounds of sugar, nine pounds of figs, and two tablespoonfuls of mixed spices, cloves, cinnamon, and a little mace; simmer the fruit in the liquor until tender. Either the purple or the best white figs are delicious prepared in this manner.

LADIES' AID SOCIETY, *Los Angeles Cookery,* 1881

Spitted Fruit

Hastletes* of fruyt: Take figs quartered, raisins whole, dates and almonds whole; and run them on a spit, and roast them; and endore† them yellow with yolks of eggs, and flour, and saffron, mixed together.

The Forme of Cury [c. 1390]

* Hastletes = skewers.

† Endore = gild or baste.

Fig Marmalade

Take fine fresh figs that are perfectly ripe, such as can only be obtained in countries where they are cultivated in abundance. Weigh them, and to every two pounds of figs allow a pound and a half of sugar, and the grated yellow rind of a large orange or lemon. Cut up the figs, and put them into a preserving kettle with the sugar, and orange or lemon rind, adding the juice. Boil them till the whole is reduced to a thick smooth mass, frequently stirring it up from the bottom. When done, put it warm into jars, and cover it closely.

PRESERVING-PAN

Miss Leslie's New Cookery Book, 1857

Inula or Elecampane
(inula helenium)

Natural family, *compositæ; syngenesia polygamia,* of Lennæus. This plant is a native of England, and grows in moist meadows; it is also not unfrequently met with in the cottage garden. The root is perennial, large, thick, branched, externally brown and of a whitish gray within. The stalk is upright, strong, round, striated, hairy, and about four feet in height. The leaves are large, ovate, serrated, crowded with a net-work of veins, with a strong fleshy mid-rib. The flower is very large and yellow. This plant is described as medicinal by Dioscorides and Pliny. The root is the part used; when dried and kept for some time it has a pleasant odour, like that of orris root. Its taste is aromatic, bitter, and pungent.

Elecampane

It yields these qualities to spirits more readily than to water. Its virtues were much extolled by the older physicians; but it has not been found so deserving of praise in modern practice. Indeed, it is now fallen entirely into disuse. Its action, however, is similar to that of the other stimulating and aromatic bitters, and it is used in similar complaints; as in cases of weak digestion, hysterical and nervous complaints.

WILLIAM RHIND, *A History of The Vegetable Kingdom* [c. 1842]

* According to William Rhind (*The Vegetable Kingdom* [c. 1842]), the Eringo roots "formerly used to be candied, and sold in the shops under the name of kissing comfits. They are thus alluded to by Shakespeare."

How to preserve Eringo roots,* Elecampane, and so of others in the same manner

Boil them till they be tender, then take away the piths of them, and leave them in a colander till they have dropped as much as they will. Then having a thin syrup ready, put them being cold into the syrup being also cold, and let them stand so three days. Then boil the syrup (adding some more fresh syrup unto it to supply that which the roots have drunk up) a little higher, and at three days end boil the syrup again without any new addition, unto the full height of a preserving syrup, and put in your roots, and so keep them. Roots preserved in this manner will eat very tender, because they never boiled in the syrup.

[HUGH PLATT], *Delightes for Ladies,* 1603

Male Costume, time of Richard II

Cowardy cowardy custard,
Eat your father's mustard.

Mustard

(sinapis alba, s. nigra)

There are two species of mustard in common use, the white and the black, both annual plants, indigenous to Britain, and found in abundance growing in the fields. Mustard seeds are characterized by a pungent aromatic taste, which is derived from an essential oil of a peculiar kind. The tender leaves are used as a salad, and the ground seed as a condiment to food. Mustard is easily raised in a light soil, and repeated sowings give a succession of tender salad leaves in spring. The seeds strewed in moist flannel, put over a cup, will also quickly germinate, and will afford an agreeable salad in winter, or on board of a ship at sea.

WILLIAM RHIND, *A History of The Vegetable Kingdom* [c. 1842]

Though Mustard-seed is held the
  smallest grain,
His powerful heat and strength
  is not in vain.
By causing tears it purges well
  the brain,
And takes away infecting poisonous pain.

(*The Regiment of Health*, 1617)

MUSTARD PLANT

To make Mustard diverse ways

Have good seed, pick it, and wash it in cold water, drain it, and rub it dry in a cloth very clean; then beat it in a mortar with strong wine-vinegar; and being fine beaten, strain it and keep it close covered. Or grind it in a mustard quern, or a bowl with a cannon bullet.

SYPHON BEER TAP

Otherways

Make it with grape-verjuice, common-verjuice, stale beer, ale, butter, milk, white-wine claret, or juice of cherries.

ROBERT MAY, *The Accomplisht Cook,* 1678

Durham Mustard

A GRINDING MILL

Prior to the year 1720, there was no such luxury as Mustard in its present form at our tables. At that time the seed was coarsely pounded in a mortar, as coarsely separated from the integument, and in that rough state prepared for use. In the year mentioned, it occurred to an old woman of the name of Clements, residing in Durham, to grind the seed in a mill, and pass it through the several processes which are resorted to in making flour from wheat. The secret she kept for many years to herself; and in the period of her exclusive possession of it supplied the principal parts of the kingdom, and in particular the metropolis, with this article. George I.

stamped it with fashion by his approval. (Hence the pots in which the mustard is sold bear the royal initials in a medallion.) Mrs. Clements twice a year travelled to London and the principal towns throughout England for orders. From her residing in Durham, the article acquired the name of "Durham mustard."

JOHN TIMBS, F.S.A., *Things Not Generally Known,* 1856

Mustard of Dijon, or French Mustard

The seed being cleansed, stamp it in a mortar with vinegar and honey. Then take eight ounces of seed, two ounces of cinnamon, two of honey, and vinegar as much as will serve good mustard not too thick. And keep it close covered in little oyster-barrels.

ROBERT MAY, *The Accomplisht Cook,* 1678

Fine French Mustard

Take a gill or two large wine-glasses of tarragon vinegar, (strained from the leaves,) and mix with it an equal quantity of salad oil, stirring them well together. Pound in a mortar, two ounces of mustard seed till it becomes a fine smooth powder, and mix it thoroughly. Add to it one clove of garlic (not more) peeled, minced and pounded. Make the mixture in a deep white-ware dish. If the mustard affects your eyes, put on glasses till you have finished the mixture. When done, put it up in white bottles, or gallipots.

OLIVE OIL

Good olive oil is not over abundant; and that is indeed one of the reasons why many people in England cannot bear it. About 1000 years ago (A.D. 817) it was so scarce in Europe that the council of Aix la Chapelle authorised the priests to manufacture anointing oil from bacon. Imagine divine right shed over kings in the essential oil of swine; and imagine how, as the Hindoo now dies happy with the tail of a cow in his hand, the good Christian of those days went shining to heaven in the extreme unction dropped from a flitch of bacon. We are driven to no such straits in these days, when oil bubbles up in wells, and fortunes are made by striking it from the rock; but still it is not easy to get the oil of Lucca good, and it is much adulterated with inferior kinds. ([E. S. DALLAS], *Kettner's Book Of The Table,* 1877)

THE OLIVE

Cork them tightly, and seal the corks. Send it to table in those bottles.

This mustard is far superior to any other, the tarragon imparting a peculiar and pleasant flavor. It is excellent to eat with any sort of roast meat, particularly beef or mutton, and an improvement to almost all plain sauces, stews, soups, &c.

French mustard is to be purchased very good, at all the best grocery stores.

Miss Leslie's New Cookery Book, 1857

SPOON-WARMER

German Mustard

Take 8 tablespoons of mustard, 4 tablespoons white sugar, 4 tablespoons salt, 1 saltspoon of cayenne pepper, 4 tablespoons of butter, and the juice of 1 large raw onion; mix all well together, and moisten with a little vinegar.

Smiley's Cook Book, 1896

Lumbard Mustard

Take mustard seed and wash it, and dry it in an oven. Grind it dry. Sift it through a sieve. Clarify honey with wine, and vinegar, and stir it all well together, and make it thick enough. And when you will spend it, make it thin with wine.

The Forme of Cury [c. 1390]

Dance to your daddy,
My little babby,
Dance to your daddy, my little lamb!
You shall have a fishy,
In a little dishy,
You shall have a fishy when the boat comes in.

To Seeth a Carp

First take a Carp and boil it in water and salt.
Then take of the broth and put it in a little pot,
then put thereto as much Wine as there is broth,
with Rosemarie, Parsley, Thyme, and marjoram
bound together, and put them into the pot, and
put thereto a good many of sliced Onions, small

Such nursery rhymes as this
were as much to comfort the
mother as to please the child.
Fishing could be hazardous and
sometimes the men did not return. But food was needed and
fish were plentiful, so the boats
continued to go out.

The boats went to sea for other reasons, too. The eating of fish was made compulsory on Fridays, Saturdays, and certain other days during the early reign of Queen Elizabeth (1558–1603). And, according to André Simon in *The Star Chamber Dinner Accounts* (1959), in those early days it was made abundantly clear that "there was no papist superstition about it and that the eating of fish by everybody was a national obligation to support and increase the home fishing fleet, the only nursery there was for recruits for the Queen's Navy."

* A dish of butter = a cup of butter.

† Soppes = small pieces of bread, fried bread, or toast sometimes cut into triangles; also called sops or sippets.

Fish Scaler.

raisins, whole mace, a dish of butter,* and a little sugar, so that it be not too sharp nor too sweet, and let all these seeth together: if the wine be not sharp enough then put thereto a little Vinegar, and so serve it upon soppes† with broth.

[THOMAS DAWSON], *The Second Part of the Good Hus-wives Jewell,* 1597

Bacallao a Viscaino

Take the best of codfish (not haddock) and soak over night in fresh water; take the bones out, then take fresh tomatoes, slice fine into an ordinary stewpan, with just a sprinkling of garlic, onion, parsley, and butter. Then put in a layer of the codfish, then again another layer of tomatoes, etc.—alternately codfish and tomatoes until the stewpan is filled. Set on a slow fire and cook, or rather simmer, for two hours with tight lid. This is a famous Spanish dish.

MAY PERRIN GOFF, ED., *The Household,* 1881

Sauce for stockfish
(cod, haddock, or other air-dried fish)

Take kernels of walnuts, and cloves of garlic, and pepper, bread, and salt, and cast all in a mortar. Grind it small, & mix it up with the same broth that the fish was boiled in and serve it forth.

ASHMOLE MS. 1429 [c. 1430]

Blanche porrey

(White Porridge with Eel)

Take blanched almonds. And grind them, and
draw them with sugar water through a strainer
into a pot making a good thick milk. And then
take the whites of leeks, and cut them small, and
grind them in a mortar with bread. Then add all
to the milk in the pot, and cast thereto sugar and
salt and let boil. Also boil good salted eels in
enough good water, then broil them on a gridiron.
Cut them in good long pieces and lay two or three
in a dish together as you do venison with
furmenty. And serve it forth.

HARLEIAN MS. 4016 [c. 1450]

FISH KETTLE AND DRAINER.

Flounders Boiled

Take a flounder. Cut it open at the side of the
head, and clean it out. Make a sauce of water and
salt, and a good quantity of ale. And when it
begins to boil, skim it and cast the fish thereto.
And let it boil and serve it forth hot; and no sauce
but salt or as a man lust.

HARLEIAN MS. 4016 [c. 1450]

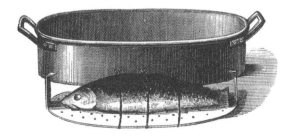

THE COMMON EEL

This fish is known frequently to
quit its native element, and to
set off on a wandering expedition
in the night, or just about the
close of day, over the meadows,
in search of snails and other
prey. It also, sometimes, betakes
itself to isolated ponds, apparently for no other pleasure than
that which may be supposed to
be found in a change of habita-
tion. This, of course, accounts
for eels being found in waters
which were never suspected to
contain them. This rambling disposition in the eel has been long
known to naturalists, and, from
the following lines, it seems to
have been known to the ancients:

"Thus the mail'd tortoise, and
the wand'ring eel,

Oft to the neighbouring beach
will silent steal."

(MRS. ISABELLA BEETON, *The
Book of Household Management,*
1861)

59

LETTUCE

Lettuce is not much cooked in England, and when cooked is not much better than a cabbage; but when raw, and eaten in salad, it has a peculiarly pleasant taste, and has a sedative action upon the nervous system which makes one return to it eagerly, as one returns to tobacco and to opium. The chemists obtain from the lettuce an inspissated juice—called sometimes lactucarium, sometimes lettuce-opium—which is said to allay pain, to slacken the pulse, to reduce animal heat, and to conduce to sleep. When Adonis died, it is reported that Venus threw herself on a lettuce-bed to lull her grief and cool her desires. ([E. S. DALLAS], *Kettner's Book Of The Table*, 1877)

FISHERMAN'S DAUGHTER

Lobster Salad

We almost hesitate to give a recipe for this, because everybody thinks he knows how to make it best; and, indeed, with good materials, it is not easy to go far wrong. Not a bad plan is this: Pick the shells clean; arrange them, empty, handsomely, on a dish, and garnish them with parsley, nasturtium flowers, &c. Put the contents of the shells, properly divided and mixed, into the bottom of a salad bowl; pour over them a liberal quantity of not too piquant sauce, or approved salad mixture. Then hide them under a coverlid of choicest salad hearts, picked leaf by leaf, and augmented with whatever suits your taste. When the soup is removed, announce the lobster salad as the bouquet of the feast; everybody will keep a corner for it. When its turn comes, and the salad-bowl and the dish of shells are placed on the table, you indignantly exclaim, "What a pity! what a shame! what an irremediable misfortune! The cats have eaten the lobster, and left us the shells! I could eat the cats, if caught, out of very spite. As it is, we must eat the salad, and smell of the shells, as canny folk do with their bread and cheese. Brown, will you have the goodness to mix the salad? The dressing, I suppose, is at the bottom. *I* haven't the heart to do it!" Whereupon, to the general comfort, Brown discovers that the lobster salad is *nearly* as good as if he had compounded it himself.

Cassell's Household Guide vol. II [c. 1885]

Oysters à l'Alexandre Dumas

Place in a sauce-bowl a heaped teaspoonful of salt, three-quarters of a teaspoonful of very finely crushed white pepper, one medium-sized, fine, sound, well-peeled, and very finely chopped shallot, one heaped teaspoonful of very finely chopped chives, and half a teaspoonful of parsley, also very finely chopped up. Mix lightly together, then pour in a light teaspoonful of olive oil, six drops of Tabasco sauce, one saltspoonful of Worcestershire sauce, and lastly one light gill, or five and a half tablespoonfuls, of good vinegar. Mix it thoroughly with a spoon; send to the table, and with a teaspoon pour a little of the sauce over each oyster just before eating them.

FILIPPINI OF DELMONICO'S, *The Table*, 1891

DUMAS

Angels on Horseback

Ingredients for dish for 4 persons.—3 thin slices of stale bread, 1 dozen oysters, a few very thin slices of bacon, some finely chopped parsley, a few drops of lemon juice, Nepaul pepper* or cayenne, butter for frying.

Cut the bacon into little squares each large enough to roll round an oyster, sprinkle over each the chopped herbs, lay on the oysters, season with the pepper and a drop of lemon juice, roll up and run on a skewer and fry in butter till the bacon is cooked. Cut the bread into squares or stamp out small rounds and fry them a bright golden colour and on each lay an oyster. Serve very hot garnished with lemon and parsley.

Time.—3 minutes to fry the oysters.

Beeton's Every-Day Cookery and Housekeeping Book [c. 1865]

*Nepaul pepper = a flavorful variety of cayenne from Nepal.

61

"Another bivalve," says Dr. Lancaster, "sometimes eaten by the inhabitants of our coasts is the Razor-Fish (*Solen maximus*). This creature would be interesting enough to us if it were not eaten, on account of its long, slightly-curved, and truncated shells, which resemble the blade of a razor. It is not uncommon on our sandy shores, where it lives buried in the sand. It is not difficult to find, as above the spot into which it has retired it leaves an impression of two holes united, something like a keyhole. It is, however, almost useless to attempt to dig them up, they back away from you so skillfully. After many vain efforts to secure one of these creatures alive, I mentioned my failures to the late Professor Edward Forbes. 'Oh,' he said, with a waggish smile, 'all you have to do is to put a little salt over their holes, and they will come out.' I remembered the story of putting salt on birds' tails; and although I resolved secretly to follow my friend's plan, it was so simple I had not the courage to tell him that I

To pickle Oysters

Take a quart of oysters, and wash them in their own liquor very well, till all the grittiness is out; put them in a sauce-pan or stew-pan, and strain the liquor over them, set them on the fire, and scum them; then put in three or four blades of mace, a spoonful of whole pepper-corns; when you think they are boiled enough, throw in a glass of white-wine; let them have a thorough scald; then take them up, and when they are cold, put them in a pot, and pour the liquor over them, and keep them for use. Take them out with a spoon.

E. SMITH, *The Compleat Housewife*, 1739

Prairie Oyster

serves as a valuable restorative of vital power. The origin of this popular pick-me-up is said to be as follows:

"Some years since three men were encamped on Texas Prairie, 500 miles from the sea-coast, when one of them was sick unto death with fever, and was frantically crying out for oysters; he was quite sure that if he could only have an oyster or two he would be cured. After much thought as to how they were to procure what he wanted, one of them, having procured some prairie hens' eggs, not far from camp, broke one, and putting the yolk into a glass, sprinkled it with a little salt and pepper, adding a little vinegar, and gave it to his sick companion, who declared it was just the thing he wanted; and from that hour he began to get better, and eventually got quite well."

EDWARD SPENCER, *The Flowing Bowl*, 1898

To boil a Pike with Oranges

(a banquet dish)

Take your Pike, split him, and boil him alone with water, Butter, and Salt. Then take an earthen pot and put into it a pint of water, and another of Wine, with two Oranges or Lemons if you have them, if not, then take four or five Oranges, the Rinds being cut away, and sliced, and so put to the licour, with six Dates, cut long ways, and season your broth with Ginger, Pepper, and Salt, and two dishes of sweet Butter, boiling these together, and when you will serve him, lay your Pike upon soppes, casting your broth upon it. You must remember that you cut off your Pikes head hard by the body and have his body split, cutting each side in two or three parts, and when he is done, set the body of the fish back in order: then take his head & set it at the foremost part of the dish, standing upright with an Orange in his mouth, and so serve him.

[THOMAS DAWSON], *The Second Part of the Good Hus-wives Jewell*, 1597

Pike, Stuffed and Roasted

First, open your Pike at the gills, and if need be, cut also a little slit towards the belly: out of these take his guts and keep his liver, which you are to shred very small with thyme, sweet-marjoram, and a little winter-savory: to these put some pickled oysters, and some anchovies, two or three, both these last whole, for the anchovies will melt, and the oysters should not; to these you must add also a pound of sweet butter, which you are to mix with the herbs that are shred, and let them all be well salted: if the Pike be more than a yard

would. I had, however, no sooner got to the seaside than I quietly stole to the pantry, and pocketed some salt, and then went alone at low tide to the sandy shore. As soon as I espied a hole I looked round, for I almost fancied I heard my friend chuckle over my shoulder; however, nobody was there, and down went a pinch of salt over the hole. What I now beheld almost staggered me. Was it the ghost of some razor-fish whose head I had chopped off in digging that now rose before me to arraign me for my malice, or was it a real live razor-fish that now raised its long shell at least half out of the sand? I grasped it, fully expecting it would vanish, but I found I had won my prize. It was a real solid specimen of the species *Solen maximus* that I had in my hand. I soon had a number of others, which were all carried home in triumph. Of course, there were more than were required for the purposes of science, and at the suggestion of a Scotch friend the animals not wanted were made into soup. When the soup was brought to table, our Scotch friend vowed it particularly fine, and ate a basinful with at least twenty razor-fish in it. One tablespoonful satisfied the ladies, whilst I and an English friend declared —against our consciences, I do verily believe—that we had never eaten anything so excellent. I counted the number of the creatures I was able to swallow; it amounted to exactly three. After a tumbler of whisky and water—taken, of course, medicinally—arrangements were made for a dredge in the morning. The Scotchman was up at five, but I and my English friend could not make our appearance. Nightmare and other symptoms of indigestion had fairly upset us, and unfitted us for anything so ticklish as a dredging excursion. Now, I do not wish to say anything against razor-fish as an article of diet, but, from what I have told, they would seem to possess an amount of resistance to the ordinary digestive activity of the stomach that would make it highly desirable to ensure before taking them, such a digestion as a Highlander fresh from his mountain-wilds is known to possess.'' (*Cassell's Dictionary of Cookery* [c. 1877])

THE PIKE

long, then you may put into these herbs more than a pound, or if he be less, then less butter will suffice: these, being thus mixed with a blade or two of mace, must be put into the Pike's belly, and then his belly sewed up, as to keep all the butter in his belly if it be possible; if not, then as much of it as you possibly can, but take not off the scales. Then you are to thrust the spit through his mouth out at his tail; and then take four, or five, or six split sticks or very thin laths, and a convenient quantity of tape or filleting; these laths are to be tied round about the Pike's body from his head to his tail, and the tape tied somewhat thick, to prevent his breaking or falling off from the spit: let him be roasted very leisurely, and often basted with claret wine, and anchovies, and butter mixed together, and also with what moisture falls from him into the pan. When you have roasted him sufficiently, you are to hold under him, when you unwind or cut the tape that ties him, such a dish as you purpose to eat him out of; and let him fall into it with the sauce that is roasted in his belly, and by this means the Pike will be kept unbroken and complete: then to the sauce which was within, and also that sauce in the pan, you are to add a fit quantity of the best butter, and to squeeze the juice of three or four oranges. Lastly, you may either put into the Pike with the oysters two cloves of garlick, and take it out whole when the Pike is cut off the spit; or, to give the sauce a *haut-gout*, let the dish into which you let the Pike fall be rubbed with it: the using or not using of this garlick is left to your discretion.

This dish of meat is too good for any but Anglers, or very honest men; and I trust you will prove both, and therefore I have trusted you with this secret.

IZAAK WALTON, *The Complete Angler,* 1653

Soles in the Portuguese Way

Take one large or two small: if large, cut the fish
in two; if small, they need only be split. The
bones being taken out, put the fish into a pan
with a bit of butter and some lemon juice, give a
fry, then lay the fish on a dish, and spread a
forcemeat over each piece, and roll it round,
fastening the roll with a few small skewers. Lay
the rolls into a small earthen pan, beat an egg
and wet them, then strew crumbs over; and put
the remainder of the egg, with a little meat gravy,
a spoonful of caper liquor, an anchovy chopped
fine, and some parsley chopped into the bottom
of the pan; cover it close, and bake till the fish are
done enough in a slow oven. Then place the rolls
in the dish for serving, and cover it to keep them
hot till the gravy baked is skimmed: if not
enough, a little fresh, flavoured as above, must be
prepared and added to it.

A FISHMONGER

Portuguese stuffing for Soles baked

Pound cold beef, mutton, or veal, a little; then
add some fat bacon that has been lightly fried,
cut small, and some onions, a little garlic, or
shallot, some parsley, anchovy, pepper, salt, and
nutmeg; pound all fine with a few crumbs and
bind it with two or three yolks of eggs.

The heads of the fish are to be left on one side
of the split part, and kept on the outer side of the
roll; and when served the heads are to be turned
towards each other in the dish.

Garnish with fried or dried parsley.

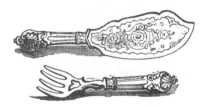

Fish Knife and Fork.

Mrs. Rundell, *Domestic Cookery* [c. 1850]

To Souse or Pickle a Turkey, in Imitation of Sturgeon

Take a fine large Turkey, dress it very clean, dry, and bone it, then tie it up; put into the Pot you boil it in, one Quart of White-wine, one Quart of Water, and one Quart of good Vinegar, and a very large Handful of Salt; let it boil, and scum it well, and then put in the Turkey; when 'tis enough, take it out, and tie it tighter; let the Liquor boil a little longer; and if it wants more Vinegar or Salt, add it when 'tis cold; pour it upon the Turkey, 'twill keep some Months; you eat it with Oil and Vinegar, or Sugar and Vinegar; 'tis more delicate than Sturgeon, and makes a pretty Variety, if that is not to be had; cover it with Fennel, when it is brought to the Table.

[MARY KETTILBY], *A Collection Of above Three Hundred Receipts, By Several Hands,* 1734

FISH-WOMAN OF ABERDEEN

Sweet Sour Fish With Wine

Put on to boil in fish kettle 1 glass water, ½ glass vinegar, 2 tablespoonfuls brown sugar, ½ dozen cloves, ½ teaspoonful ground cinnamon, 1 onion cut in round slices. Boil thoroughly, then strain and add to it 1 lemon cut in round slices, 1 goblet red wine, 1 dozen raisins, 1 tablespoonful pounded almonds; put on stove again, and when it comes to a boil, add fish that has been cut up and salted. Cook until done, remove fish to a platter, and to the liquor add a small piece Lebkucken or ginger cake, and stir in the well-beaten yolks of 4 eggs; stir carefully or it will curdle. If not sweet enough add more sugar.

Pour over fish. Shad or trout is the best fish to use.

MRS. C. F. MORITZ AND MISS ADÈLE KAHN, *The Twentieth Century Cook Book,* 1898

Carved Hunting-Horn of the Sixteenth Century, belonging to Earl Ferrers

Doodledy, doodledy, doodledy, dan;
I'll have a piper to be my good-man;
And if I get less meat, I shall have game,
Doodledy, doodledy, doodledy, dan.

General Observations on Game

The Common Law of England has a maxim, that goods, in which no person can claim any property, belong, by his or her prerogative, to the king or queen. Accordingly, those animals, those *feræ naturæ*, which come under the denomination of game, are, in our laws, styled his or her majesty's, and may therefore, as a matter of course, be granted by the sovereign to another; in consequence of which another may prescribe to possess the same within a certain precinct or lordship. From this circumstance arose the right of lords of manors or others to the game within their respective liberties; and to protect these species of animals, the game laws were originated, and still remain in force. There are innumerable acts of parliament inflicting penalties on persons who may illegally kill game, and some of them are very severe; but they cannot be said to answer their end, nor can it be expected that they ever will, whilst there are so many persons of great wealth who have not otherwise the

A RULE FOR GAMEKEEPERS

Sportsmen will find the following rule of very great advantage to themselves and their Cooks, —to order their gamekeepers (and observe the same themselves) to cut off a Claw of each Bird they kill, denoting the day of the week, thus

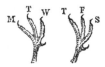

and the Cook should be particular in keeping each week's killing separate. The claws should not be cut off when the Bird is dressed for Table, as they serve to show the Company when it was killed, and consequently how long it has been kept. [Dr. WILLIAM KITCHINER], *The Cook's Oracle*, 1823

67

means of procuring game, except by purchase, and who will have it. These must necessarily encourage poaching, which, to a very large extent, must continue to render all game laws nugatory as to their intended effects upon the rustic population.

That hunting has in many instances been carried to an excess is well known, and the match given by the Prince Esterhazy, regent of Hungary, on the signing of the treaty of peace with France, is not the least extraordinary upon record. On that occasion, there were killed 160 deer, 100 wild boars, 300 hares, and 80 foxes: this was the achievement of one day. Enormous, however, as this slaughter may appear, it is greatly inferior to that made by the contemporary king of Naples on a hunting expedition. That sovereign had a larger extent of ground at his command, and a longer period for the exercise of his talents; consequently, his sport, if it can so be called, was proportionably greater. It was pursued during his journey to Vienna, in Austria, Bohemia, and Moravia; when he killed 5 bears, 1,820 boars, 1,950 deer, 1,145 does, 1,625 roebucks, 11,121 rabbits, 13 wolves, 17 badgers, 16,354 hares, and 354 foxes. In birds, during the same expedition, he killed 15,350 pheasants and 12,335 partridges. Such an amount of destruction can hardly be

Ladies hunting Deer

called sport; it resembles more the indiscriminate slaughter of a battle-field, where the scientific engines of civilized warfare are brought to bear upon defenceless savages.

Mrs. Isabella Beeton, *The Book of Household Management*, 1861

Grace Before Meat

The custom of saying grace at meals had, probably, its origin in the early times of the world, and the hunter-state of man, when dinners were precarious things, and a full meal was something more than a common blessing! when a belly-full was a wind-fall, and looked like a special providence. In the shouts and triumphal songs with which, after a season of sharp abstinence, a lucky booty of deer's or goat's flesh would naturally be ushered home, existed, perhaps, the germ of the modern grace. It is not otherwise easy to understand, why the blessing of food—the act of eating—should have had a particular expression of thanksgiving annexed to it, distinct from the implied and silent gratitude with which we are expected to enter upon the enjoyment of the many other various gifts and good things of existence.

I own that I am disposed to say grace upon twenty other occasions in the course of the day besides my dinner. I want a form for setting out upon a pleasant walk, for a moonlight ramble, for a friendly meeting, or a solved problem. Why have we none for books, those spiritual repasts—a grace before Milton—a grace before Shakespeare—a devotional exercise proper to be said before reading the Faerie Queene?

SAYING GRACE

Charles Lamb, *Essays of Elia*, 1823

* Butter was thickened by heating it with either flour or egg yolks.

To boyle a Rabbet, Capon, or Chickins with Turneps

Boil your Rabbet, Capon, or Chickins very tender in fair water and strained Oatmeal to make them look white. Take half a pint of very good Cream being boiled with whole Mace, likewise put to it a quarter of a pint of thick butter,* a ladle full of stewed Turnips, mingle them well together in a dish, then presently you shall dish up your Rabbet, Capon, or Chickins upon sippets. Then pour your broath upon them, and so let it be served hot to the Table.

JOHN MURRELL, *A Delightfull Daily Exercise,* 1621

† According to the *Oxford English Dictionary,* the word "barbecue" is from the Spanish or Haitian meaning a framework of sticks for supporting meat or fish to be smoked or dried over the fire. The *OED* adds that "the alleged French *barbe à queue* 'beard to tail,' is an absurd conjecture suggested merely by the sound of the word."

Brunswick Stew, Easy

The large gray squirrel is seldom eaten at the North, but is in great request in Virginia and other Southern States. It is generally barbecued, precisely as are rabbits; broiled, fricasseed, or—most popular of all—made into a Brunswick stew. This is named from Brunswick County, Virginia, and is a famous dish—or was—at the political and social pic-nics known as barbecues.† I am happy to be able to give a receipt for this stew that is genuine and explicit, and for which I am indebted to a Virginia housekeeper.

2 squirrels—3, if small.
1 quart of tomatoes —peeled and sliced.
1 pint butter-beans, or Lima.

6 potatoes, parboiled and sliced.
6 ears of green corn cut from the cob.
½ lb. butter.

½ lb. fat salt pork.
1 teaspoonful
ground black
pepper.
Half a teaspoonful
cayenne.

1 gallon water.
1 tablespoonful salt.
2 teaspoonfuls
white sugar
1 onion, minced
small.

Put on the water with the salt in it, and boil five minutes. Put in the onion, beans, corn, pork or bacon cut into shreds, potatoes, pepper, and the squirrels, which must first be cut into joints and laid in cold salt and water to draw out the blood. Cover closely and stew two and a half hours very slowly, stirring frequently from the bottom. Then add the tomatoes and sugar, and stew an hour longer. Ten minutes before you take it from the fire add the butter, cut into bits the size of a walnut, rolled in flour. Give a final boil, taste to see that it is seasoned to your liking, and turn into a soup-tureen. It is eaten from soup-plates. Chickens may be substituted for squirrels.

Marion Harland, *Common Sense in the Household,* 1877

A Coated Hare, or Large Rabbit

The hare, or rabbit, should be large and fat. Save the liver and heart to assist in the gravy, which ought to be made of some pieces of the lean of good fresh beef, seasoned with pepper, salt, and nutmeg, stewed in a small sauce-pan, till all the essence is extracted, adding the chopped liver and heart, and a bit of fresh butter, rolled in flour. Cold fresh meat, or meat that has to be recooked, is unfit for gravy, and so it is for soup. Line the inside of the hare with small thin slices of fat ham, or bacon, and then fill the cavity with a stuffing made of grated bread-crumbs, the

THE BARBECUE

According to Federick Hackwood (*Good Cheer,* 1911):

"Never were more substantial repasts spread than in the baronial halls of our ancient feudal mansions, or in the spacious refectories of old English monasteries. But the barbecue—the animal cooked whole—was the fare provided for the open-air entertainment at great rejoicings.

"When the meat was roasted, it was placed in front of the fire on a spit which needed constant turning. This service was performed by a smoke-jack in the chimney actuated by the ascending current of air, or by a long-bodied 'turn-spit' dog in a wheel-cage, or by a small boy turning a handle. The pulley-wheel which was on the spit was connected to one or other of these motive 'engines' by means of ropes or chains.

"In old kitchens the dog-wheel was generally over the right corner of the chimney-piece, and the dogs employed were long-bodied, crooked-legged creatures. In large establishments, where one dog was insufficient to do all the turning, several were kept, and worked in relays. And some of them were intelligent enough not to do more than their stint.

"With eagerness he still does
    forward tend,
Like Sisyphus, whose journey
    had no end."

"It is related that consternation once reigned in the kitchens and dining-rooms of Bristol, when a sea-captain, to spite the inhabitants, who had been pointedly inhospitable to him, sent out his men one night and stole every turnspit dog that was to be found. The dog it was that 'ruled the roast' in those days.

"The most singular spit in the world was that of the Count de Castel Maria, one of the most opulent lords of Treviso. This spit turned one hundred and thirty different roasts at once, and played twenty-four tunes, and whatever it played, corresponded to a certain degree of cooking, which was perfectly understood by the cook. Thus, a leg of mutton *a l'Anglaise* would be excellent at the twelfth air; a fowl *a la Flamande* would be juicy at the eighteenth, and so on. It would be difficult, perhaps, to carry farther the love of music and gormandising.''

ROYAL PARTY HUNTING RABBITS

grated yellow rind and juice of a lemon, or orange, a piece of fresh butter, some minced sweet marjoram, and the crumbled yolk of one or two hard-boiled eggs. Season the stuffing with a little pepper and salt, and some powdered nutmeg and mace. Fill the body of the hare with this mixture, and sew it up, to keep in the stuffing. Spit the hare, and roast it well, keeping it for a while at a moderate distance from the fire. To baste it, while roasting, make a dressing of the beaten yolks of four eggs, four spoonfuls of flour, a pint of milk, and three tablespoonfuls of salad oil, all well-beaten together. Baste the hare with this till it is thickly coated all over with the batter, taking care it does not burn. Send the gravy to table in a sauce-boat, accompanied by currant, or cranberry jelly.

A very young fawn, or a kid, may be drest in a similar manner. Kids are not eaten after three months old. Till that age their meat is white and delicate. Their flesh, *after* that time, gradually becomes coarse and dark-colored. A very young kid, before it is weaned, is very delicious; but no longer. In the oriental countries, young kids are stuffed with chopped raisins and almonds, or pistachio nuts, previous to roasting; and basted with rich milk, or cream.

For sauce to a kid or fawn, use orange marmalade, or grape jelly.

Miss Leslie's New Cookery Book, 1857

To make Miraus of Spaine

First take Pigeons, Pullets, or Capons, and dress them as if they were to be roasted, and so spit them, and when they are half roasted, take them from the spit, cut them in pieces, which done, put them into an earthen pot. Then take almonds scorched on hot embers, and wipe clean, & without more wiping of them stamp them in a mortar: then take toasted bread with three or four yolks of eggs, and stamp them with the almonds, and mix them with a little vinegar and broth strained through a cloth, and then put them into the meat, and set them on the coals with a good store of spice, especially Cinnamon and Saffron, and Sugar enough, and let it boil for the space of an hour, stirring it with a spoon, and when it is boiled, send it to the table in a flat dish or platter, or else in pottage which is most convenient.

Epulario, Or, The Italian Banquet, 1598

A NOTE ON THE CAPON

According to Frederick Hackwood (*Good Cheer,* 1911), "The cock, always honoured as a warlike bird, did not at first enjoy a high culinary reputation in Rome. And when that tyrant of the kitchen, C. Fannius, the Consul, thought that hens, owing to the enormous consumption of them, would soon become extinct, he ordered that for the future Romans should dispense with fattening and eating this delicious table bird. But the law said nothing about cocks, a silence which saved Roman gastronomy, for the capon was invented."

Pheasant à la Gitana

Truss a pheasant as for boiling, put it in a stewpan with half a pound of streaky bacon cut in squares of about an inch; add an ounce of butter and a clove of garlic; fry all together over the fire, until the pheasant has become equally browned all over; then pour off all grease, add two Portugal onions, and four ripe tomatas, sliced thin, and two glasses of sherry; put the lid on, and set the stewpan to stew gently over a slow fire for about three-quarters of an hour, gently shaking the pheasant round occasionally; just before dishing up, add a teaspoonful of sweet red Spanish pepper.*

NOTE: All kinds of game and poultry, or indeed, all kinds of meat, or firm-fleshed fish, are most excellent when dressed à la Gitana, or gipsy fashion.

CHARLES ELMÉ FRANCATELLI, *The Cook's Guide,* 1884

CROSS-BOW SHOOTING AT SMALL BIRDS

* Sweet red Spanish pepper = paprika.

73

The Bison.

* Indian meal = corn meal.

Squatter's Soup

Take plenty of *fresh-killed* venison, as fat and juicy as you can get. Cut the meat off the bones and put it (with the bones) into a large pot. Season it with pepper and salt, and pour on sufficient water to make a good rich soup. Boil it slowly (remembering to skim it well) till the meat is all in rags. Have ready some ears of young sweet corn. Boil them in a pot by themselves till they are quite soft. Cut the grains off the cob into a deep dish. Having cleared the soup from shreds and bits of bone left at the bottom of the pot, stir in a thickening made of indian meal* mixed to a paste with a little fresh lard, or venison gravy. And afterwards throw in, by degrees, the cut corn. Let all boil together, till the corn is soft, or for about half an hour. Then take it up in a large pan. It will be found very good by persons who never were squatters. This soup, with a wild turkey or a buffalo hump roasted, and stewed grapes sweetened well with maple sugar, will make a good backwoods dinner.

Miss Leslie's New Cookery Book, 1857

Venison Pasty

The venison pasty stands aloof from all other game pies, inasmuch as it should contain venison only. The mixture of other game, of forcemeat, of eggs, degrades the pasty from its high, ancient dignity. It is no longer the venison pasty dear to the knights of the age of chivalry, and to Robin Hood, in the forest of Sherwood; but a modern game pie. The neck and breast of venison are the best parts for the pasty; these should be washed in vinegar, sprinkled with sugar, and hung in a

ROBIN HOOD'S GRAVE.

cool dry place for a fortnight, being often taken down and wiped with a clean dry cloth. Before using the venison, dip it into warm water, and dry it; bone it, and then cut it up for the pie. Make a stiff short paste, very good; line the baking-dish entirely; then lay in the breast at the bottom, cut into two pieces, with some thin slices of fat over it; season with pepper and salt only; then lay in small steaks from the neck, always laying the fat in thin slices over, that in cutting the pieces may be sliced through to the bottom of the pasty, each slice having the due proportion of fat and lean. When the dish is filled, put in from half to a whole pound of butter, as may be needed, and a quarter of a pint of water; cover with the paste, and make an opening and a small chimney of paste in the middle; put a rolled card in it to keep it open; brush the pie over with egg and ornament it. Then bake it in a well-heated oven from three to four hours, according to size. In the meantime put the bones into a stewpan, with a dozen peppercorns, two teaspoonfuls of salt, a quarter of an ounce of mace, and three pints of cold water, and let them stew gently till half reduced; then strain the liquor, leave it to cool, that the fat may be removed, and when the pie is baked, heat this gravy in a stewpan with a glass of port wine and a teaspoonful of lemon-juice; take the card from the chimney of the pasty, and through a funnel pour it in, shaking the dish round that it may penetrate to all parts. This pie will keep well, and be good, if properly carved, cold as hot.

ANNE BOWMAN, *The New Cookery Book*, 1869

HUNTING STAG

Pastry for Venison Pasty

Pastry for venison pasty* should be good and short, but stiff. For a rich pastry, it may be made in the proportion of ten ounces of butter to one pound of flour, and worked to a smooth stiff paste with two eggs and a little lukewarm water. For an ordinary pasty, rub three or four ounces of butter into a pound of flour, and work it to a smooth stiff paste with a beaten egg and a little lukewarm water.

Cassell's Dictionary of Cookery [c. 1877]

* Giles Rose (*The Officers of the Mouth*, 1682) recommends using rye flour.

Agra Dolce

(Sour Sweet)
(An Italian Sauce Used with Venison, Sweetbreads, Calf's-Head, and Mutton)

Mix together two heaping tablespoonfuls of brown sugar, one quarter bar of grated chocolate, one tablespoonful each of shredded candied orange and lemon-peel, ten blanched almonds shredded, one half cupful of currants, and one cupful of vinegar. Let them soak for two hours. Then pour it over the cooked meat, and simmer for ten minutes.

This receipt was obtained in Florence, and is a well-known and favorite sauce.

Mary Ronald, *The Century Cook Book*, 1895

The old Currant-Sauce for Venison

Boil an ounce of dried currants in half a pint of water a few minutes; then add a small tea-cupful of bread-crumbs, six cloves, a glass of port wine, and a bit of butter. Stir it till the whole is smooth.

[MARIA ELIZA RUNDELL], *The Experienced American House-keeper*, 1836

GRAVY KETTLE

Pevorat* for veal and venison

Take bread and fry it in grease. Mix it up with broth and vinegar. Take powder of pepper and salt, add to it, and set it on the fire. Boil it and serve it forth.

The Forme of Cury [c. 1390]

* Pevorat = peverade, from the pepper of which it is principally composed.

Hunting-flask

As to the best compound for a hunting-flask, it will seldom be found that any two men perfectly agree; yet, as a rule, the man who carries the largest, and is most liberal with it to his friends, will be generally esteemed the best concocter. Some there are who prefer to all others a flask of gin into which a dozen cloves have been inserted, while others, younger in age and more fantastic in taste, believe in equal parts of gin and noyeau, or of sherry and Maraschino. For our own part, we must admit a strong predilection for a pull at a flask containing a well-made cold punch, or a dry Curaçoa. Then, again,

Robert Burns

According to Frederick Hackwood (*Good Cheer,* 1911), "While alive, animals reared and fattened for food retained their Saxon names, being tended by Saxon servants; but when they were killed and cooked and brought to table, they were dignified with Norman names. Bacon retained its Saxon name because the Normans despised it. In *Ivanhoe* we read: 'Swine is called pork when carried to the castle hall to feed the nobles.'"

Saxon	*Norman*
cow, ox, or steer	beef
sheep	mutton
sow or swine	pork
fowl	pullet
calf	veal
deer	venison

if we take the opinion of our huntsman, who (of course) is a *spicy* fellow, and ought to be up in such matters, he recommends a piece of dry ginger always kept in the waistcoat pocket; and does not care a *fig* for anything else. So much for difference of taste: but as we have promised a recipe, the one we venture to insert is specially dedicated to the lovers of usquebaugh, or "the crathur:" it was a favourite of no less a man than Robert Burns, and one we believe not generally known; we therefore hope it will find favour with our readers.

To a quart of whisky add the rinds of two lemons, an ounce of bruised ginger, and a pound of ripe white currants stripped from their stalks. Put these ingredients into a covered vessel, and let them stand for a few days; then strain carefully, and add one pound of powdered loaf sugar. This may be bottled two days after the sugar has been added.

Cups and Their Customs, 1869

Nutritious Soup for the Laborious Poor

The Cook should save the boiling of every piece of Meat, Ham and Tongue, however salt, and by adding bones, barley, the Trimmings of the Vegetables and the odds and ends otherwise wasted, and by putting them on as soon as the dinner is served, to save a second fire, very nutritious Soups for the laborious Poor can be obtained, affording them better Nourishment than they would otherwise get. What a Relief to the labouring Husband instead of Bread and Cheese, to have a warm comfortable Meal! to the sick, aged and infant branches how important an advantage! nor less to the industrious Mother, who often forbears that others may have a larger Share.

MARGARET HUNTINGTON HOOKER, Yᵉ Gentlewoman's House-wifery, 1896

Russian Balorine

(Time, a few minutes)

Roast or boiled beef; spring onions; boiled beetroot; a small quantity of caraway seeds; a bunch of spinach or sorrel; eggs; whiskey.

Cut some cold roast or boiled beef into small pieces; add to them some spring onions cut small, some slices of boiled beetroot, and a small quantity of caraway seeds; place all these in a *purée* of spinach or of sorrel, and add half a glass of whiskey. Serve with hard-boiled eggs chopped up in it.

AGATE SEAMLESS STOVE-POT

MARY JEWRY, ED., *Warne's Model Cookery,* 1893

DINNER PARTY

To farce a Cabbage for a banquet dish

Take a little round cabbage cutting off the Stalk, then make a round hole in your cabbage, as much as will receive your forcing meat. Take heed you break not the brims thereof with your knife, for the hole must be round and deep. Then take the Kidney of a mutton or more, and chop it not small. Then boil six Eggs hard, taking the yolks of them and also take raw Eggs and a manchet* grated fine. Then take a handful of prunes, as many great raisins, seasoning all these with Salt, pepper, Cloves and Mace, working all these together, and stuff your Cabbage. But if you have Sausage you may put it among your meat at the putting in of your stuff, but you must leave out both the ends of your sausage at the mouth of the Cabbage when you shall serve it out. In the boiling, it must be within the Cabbage, and the cabbage must be stopped close with his cover in the time of his boiling, and bound fast round for fear of breaking; the cabbage must be boiled in a deep pot with fresh beef broth or mutton broth, and no more than will lie up to the top of the cabbage. And when it is enough, take away the thread, and so set it in a platter, opening the head and laying out the sausage ends, and so serve it forth.

[THOMAS DAWSON], *The Second Part of the good Hus-wives Jewell*, 1597

* Manchet = "The finest kind of wheaten bread" (*Oxford English Dictionary*)

80

Beef Cheese

Take three parts* of beef steak from any fleshy part of the animal, and one part equally composed of lean veal and uncooked ham; chop them together as finely as possible; cut a piece of white bacon into small dice, and mix it with the minced meat; season with salt, pepper, allspice, chopped parsley, and chives or green onions, half a clove of garlic, bay-leaf, sprig of thyme, and half a wine-glassful of brandy. Line the bottom of an earthen pâté-dish with thin slices of bacon; on this place the seasoned mincemeat; cover with more thin slices of bacon. Put the cover on the dish; lute it down with paste made of flour and vinegar, and send it to pass the night in a very slow baker's oven. Let the beef cheese cool and stiffen in the celler for twenty-four hours before opening or cutting it up. This makes a useful, nutritious, and economical dish to help out a cold dinner, where there are many children, or guests to serve in a hurry, and where bones are inconvenient, as in travelling, and on many occasions of an active and busy life.

Cassell's Dictionary of Cookery [c. 1877]

Gravey

Cut a piece of beef into thin slices and fry it brown in a stew-pan with 2 or 3 onions, 2 or 3 lean slices of bacon, then pour to it a ladle or 2 of strong broth, rubbing the brown off from the pan very clean, add to it more Strong broth, claret, white wine, anchovies, a faggot of sweet-herbs, season it and let it stew very well, then strain it off.

E. KIDDER, *Receipts of Pastry and Cookery* [c. 1730]

* Parts = pounds.

ANCIENT FORKS

From a passage in that curious work, Coryate's *Crudities,* it has been imagined that its author, the strange traveller of that name, was the first to introduce the use of the fork into England, in the beginning of the seventeenth century. He says that he observed its use in Italy only "because the Italian cannot by any means endure to have his dish touched with fingers, seeing all men's fingers are not alike clean." These "little forks" were usually made of iron or steel, but occasionally also of silver. Coryate says he "thought good to imitate the Italian fashion by this forked cutting of meat," and that hence a humorous English friend, "in his merry humour, doubted not to call me *furcifer,* only for using a fork at feeding." This passage is often quoted as fixing the earliest date of the use of forks; but they were, in reality, used by our Anglo-Saxon forefathers, and throughout the middle ages. In 1834, some labourers found, when cutting a deep drain at Sevington, North Wilts, a deposit of seventy Saxon pennies,

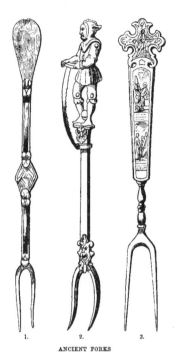

ANCIENT FORKS

Beef à la Mode

(L. S. Williston, Heidelberg, Germany)

In a piece of the rump, cut deep openings with a sharp knife; put in pieces of pork cut into dice, previously rolled in pepper, salt, cloves and nutmeg. Into an iron stew-pan lay pieces of pork, sliced onions, slices of lemon, one or two carrots and a bay-leaf; lay the meat on and put over it a piece of bread-crust as large as the hand, a half-pint wine and a little vinegar, and afterwards an equal quantity of water or broth, till the meat is half covered; cover the dish close and cook till tender. Then take it out, rub the gravy thoroughly through a sieve, skim off the fat, add some sour cream, return to the stew-pan and cook ten minutes. Instead of the cream, capers or sliced cucumber pickles can be added to the gravy if preferred, or a handful of grated ginger-bread or rye bread. The meat can also be laid for some days before in a spiced vinegar or wine pickle.

Buckeye Cookery, 1883

of sovereigns ranging from Cœnwulf, king of Mercia (796 A.D.), to Ethelstan (878–890 A.D.); they had been packed in a box of which there were some decayed remains, and which also held some articles of personal ornament, a spoon, and *the fork,* which is first in the group here engraved. The fabric and ornamentation of this fork and spoon would, to the practised eye, be quite sufficient evidence of the approximate era of their manufacture, but their juxtaposition with the coins confirms it. It must not, however, be imagined that they were frequently used;

Ham Pasty

One pound fine flour, two ounces of butter, one egg, a quarter of a pint of thick sour cream: mix this together with a knife into a paste, cut it into several pieces, which roll out quite thin. Butter a mould or an iron saucepan, and cover it at the bottom and round the sides with the paste. Take the remains of a boiled ham, lean and fat, mince it fine, with an onion, beat five eggs up with half a pint of thick cream, stir a large soup-plateful of the minced ham and onion up with this, season with a little pepper and nutmeg, spread a layer of this purée on the paste at the bottom of the mould about as thick as a finger, then cover this with a round leaf of the paste, rolled quite thin, then another layer of the ham, and so on to the end, finishing with the paste. Bake one hour in a hot oven, turn it out and serve. It is excellent.

LADY HARRIET ST. CLAIR (LATE COUNTESS MÜNSTER), *Dainty Dishes* [1884]

Lancashire Hot-Pot

Procure a ''hot-pot dish,'' or wide brown stew-pot. Take 2 or 3 lbs. of mutton chops freed from most of the fat and the long bones, 4 mutton kidneys, 3 small onions, and 25 oysters. Put chops at the bottom of the pot, then a layer of sliced kidney (previously soaked for an hour in warm water), some shred onion, 4 or 5 bearded oysters, a sprinkling of pepper, salt, and a good pinch of currie powder; upon these place a layer of sliced potatoes; repeat this till all the ingredients are in. Put potatoes at the top. Add the strained liquor from the oysters and half-a-pint of water or unsalted gravy; cover the pot close, and bake it in a moderate oven till the meat is tender; add (by degrees) if required, a little more gravy or water to prevent it getting too dry. When done, have ready some good gravy (if possible, made of the remains of game or poultry), boil the gravy, and just before serving pour it into the dish. The potatoes at the top are sometimes left whole. Serve in the dish in which it is cooked; a brown pot may have a napkin pinned round it. TIME—About 3 hours.

B. M., *Cookery for the Times*, 1870

indeed, throughout the middle ages, they seemed to have been kept as articles of luxury, to be used only by the great and noble in eating fruits and preserves on state occasions. A German fork, believed to be a work of the close of the sixteenth century is the second of our examples. It is surmounted by the figure of a fool or jester, who holds a saw. This figure is jointed like a child's doll, and tumbles about as the fork is used, while the saw slips up and down the handle. It proves that the work was treated merely as a luxurious toy. Indeed, as late as 1652, Heylin, in his *Cosmography*, treats them as a rarity: "the use of silver forks, which is by some of our spruce gallants taken up of late," are the words he uses. A fork of this period is the third of our selected examples; it is entirely of silver, the handle elaborately engraved with subjects from the New Testament. It is one of a series so decorated, the whole of our engraved examples being at present in the collection of Lord Londesborough. In conclusion, we may observe that the use of the fork became general by the close of the seventeenth century. (R. CHAMBERS, ED., *The Book of Days*, vol. II, 1862–4)

Gravy Strainer

* Instead of the caul, the liver may be larded.

Calf's Liver roasted and stuffed

Having washed and wiped the liver, cut a long hole in it, and fill with a forcemeat of grated bread, an anchovy chopped, fat bacon chopped, sweet herbs and an onion finely shred, a bit of butter, the yolk of an egg, salt and pepper: sew up the hole, and having covered the liver with a caul,* roast it gently: serve with gravy made from bones of any kind, with an onion, sweet herbs, a gill of table beer, and the same of water; all well stewed, and strained over the liver.

JOHN FARLEY, *The London Art of Cookery*, 1811

Minced Veal, Plain

(Second dressing)

Chop three-quarters of a pound of cold veal, season with the tenth part of a nutmeg, grated, a saltspoonful of white pepper, a piled saltspoonful of salt, the grated rind of half a lemon, a tablespoonful of baked flour. Rub a stewpan three times across the bottom with a piece of garlic; put in the veal, with a teacupful of gravy and a tablespoonful of mushroom ketchup; simmer very gently for twenty minutes, keeping the mince stirred; add the juice of half a lemon, and serve. Garnish with rolled thin rashers of bacon toasted before the fire, or with three cornered bread sippets fried to a pale brown colour in good butter.

Minced Veal White

Prepare and season the veal as directed in the preceding receipt; put it in a stewpan, with a gill of new milk, and simmer gently for twenty minutes, stirring constantly; add half a gill of thick cream, and serve. Garnish with cut lemon.

Cre-Fydd's Family Fare, 1874

Mushroom Catsup

If you love GOOD CATSUP, gentle reader, make it yourself, after the following directions, and you will have a delicious Relish for Made dishes, Ragouts, Soups, Sauces, or Hashes.

Look out for Mushrooms from the beginning of September.

Take care they are the right sort, and *fresh gathered*. Full grown Flaps are to be preferred: put a layer of these at the bottom of a deep earthen pan, and sprinkle them with Salt, then another layer of Mushrooms, and some more salt on them, and so on alternately, salt and mushrooms;—let them remain two or three hours, by which time the salt will have penetrated the mushrooms, and rendered them easy to break;—then pound them in a mortar or mash them well with your hands, and let them remain for a couple of days, not longer, stirring them up, and mashing them well each day;—then pour them into a stone jar, and to each quart add an ounce of whole Black Pepper; stop the jar very close, and set it in a stew-pan of boiling water, and keep it boiling for two hours at least.—Take out the jar, and pour the juice clear from the settlings through a hair sieve (without squeezing the mushrooms) into a clean stewpan; let it boil very gently for half an hour; those who are for SUPERLATIVE CATSUP, will continue the boiling till the Mushroom juice is reduced to half the quantity, it may then be called *Double Cat*-sup or DOG-sup.

[DR. WILLIAM KITCHINER], *The Cook's Oracle*, 1823

Double Mincing Knife

† Robert May, in 1678, suggested that bacon could be used instead of the beef suet.

Neats-tongue roasted

Take a Neats-tongue* tenderly boiled, blanched, and cold. Cut a hole in the butt-end, and mince the meat that you can take out. Then put some sweet Herbs finely minced to it, with a minced Pippin or two, the yolks of Eggs sliced, some minced Beef-suet,† beaten Ginger and Salt. Fill the Tongue and stop the end with a Caul of Veal, lard it and roast it. Make your Sauce with Butter, Nutmeg, Gravy, and juice of Oranges: Garnish the Dish with sliced Lemon and Barberries.

HANNAH WOOLLEY, *The Gentlewomans Companion*, 1673

French Pot au Feu

This is one of the national dishes of France. The following is a genuine French receipt, and it would be found very palatable and very convenient if tried in our own land of plenty. The true French way to cook it is in an earthen pipkin, such as can be had in any pottery shop. The French vessel has a wide mouth, and close-fitting lid, with a handle at each side, in the form of circular ears. It is large and swelling in the middle, and narrows down towards the bottom. The American pipkin has a short thick spout at one side, and stands on three or four low feet. No kitchen should be without these vessels, which are cheap, very strong, and easily kept clean. They can sit on a stove, or in the corner of the fire, and are excellent for slow cooking.

The wife of a French artisan commences her pot au feu soon after breakfast, prepares the ingredients, puts them, by degrees, into the pot, attends to it during the day; and when her hus-

French *Pot-au-Feu*; or, Earthen Soup Pot

band has done his work she has ready for him an excellent and substantial repast, far superior to what in our country is called a *tea-dinner*. Men frequently indemnify themselves for the poorness of a tea-dinner by taking a dram of whiskey afterwards. A Frenchman is satisfied with his excellent pot au feu and some fruit afterwards. The French are noted as a temperate nation. If they have eaten to their satisfaction they have little craving for drink. Yet there is no country in the world where so much good eating might be had as in America. But to live well, and wholesomely, there should also be good cooking, and the wives of our artisans must learn to think more of the comfort, health, and cheerfulness of him who in Scotland is called the *bread-winner*, than of their own finery, and their children's uncomfortable frippery.

I   Coupe perpendiculaire.

Receipt. — For a large pot au feu, put into the pipkin six pounds of good fresh beef cut up, and pour on it four quarts of water. Set it near the fire, skim it when it simmers, and when nearly boiling, add a tea-spoonful of salt, half a pound of liver cut in pieces, and some black pepper. Then add two or three large carrots, sliced or grated on a coarse grater; four turnips, pared and quartered; eight young onions peeled and sliced thick, two of the onions roasted whole; a head of celery cut up; a parsnip split and cut up; and six potatos, pared, sliced, or quartered. In short any good vegetables now in season, including tomatos in summer and autumn. Also a bunch of sweet herbs, chopped small. Let the whole continue to boil slowly and *steadily;* remembering to skim well. Let it simmer slowly five or six hours. Then, having laid some large slices of bread in the bottom of a tureen, or a very large pan or bowl, pour the stew or soup upon it; all the meat, and all the vegetables. If you have any

II   Coupe horizontale.

III   Coupe transversale.

left, recook it the next morning for breakfast, and *that day* you may prepare something else for dinner.

For beef you may substitute mutton, or fresh venison, if you live in a venison country, and can get it newly killed.

Miss Leslie's New Cookery Book, 1857

Ancient Salt-Cellar at New College, Oxford

To Make Sausages Without Guts

Take a Pound of lean Mutton, and a Quarter of a Pound of Beef-suet shred very small, and beat it in a Mortar to a fine Paste, season it with *Jamaica** and Black-pepper, Nutmeg, Salt, Thyme, Sweet-marjoram and Parsley; then drudge Flour on the Table, and roll the Sausage with your Hands into Rolls the Thickness of Sausages, and make them into various Shapes, as O, S, C, X, or in any other Shape as your Fancy directs: And when you have Turkey-pouts or Chickens roasted or boiled, lay these Sausages on a Tin-pan and set them in a quick Oven, or before the Fire and broil them, and lay round and over the Fowl or Fowls, with Gravy on the Dish.

Ann Cook, *Professed Cookery,* 1760

* Jamaica = allspice.

PARAGON MINCING MACHINE.

An Irish Stew

Take three pounds of thick mutton cutlets from the loin, and remove the fat. Slice thick five pounds of fine potatos that have been previously pared. Place a layer of meat in the bottom of a stew-pan, or an iron pot, and lay some of the potatos upon it. Season all with salt and pepper. Upon this another layer of meat—then some potatos again, then meat, and so on till all is in, finishing with potatos at the top. Pour in a pint of cold water. Let it simmer gently for two hours or more, till the meat and potatos are thoroughly done. Serve it up very hot, meat and potatos, on the same dish. If approved, you may add, from the beginning, one or two sliced onions.

A similar stew may be made of beef steaks and potatos.

You may stew pork cutlets in the same manner, but with *sweet* potatos, split and cut in long pieces, or with yams. The seasoning for the pork should be minced sage.

This is a very plain, but very good dish, if made of nice fresh meat and good potatos, and well cooked.

Miss Leslie's New Cookery Book, 1857

White Scotch Collops

(Lady Clarke)

Cut your veal thin, and hack it well with a rolling pin. Then beat up the yolks of three or four Eggs, and dip every piece in. Then have ready your Stew-pan with a piece of butter in it, and put them into it to fry. You must put one Onion into the butter whole before you put in the meat; when they are fried enough, which they will soon be, for if they are long a-doing they turn brown, then put in one Anchovy; when that is melted, put in some Cream, which must be proportioned according to the quantity you make, and roll some butter in some flour and thicken it up *&* serve it.

The Receipt Book of Mrs. Ann Blencowe, 1694

Irish stew is a white ragout of mutton with potatoes for the chief garnish. The beautiful simplicity of the Irish stew would be lost if it were allowed in any way to brown. The potatoes are so important in it that they are always double the weight of the meat, and the only other vegetable that they go with is the onion —which may be much or little according to taste. In the true Irish stew, too, both potatoes and onions are exceedingly well done, so that they are half reduced to a mash.

In Scotland they produce exactly such a stew, cover it over with a crust, and call it Shepherd's pie. In Devonshire and Cornwall they make this pie, put apples into it instead of potatoes, and announce it as Devonshire, Cornish, or Squab pie. ([E. S. DALLAS], *Kettner's Book Of The Table,* 1877)

Far from home across the sea
    To foreign parts I go;
When I am gone, O think of me
    And I'll remember you.
Remember me when far away,
    Whether asleep or awake,
Remember me on your wedding day
    And send me a piece of your cake.

Marriage Customs in Old New England

The "coming out," or, as it was called in New-buryport, "walking out" of the bride was an important event in the little community. Cotton Mather wrote in 1713 that he thought it expedient for the bridal couple to appear as such publicly, with some dignity. We see in the pages of Sewall's diary one of his daughters with her new-made husband leading the orderly bridal procession of six couples on the way to church, observed of all in the narrow Boston street and in the Puritan meeting-house. In some communities the bride and groom took a prominent seat in the gallery, and in the midst of the sermon rose to their feet and turned around several times slowly, in order to show from every point of view their bridal finery to the admiring eyes of their assembled friends and neighbors in the congregation.

Throughout New England, except in New Hampshire, the law was enforced for nearly two centuries, of publishing the wedding banns three times in the meeting-house, at either town meeting, lecture, or Sunday service. Yet in the early days of the colonies the all-powerful minister could not perform the marriage ceremony—a magistrate, a captain, any man of dignity in the community could be authorized to marry Puritan lovers, save the parson. Not till the beginning of the eighteenth century did the Puritan minister assume the function of solemnizing marriages. Gov. Bellingham married himself to Penelope Pelham when he was a short time a widower and forty-nine years old, and his bride but twenty-two. When he was "brought up" for this irregularity he arrogantly and monopolizingly persisted in remaining on the bench to try his own case. "Disorderly marriages" were punished in

MRS.

An old custom of the last century is being revived—the custom of calling all women Mrs., the abbreviation of Mistress—whether married or single. This was the general custom in England in the olden time. "Miss" was confined to boarding-schools and to young ladies under twenty-five. (*Godey's Lady's Book*, October, 1874)

BRIDE CAKE.

many towns; doubtless many of them were between Quakers. Some couples were fined every month until they were properly married. A very trying and unregenerate reprobate in New London persisted that he would "take up" with a woman in the town and make her his wife without any legal or religious ceremony. This was a great scandal to the whole community. A pious magistrate met the ungodly couple on the street and serenely reproved them thus: "John Rogers, do you persist in calling this woman, a servant, so much younger than yourself, your wife?"

"Yes, I do," violently answered John.

"And do you, Mary, wish such an old man as this to be your husband?"

"Indeed I do," she answered.

"Then," said the governor, coldly, "by the laws of God and this commonwealth, I as a magistrate pronounce you man and wife."

"Ah! Gurdon, Gurdon," said the groom, married legally in spite of himself, "thee's a cunning fellow."

ALICE MORSE EARLE, *Customs and Fashions in Old New England,* 1893

The Countess of RUTLANDS Receipt of making the rare Banbury Cake, which was so much praised at her Daughter (the right Honourable the Lady CHAWORTHS) Wedding

Take a peck of fine Flour, and half an Ounce of large Mace, half an Ounce of Nutmegs, and half an Ounce of Cinnamon, your Cinnamon and Nutmegs must be sifted through a Sieve, two pounds of Butter, half a score of Eggs, put out four of the whites of them, something above a pint of good Ale-yeast. Beat your Eggs very well and strain them with your Yeast, and a little warm water into your Flour, and stir them together. Then put your Butter cold in little Lumps: The water you knead with must be scalding hot, if you will make a good Paste, which having done, lay the Paste to rise in a warm Cloth, a quarter of an hour, or thereupon. Then put in ten pounds of Currants, and a little Muske and Ambergreece dissolved in Rosewater. Your Currants must be very dry, or else they will make your Cake heavy. Strew as much Sugar finely beaten amongst the Currants, as you shall think the water hath taken away the sweetness from them. Break your Paste into little pieces, into a Kimnell,* or such thing, and lay a Layer of Paste broken into little pieces, and a Layer of Currants, until your Currants are all put in. Mingle the Paste and the Currants very well, but take heed of breaking the Currants. You must take out a piece of Paste after it hath risen in a warm cloth, before you put in the Currants, to cover the top and the bottom. You must roll the Cover somewhat thin, and the bottom likewise, and wet it with Rosewater, and close them at the bottom of the side, or the middle which you like best. Prick the top and the sides with a small long pin. When your Cake is ready to go into the Oven, cut it in the middle of the top round about with a Knife an inch deep. If your Cake be of a peck of Meal, it must stand two hours in the Oven. Your Oven must be as hot as for manchet.†

The Compleat Cook, 1659

MACE AND NUTMEG

* Kimnel = a large tub or a very large bowl. Chaucer's "Miller's Tale" contains the line, "Anon go gete vs a knedying trogh or ellis a kymelyn."

† As hot as for manchet = gentle heat.

Bride Cake

Presuming that this work may fall into the hands of some persons who may occasionally have a wedding amongst them, it would be imperfect without a "wedding cake," and as I have lately had an opportunity to test this one, upon "such an occasion," in my own family, I can bear testimony, so can the "printer," to its adaptation for all similar displays.

Take butter 1½ lbs.; sugar 1¾ lbs., half of which is to be Orleans sugar;* eggs well beaten 2 lbs.; raisins 4 lbs.; having the seeds taken out and chopped; English currants having the grit picked out and nicely washed 5 lbs.; citron, cut fine, 2 lbs.; sifted flour 2 lbs.; nutmegs 2 in number, and mace as much as in bulk; alcohol 1 gill to ½ pint, in which a dozen or fifteen drops of oil of lemon have been put.

When ready to make your cake, weigh your butter and cut it in pieces, and put it where it will soften, but not melt. Next, stir the butter to a cream, and then add the sugar, and work till white. Next beat the yolks of the eggs, and put them to the sugar and butter. Meanwhile another person should beat the whites to a stiff froth and put them in. Then add the spices and flour, and, last of all, the fruit, except the citron, which is to be put in about three layers, the bottom layer about one inch from the bottom, and the top one an inch from the top, and the other in the middle, smoothing the top of the cake by dipping a spoon or two of water upon it for that purpose.

The pan in which it is baked should be about thirteen inches across the top, and five and a half or six inches deep, without scollops, and two three-quart pans also, which it will fill; and they will require to be slowly baked about three to four hours. But it is impossible to give definite

NORWEGIAN BRIDE.

* Orleans sugar = molasses or brown sugar.

94

rules as to the time required in baking cake. Try whether the cake is done, by piercing it with a broom splinter, and if nothing adheres it is done.

Butter the cake pans well; or if the pans are lined with buttered white paper, the cake will be less liable to burn. Moving cakes while baking tends to make them heavy.

The price of a large "Bride Cake," like this, would be about twelve dollars, and the cost of making it would be about three dollars only, with your two small ones, which would cost as much to buy them as it does to make the whole three.

The foregoing was written and printed over a year ago. The daughter came home and took dinner with us, one year from the marriage; and her mother set on some of the cake as nice and moist as when baked.

A. W. Chase, M.D., *Dr. Chase's Recipes*, 1880

Groom's Cake

(Mary Wilcox, Dalton)

Ten eggs beaten separately, one pound butter, one of white sugar, one of flour, two of almonds blanched and chopped fine, one of seeded raisins, half pound citron, shaved fine; beat butter to a cream, add sugar gradually, then the well-beaten yolks; stir all till very light, and add the chopped almonds; beat the whites stiff and add gently with the flour; take a little more flour and sprinkle over the raisins and citron, then put in the cake-pan, first a layer of cake batter, then a layer of raisins and citron, then cake, and so on till all is used, finishing off with a layer of cake. Bake in a moderate oven two hours.

Buckeye Cookery, 1883

MARRIED *en chemisette*

Some of the most remarkable marriages that have ever taken place are those in which the brides came to the altar partly, or in many cases entirely, divested of clothing. It was formerly a common notion that if a man married a woman *en chemisette* he was not liable for her debts; and in *Notes and Queries* there is an account by a clergyman of the celebration of such a marriage some few years ago. He tells us that, as nothing was said in the rubric about the woman's dress, he did not think it right to refuse to perform the marriage service. (R. Chambers, ED., *The Book of Days*, 1862–4)

A MARRIAGE SETTLEMENT

"There was recorded at the Register's office yesterday a marriage settlement made by Leonard W. Jerome and wife in favor of their daughter Jennie, who is about to marry Lord Randolph Henry Spencer Churchill, son of the Marquis of Blandford. Thomas M. Foote, of this city, and George Charles Spencer Churchill, Marquis of Blandford are made trustees, to receive an annuity of $10,000 in gold. A portion of $125,000 is allotted to Lord Churchill, in case of the death of his wife, leaving no issue surviving, and a further allotment of $250,000 is made for the issue of this marriage, in case of the death of both of the parties thereto. The property known as the Union League Club House is the security for this settlement."—*N.Y. Herald.*

Here we get at the exact price that an American citizen pays for a foreign title for his daughter. We think it rather expensive, but it is a great thing to have a daughter a Marchioness in expectancy. (*Godey's Lady's Book and Magazine,* October, 1874)

Wedding Punch

1 tumbler of currant jelly	3 quarts of Apollinaris
1 tumbler of raspberry jelly	1 bottle of sarsaparilla
1 tumbler of black-berry jelly	1 pint of grated pine-apple
12 lemons	1 pint of preserved strawberries
2 oranges	1 quart of canned peaches
1 pint of grape juice	¼ pound of conserved cherries
1 quart bottle of ginger ale	2 pounds of sugar

Grate the yellow rind from the oranges and lemons into the sugar, put them into a porcelain-lined kettle, and add one quart of water. Stir until the sugar is dissolved, and boil ten minutes. Strain. While hot, add all the jellies and stand aside to cool. When cool, add the grated pineapple, strawberries and conserved cherries cut into quarters. Cover and stand aside all night. At serving time, turn the mixture in the punch bowl, add one quart of shaved ice and all the other ingredients.

SARAH TYSON RORER, *Mrs. Rorer's New Cook Book,* 1898

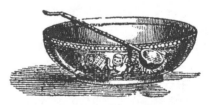

PUNCH-BOWL AND LADLE

MARY TUDOR

PHILIP II OF SPAIN

A RIDDLE:

Flour of England, fruit of Spain,

Met together in a shower of rain;

Put in a bag, tied round with a string

If you'll tell me this riddle,

I'll give you a ring.

Plum-pottage

Take two gallons of strong broth; put to it two pound of currants, two pound of raisons of the Sun, half an ounce of Sweet Spice, a pound of Sugar, a quart of claret, a pint of Sack, the juice of three oranges and three lemons; thicken it with grated biskets, or rice flour with a pound of pruants.*

Sweet Spice is Cloves, Mace, Nutmeg, Cinnamon, Sugar & Salt.

E. KIDDER, *Receipts of Pastry and Cookery* [c. 1730]

THE ANSWER to this nineteenth-century riddle is the plum pudding. This famous dish is a direct descendant of the older plum porridge, which has been traced back to the Danish-German borderland and may have been introduced into England by the Danes who, under their king, Sweyn, conquered England in

* Pruants = prunes.

1013. Eaten hot or cold, it began as a stewed "broth," developed into a thickened "pottage" or "porridge," and by the mid 1700s had finally become a "plum pudding"; the "plums" were usually not plums at all, but currants or raisins—the "fruit of Spain."

Katherine Elwes Thomas (*The Real Personages of Mother Goose,* New York, 1930) reads a more romantic-political meaning into the rhyme: The "Flour (flower) of England" is Mary Tudor (1516–1558), who was the daughter of Henry VIII and became the first reigning queen of England in more than 1500 years; and the "fruit of Spain" is her cousin Philip II (1527–1598), later King of Spain. There was, in fact, a great shower of rain when Philip rode to meet Mary. She sent a ring to him and asked him to delay his visit until the downpour had ceased, but he continued his journey. Although many of her subjects rebelled against the union—for both political and religious reasons—the royal cousins were married in Winchester Cathedral on July 25, 1554. Within seven months Mary began her persecution of the Protestants, which eventually earned her the name "Bloody Mary." About a year and a half after their marriage, Philip left her.

GREAT SEAL OF QUEEN MARY

Christmas Plum Pudding

The plum pudding is a national dish, and is despised by foreign nations because they never can make it fit to eat. In almost every family there is a recipe for it, which has been handed down from mother to daughter through two or three generations, and which never has been and never will be equalled, much less surpassed, by any other. Every ingredient composing these puddings should be fresh and good, as one bad article, and especially one bad egg, will spoil the whole. The puddings are, we think, better when boiled in moulds, which should be well buttered before the mixture is put in, should be quite full, and should be covered with one or two folds of paper floured and buttered, and then with a floured pudding-cloth. When bread is used, which makes a pudding lighter than flour, a little room should be allowed for swelling. A pinch of salt should always be remembered, as it brings out the flavour of the other ingredients. After it is tied in the cloth the pudding should be put into boiling water, and kept boiling until it is taken off, when it should be plunged quickly into a basin of cold water; by this means it will be less likely to break when turning out of the mould. It is usual, before sending it to table, to make a little hole in the top and fill it with brandy, then light it, and serve it in a blaze. In olden time a sprig of arbutus, with a red berry on it, was stuck in the middle, and a twig of variegated holly, with berries, placed on each side. This was done to keep away witches. It is a good plan to mix much more than is needed, and to make several puddings instead of one, boil all together, and warm one up when necessary. If well made, Christmas plum pudding will be good for twelve months. It should be boiled for eight or nine hours some days before it is wanted; and when it is to be used, plunged again into boiling water, and boiled for at least two hours.

Cassell's Dictionary of Cookery [c. 1877]

Christmas Plum-Pudding

(Mrs. Acton's Receipt)

To three ounces of flour, and the same weight of fine lightly grated bread-crumbs, add six of beef kidney-suet chopped small, six of raisins weighed after they are stoned, six of well cleaned currants, four ounces of minced apples, five of sugar, two of candied orange-rind, half a teaspoonful of nutmeg mixed with powdered mace, a very little salt, a small glass of brandy, and three whole eggs. Mix and beat these ingredients well together, tie them lightly in a thickly floured cloth, and boil them for three hours and a half. We can recommend this as a remarkably light small rich pudding. It may be served with German wine or punch sauce.

TABITHA TICKLETOOTH, *The Dinner Question,* 1860

ENGLISH HOLLY

HOLLY AND MISTLETOE

It was believed by some nations that if the branches of holly, with their prickly leaves, were cut on Christmas Eve, and hung up in houses and stables, it would capture all the little devils and witches hanging around, or else drive them away, so that they could do no harm. Witches were said to particularly detest holly, because in its name they saw but another spelling of the word Holy, and in its thorny foliage and blood-red berries so many Christian suggestions.

Mistletoe is not used in Christian connections on account of its having been the sacred plant of the Druids.

An old English superstition was that elves and fairies joined in the social gatherings at Christmas, and branches were hung in hall and bower, so that the fays might "hang in each leaf and cling on every bough during that sacred time when spirits have no power to harm." These evergreens were to be taken down on Candlemas Eve. (*The House-wife,* vol. X, 1895)

According to Mrs. Humphry (*Cookery Up-to-Date*, 1896), "The pudding served on Christmas Day should contain a silver coin, not smaller than a sixpence, a silver thimble, a gold or silver ring, a large Spanish nut, a large bone button. Whoever gets the money will be lucky throughout the approaching year. The thimble and button portend celibacy during the same period. The nut means wealth."

CHRISTMAS PLUM-PUDDING

This peculiarly national dish, which Lord Byron, during his sojourn in Florence, after devoting a whole morning to giving directions to his cook for its proper preparation, for an English treat to his friends on his birthday, had served up as soup in a tureen, is now so well known throughout the Continent, that in some guise or other, although it must be confessed our "home-bred youth" may often say with Hamlet, "Thou comest in such a *questionable* shape," it is to be found occupying a distinguished position among the *entremets* in the *cartes* of the highest and lowest restaurateurs. "*Blom Budin*" *au Rhum* or *Vin de Madére* being considered, like

Fine Plum Pudding

This pudding is best when prepared, (all but the milk and eggs,) the day before it is wanted. Seed and cut in half one pound of the best bloom raisins; and pick, wash, and dry before the fire, a pound of Zante currants, (commonly called plums.) Dredge the fruit well with flour, to prevent its sinking or clogging. Take one pound of fresh beef suet, freed from the skin and strings, and chopped *very fine;* a pint of grated bread-crumbs, and half a pint of sifted flour; a large quarter of a pound of the best sugar, a large table-spoonful of powdered mace and cinnamon mixed, and two powdered nutmegs—all the spice steeped in a half pint of mixed wine and brandy. Put away these ingredients separately, closely covered, and let them stand undisturbed all night. Next morning proceed to finish the pudding, which requires at least six hours boiling. Beat nine eggs till very thick and smooth, then add gradually a pint of rich milk, in turn with the bread-crumbs and flour. Mix with the sugar the grated yellow rind and juice of two large lemons or two oranges, and add gradually to the mixture all the ingredients, stirring very hard. If you find it too thick, add by degrees some more milk; if too thin, some more bread-crumbs. But take care not to have too much bread or flour, or the pudding will be solid and heavy. Dip a large strong cloth in boiling water; shake it out, and spread it in a large pan. Dredge it lightly with flour, and pour in the mixture. Tie it tightly, but leave sufficient space for the pudding to swell in boiling. Put it into a pot of fast-boiling water, and boil it steadily six hours or more, not taking it up till wanted for table. Before turning it, dip the cloth for a moment in cold water to make the pudding come out easily. Have ready some slips of citron or of blanched sweet almonds, or both, and stick them, liberally, all over the surface of the pudding after you have dished it. Serve it up with wine sauce highly flavored, or with butter and sugar beaten to a cream, and seasoned with nutmeg and rose[water]. Do not set the pudding on fire to burn out the liquor; that practice has had its day, and is over. It was always foolish.

If you wish to send it to a distant place, (for instance, to some part of the world where plum puddings are not known or not made,) you may preserve it, (after boiling it well,) by leaving it tied up in the cloth it was cooked in; hanging it up in a cool dry place, and then packing it well in a tin vessel having a close fitting cover. Paste a band of thick white paper all around the place where the lid shuts down, and put into a tight box the vessel that contains the pudding. When it arrives at its destination, the friend who receives it will pare off thinly the outside, and tying up the pudding in a fresh clean cloth, will boil it over again for an hour or more; and when done the surface may be then decorated with slips of citron or almond. It has been said that in this way a plum pudding can be kept for *six* months, as good as ever. It cannot. But it may keep six *weeks*. Do not *fry* or *broil* plum pudding that is left at dinner. The slices will be greasy and heavy. But tie the piece that remains in a small cloth, and *boil* it over again for an hour. It will then be nearly as good as on the first day. Believe in no wonders that you hear, of the long keeping of either plum pudding, plum cake, or mince meat, which are all of the same family. However long they may be preserved from absolute decomposition, these things are always best when fresh.

Miss Leslie's New Cookery Book, 1857

"*Pal-al*" and red hair, a *Britannique spécialité.*

To "make assurance doubly sure," and give the inexperienced housewife an opportunity of perfecting her *own* pudding by adapting the good points and eschewing the bad of several "old masters" and mistresses of the culinary art (as a young painter will try to retain the beauties of a Turner or a Rembrandt, while he avoids their eccentricities), I will for once depart from my usual course, and give two or three "other ways" from the works of my most talented contemporaries. (Tabitha Tickletooth, *The Dinner Question,* 1860)

Plum-Pudding

(Mrs. General Sherman)

Ingredients: One cupful of butter, one cupful of sugar, half a cupful of cream, half a cupful of rum, one cupful of ale, one cupful of suet (chopped), one cupful of fruit (currants and raisins), half a cupful of candied orange cut fine, six eggs well beaten, two grated nutmegs, one tea-spoonful of ground cinnamon, half a tea-spoonful of ground cloves, bread-crumbs.

Beat the butter and sugar together to a cream. The bread-crumbs should be dried thoroughly, and passed through a sieve. Beat all well together before adding the bread-crumbs, then add enough of them to give proper consistency. Put the pudding into a tin mold (not quite filling it), and boil it four hours.

The Sauce. Use equal quantities of butter and sugar. Cream the butter, then add the sugar, beating them both until very light. Add then the beaten yolk of an egg, and a little grated nutmeg. Heat on the fire a large wine-glassful of sherry wine diluted with the same quantity of water, and when just beginning to boil, stir it into the butter and sugar.

Mrs. Mary F. Henderson, *Practical Cooking, and Dinner Giving,* 1895

BRINGING IN THE YULE-LOG ON CHRISTMAS EVE.

Uxbridge Plum Pudding (excellent)

Shred a half-pound of suet very finely, mix with
it half a pound of flour, half a pound of sugar,
half a pound of mashed potatoes, half a pound
of grated carrots, three-quarters of a pound of
picked and dried currants, two ounces of minced
candied peel, and a little grated nutmeg. Mix the
ingredients thoroughly. Press them into a buttered basin or mould which they will quite fill,
cover the mould with a saucer, and tie it tightly
in a cloth. Plunge it into boiling water, and keep
it boiling quickly until done enough. A quarter
of an hour before the pudding is wanted take it
up, and before turning it out of the basin put
it into the oven. This will remove any moisture it
may have acquired in boiling, and cause it to
turn out better. Send brandy or wine sauce to
table with it. Time to boil the pudding, fully six
hours. Sufficient for six or eight persons.

Cassell's Dictionary of Cookery [c. 1877]

Economist's Pudding

This well-known pudding is merely a *rifaccia-
mento* of the remains of a cold boiled plum pudding. Cut the pudding in slices about half an
inch thick, and fill a buttered dish about three
parts. Make a custard of two eggs, half a pint of
milk, and two ounces of sugar; beat it well, pour
it over the pudding, and let it stand an hour
before you put it in the oven. Bake it three-
quarters of an hour, and serve it hot, with sifted
sugar over, and any good sauce.

ANNE BOWMAN, *The New Cookery Book,* 1869

JELLY-MOULD

A HOLIDAY GAME

A plan for amusing the young folks in an instructive fashion is to take some simple subject, such as the Christmas pudding, and let each one give his and her idea of how it is made and cooked, what the ingredients are, and where they are grown or manufactured. It is wonderful how much of interest is to be found even in a Christmas pudding, besides its pleasant taste —the growing of the raisins, currants, and candied peels, almonds, etc.; the cathedral-like salt mines from whence the salt is taken; the flour, made from golden wheat; the suet from the fat ox, and so on. This opens and expands the minds of children very much, and even the older people have to brush up their memories to reply to the questions asked on all sides. (*The Housewife,* vol. X, 1895)

Plum Pudding Jelly

½ box, or 1 ounce, of gelatine soaked ½ hour in 1 cupful of cold water.	1 pint of milk.
	1 cupful of raisins stoned.
1½ ounces of chocolate.	½ cupful of currants.
1 cupful of sugar.	¼ cupful of sliced citron.

Dissolve the sugar in the milk, and put it in a double boiler to scald. Melt the chocolate on a dry pan; then add a few spoonfuls of the milk to make it smooth, and add it to the scalded milk. Remove from the fire, and add the soaked gelatine. Stir until the gelatine is dissolved; then strain it into a bowl. When it begins to set, or is firm enough to hold the fruit in place, stir in the fruit, which must have stood in warm water a little while to soften. Flavor with one half teaspoonful of vanilla, or a few drops of lemon. Turn it into a mold to harden. Serve with it whipped cream, or a sauce made of the whipped white of one egg, one tablespoonful of powdered sugar, a cupful of milk and a few drops of vanilla.

MARY RONALD, *The Century Cook Book,* 1895

ROUND MOULD

Beacon Street Sauce

Beat to a cream one cup of butter and two cups of sugar, add one glass of wine, and a seasoning of nutmeg. Stir half a teaspoon of soda in a cup of thick sour milk, when it foams add it to the butter and sugar, and stir all together, then add four tablespoons of boiling water without stirring. Put it in the tureen disturbing as little as possible.

This is the best sauce on earth for a boiled fruit or Christmas pudding.

Hood's Practical Cook's Book, 1897

A Delicious German Pudding Sauce

Dissolve in half a pint of sherry or of Madeira, from three to four ounces of fine sugar, but do not allow the wine to boil; stir it hot into well-beaten yolks of six fresh eggs, and mill the sauce over a gentle fire until it is well thickened, and highly frothed; pour it over a plum, or any other kind of sweet boiled pudding, of which it much improves the appearance. Half the quantity will be sufficient for one of moderate size. A small machine, resembling a chocolate mill, is used in Germany for frothing this sauce; but a couple of silver forks, fastened together at the handles, will serve for the purpose, on an emergency. We recommend the addition of a dessertspoonful of strained lemon-juice to the wine.

For large pudding, sherry or Madeira, ½ pint; fine sugar, 3 to 4 ozs.; yolks of eggs, 6; lemon-juice (if added), 1 dessertspoonful.

Obs. The safer plan with sauces liable to curdle

Making German Sauce

is to thicken them always in a jar or jug, placed in a saucepan of water; when this is not done, they should be held over the fire, but never placed *upon* it.

Eliza Acton, *Modern Cookery,* 1852

Wine Sauce, Red

This is a Danish Sauce to be eaten with plum pudding. Take a quarter of a pint of cherry-juice and half a pint of wine. When the mixture boils put in a good spoonful of flour mixed with a gill of water and two or three spoonfuls of brandy. Just before the sauce reaches the boiling point take it off, and serve immediately.

Cassell's Dictionary of Cookery [c. 1877]

PERKINS SANITARY SEAMLESS STEEL SAUCEPAN

Girls and Boys,
Come out to play,
The Moon does shine,
As bright as Day,

Come with a Hoop,
Come with a Call,
Come with a good will,
Or not at all.

Up the Ladder
And down the Wall,
A halfpenny Loaf
Will serve us all.

Loose your supper,
And loose your Sleep,
Come to your Play fellows
In the Street,

You find milk
And I'll find flour,
And we'll have a pudding
In half an hour.

107

Sometimes we must revive our spirits after our study. Men do that by playing and other honest pastimes. The honest pastimes that pertain to children are the top and scourge, the balls, the exercises of the body, and as always, tennis and leapings. The kinds of leapings are the leap of grasshoppers with both legs, the feet joined together, and with one leg only. Men do exercise themselves with wrestling, and with the sword, if it be done in the presence of the master and without envy. As concerning swimming, better it were to be a looker on than a doer. But it is much more honorable to exercise the spirit in instruments of music, which is the most honest pleasure, and the most agreeable to muses that a man can find. Plays forbidden are these: dice, cards, and other games of hazard and swimming in the water like ruffians. These be the things that enrich the play: dignity, honest mirth, mutual friendliness, to play frankly, to win by truth, and not by deceit. (THOMAS PAYNELL, *The Civilitie of Childehode,* 1560)

American Corn Puddings

Boil a quart of milk, and stir into it gradually eight tablespoonfuls of good Indian flour, four tablespoonfuls of powdered sugar, and half a nutmeg, grated; stir it over the fire for a quarter of an hour, then turn it out to cool. Beat eight eggs very well, and stir into the batter when cold. Butter your cups, and fill them three parts; bake half an hour, and turn out. Half the quantity of batter would be sufficient for a small party. In America these puddings are eaten with butter and molasses. We would recommend port or claret sauce to be served with them.

ANNE BOWMAN, *The New Cookery Book,* 1869

Cottage Pudding
(Mrs. Denise)

One cup sugar.	One pint flour.
One cup milk.	One teaspoonful baking powder.
Three tablespoonsful melted butter.	One egg.

Bake thirty minutes. To be served with wine sauce.

MRS. D. S. SEARS, *The Practical Cook,* 1878

Baked Huckleberry Pudding

One quart of ripe, fresh huckleberries or blue-
berries; half a teaspoonful of mace or nutmeg,
three eggs well beaten, separately; two cupfuls
of sugar; one tablespoonful of cold butter; one
cupful of sweet milk, one pint of flour, two teaspoonfuls of baking-powder. Roll the berries
well in the flour, and add them last of all. Bake
half an hour and serve with sauce. There is no
more delicate and delicious pudding than this.

Mrs. F. L. Gillette and Hugo Ziemann, *The White-House
Cook-Book,* 1894

Puzzles to play while waiting for the pudding

(Answers on page 110)

(from *The Family Friend,* 1850 and 1851)

1. Draw six vertical lines as below, and by
adding five other lines to them, let the whole form
nine:

2. Having tied two strings to the wrists of two
persons, and intersected them, as in the diagram,
release the parties without untying either of the
strings.

3. Take a piece of cardboard or leather, of the shape and measurement indicated by the diagram. Cut it in such a manner that you yourself may pass through it, still keeping it in one piece!

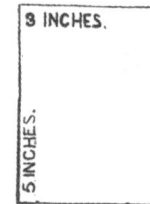

3 INCHES.

5 INCHES.

4. I have a lodging-house in which there are five boarders, all of whom have applied to me to let them cultivate the garden, but they require me to divide the ground around the house into five portions of the same shape and size, giving each two trees. Unless I can do it, I fear I shall offend my lodgers.

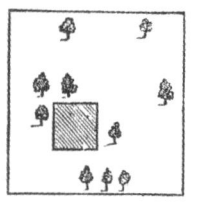

Answers to Puzzles

1.

NINE

Draw the lines in the direction of the dots.

2. Take one of the strings and pass it in a loop upward under the string which binds the wrist of the opposite person, then draw the loop through, and enlarge it, and by passing it over the hand, the release may be easily effected.

3.

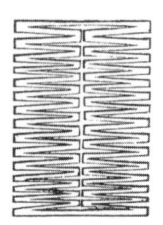

Double the cardboard or leather lengthways down the middle, and then cut it first to the right, nearly to the end (the narrow way), and then to the left, and so on to the end of the card; then open it, and cut down the middle, except the two ends. The diagram shows the proper cuttings. By opening the card or leather, a person may pass through it!

4.

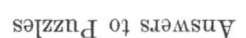

Go to bed, Tom,   Drunk or sober,
Go to bed, Tom,   Go to bed, Tom.

It may not be amiss to cite
A CURIOUS ADVERTISEMENT,
From the Bahama Gazette, June 30, 1795

WHEREAS the subscriber, through the pernicious habit of drinking, has greatly hurt himself in purse and person, and rendered himself odious to all his acquaintance, and finding there is no possibility of breaking off from the said practice, but through the impossibility to find the liquor; he therefore begs and prays that no persons will sell him, for money or on trust, any sort of spirituous liquors, as he will not in future pay it, but will prosecute any one for an action of damage against the temporal and eternal interests of the public's humble, serious, and sober servant,

JAMES CHALMERS

Witness WILLIAM ANDREWS
Nassau, June 28, 1795

WILLIAM HONE, *The Every-Day Book*, vol. II, 1827

THIS RHYME is said to be based on a military song or barracks room ballad of the eighteenth century in which the first line, "Go to bed, Tom," is a euphemism for the military tattoo, a drum or bugle signal telling the troops to return to camp. The word comes from the Dutch *taptoe*, which means literally to shut the taps on the casks. The *Oxford English Dictionary* quotes "Col. Hutchinson's Orders" (1644) as follows: "If anyone shall bee found tiplinge or drinkinge in any Taverne, Inne, or Alehouse after the houre of nyne of the clock at night, when the Tap-too beates, hee shall pay 2*s.* 6*d.*"

Drunkenness

Men, and women too, drift gradually and insensibly into drunkenness without knowing it. Sometimes the habit is formed carelessly, from the mere love of company and jovial society. Sometimes it begins by taking small sips of brandy or gin to relieve pain of different kinds. This is a way of relieving pain which some people cannot too suspiciously guard against. Women especially, both young and old, are tempted by pains they experience, to take a little spirit of some kind. But it is often a dangerous thing to do, and it must be understood that something else, such as a cup of warm tea or coffee, and a warm external application will often afford relief. We are obliged, for the mere sake of fairness, to admit that drunkenness does sometimes originate in the too carelessly given advice of medical men to their patients to take wine, beer, or spirits in considerable quantities. There has been a habit, or a fashion, common of late among doctors, of recommending liberal diet, and especially the free use of wine or brandy, and some form of beer. This medical fashion has made many a drunkard. Fortunately, medical men are now seeing this, and are acting with much greater care and sense of responsibility in ordering stimulants. We say fortunately, for not only was the fashion bad, and often frightful in its consequences, but the remedy, as prescribed, was bad and injurious. Passing over those cases in which drunkenness seems to originate in a way that can be understood and followed, we come to the genuine disease of drunkenness, or as the doctors call it, dipsomania (from the Greek words, *dipsa*, thirst, and *mania*, madness). Everybody is familiar with cases of this kind, in which the love of drink seems a madness or mania:

The Drunkard's Cloak

there is an intense craving for intoxicating liquors, accompanied with general depression of the system, and especially of the nervous system, and restlessness. Accompanying this state, there is often also a certain slyness, or untruthfulness, or deceitfulness, which is characteristic. Such people will often deny that they drink much if they are questioned on the subject; and yet the love of drink is the passion which domineers over all their life and all their other feelings. They will admit all the arguments against drinking, but they will drink again; and the habit acquires strength with indulgence. As it gets stronger the power of self-control gets weaker, self-respect grows less and less, and after a time, the power of resistance is completely gone. Now, it seems at once the kindest and the truest view of this awful state, to look upon it as a disease, and to treat it accordingly.

Cassell's Household Guide, vol. II [c. 1885]

Athol Brose

Add two wineglassfuls of Scotch whisky to a wineglassful of heather-honey; mix well, and then stir in a well-beaten new-laid egg.

The Family Friend, vol 3, 1851

Bang

Take a pint of cider, and add to a pint of warm ale; sweeten with treacle or sugar to taste, grate in some nutmeg and ginger, and add a wineglassful of gin or whisky.

The Family Friend, vol. 3, 1851

THE WHISTLE DRINKING-CUP

The drinking-customs of various nations would form a curious chapter in ethnology. The Teutonic races have, however, the most claim to be considered "potent in potting." The Saxons were great drinkers; and took with them to their graves their ornamental ale-buckets and drinking-glasses, the latter made without foot or stand, so that they must be filled and emptied by the drinker before they could be set down again on the festive-board. Mighty topers they were, and history records some of their drinking-bouts. Notwithstanding the assertion of Iago, that "your Dane, your German, and your swag-bellied Hollander, are nothing to your English" in powers of drinking, it may be doubted if the Germans have ever been outdone. Certainly no persons have bestowed more thought on quaint inventions for holding their liquors, or enforcing large consumption, than they have. The silversmiths of Augsburg and Nuremberg, in the sixteenth and seventeenth centuries, devoted a large amount of invention to the production of drinking-cups, taking the form of men, animals, birds, &c., of most grotesque design. Our engraving represents one surmounted by a wind-mill. It will be perceived that the cup must be held in the hand to be filled, and retained there till it be emptied, as then only it can be set upon the table. The drinker having swallowed the contents, blew up the pipe at the side, which gave a shrill whistle, and set the sails of the wind-mill in motion also. The power of the blow, and the length of the gyration, were indicated in a small dial upon the front of the mill, and also in some degree testified to the state of the consumer. Among the songs of Burns is one upon a whistle, used by a Dane of the retinue of Anne of Denmark, which was laid upon the table at the commencement of the orgie, and won by whoever was last able to blow it. The Dane conquered all-comers, until Sir Robert Lawrie of Maxwelton, "after three days and three nights' hard contest, left the Scandinavian under the table." On 16th October 1789, a similar contest took place, which has been immortalised in Burns's verses. (R. CHAMBERS, ed., *The Book of Days*, vol. II, 1862–4)

WHISTLE DRINKING CUP

Bhang

A dreadful East Indian drink, and a deadly intoxicant, is distilled from hemp; and if it had only been round the neck of the inventor before he invented it, society would have benefited.

EDWARD SPENCER, *The Flowing Bowl,* 1898

Bishop

Take three smooth-skinned and large Seville oranges, and grill them to a pale brown colour over a clear slow fire; then place in a small punch-bowl that will about hold them, and pour over them half a pint from a bottle of old Bordeaux wine, in which a pound and a quarter of loaf sugar is dissolved; then cover with a plate, and let it stand for two days. When it is to be served, cut and squeeze the oranges into a small sieve placed above a jug containing the remainder of the bottle of sweetened Bordeaux, previously made very hot, and if when mixed it is not sweet enough, add more sugar. Serve hot in tumblers.

Some persons make Bishop with raisin or Lisbon wine, and add mace, cloves, and nutmegs, but it is not the proper way.

Cardinal is made the same way as Bishop, substituting old Rhenish wine for the Bordeaux.

Pope is made the same as Bishop, substituting Tokay for Bordeaux.

The Family Friend, vol. 3, 1851

Beer Bishop
(Kaltschalen)

Pumpernickel is grated on a grater and put in a tureen; mix with it one-fourth of a pound of powdered sugar, one-fourth of a pound of choice raisins, a teaspoonful of powdered cinnamon, an unpeeled lemon, cut in pieces without seeds; add a quart of white beer or lager (*Franziskaner*), and serve.

The "Only William," *The Flowing Bowl*, 1892

BISHOP CUP

Bosom Caresser

Small tumbler: one wine-glassful of sherry, half a wine-glassful of brandy, the yolk of an egg, two teaspoonfuls of sugar, and two grains of cayenne pepper. Add ice, shake well, strain, and dust with nutmeg and cinnamon.

Edward Spencer, *The Flowing Bowl*, 1898

Burning Brandy

A curious recipe comes from Switzerland, an elaborate method of burning brandy or any other spirit but gin.

Cut the top off a lemon, and hollow out the interior with the handle-end of a spoon. Place the empty cone thus formed by the skin on the top of a large wine-glass. Fill the cone with brandy, rum, or whisky; take a fork, balance a piece of sugar on the prongs, set the spirit alight, and hold the sugar over the flame until it has melted into the cone. Then take a skewer, and pierce a small

115

WINE-COOLER

CHARTREUSES

According to Mary Ronald (*The Century Cook Book*, 1895), "Chartreuse is a liqueur made by the monks of the French monastery of Grande Chartreuse; but a class of dishes have also been given this name, which are made of two or more foods, one of which conceals the others. The story goes that on fast days the monks were thus able to indulge in forbidden food, and savory viands were hidden under cabbage or other severely plain articles. Chartreuses are made by lining a mold with rice, a vegetable, or a forcemeat, and filling the center with a different food. Two vegetables are sometimes so combined, but more often game or meats are inclosed in rice and served with a good sauce."

hole in the base of the cone. When all the spirit has trickled into the glass, throw the cone away, and drink the result.

EDWARD SPENCER, *The Flowing Bowl*, 1898

To Burn Wine

Take about a quart of good Burgundy Wine, and put it into a Silver Tankard, or what other vessel you please, with a pound of Sugar, two blades of large Mace, one corn of long Pepper, twelve Cloves, a sprig of Rosemary, and two Bay-leaves; set your vessel upon a good Charcoal fire, make your wine boil, and light it with a paper, and let it burn till it goes out of it self; drink this as hot as you can, the hotter the better.

GILES ROSE, *The Officers of the Mouth,* 1682

Chartreuse

The preparation of this famous cordial and its trade is monopolized by the monks of the monastery Grande Chartreuse, in the French département Isère; the monastery was built by St. Bruno in the year 1086.

The monks keep their secret very carefully; an imitation may be obtained in the following way: Take one pint of the best brandy or kirschwasser, eight drops of vermouth essence, one drop of cinnamon essence, one drop of rose essence, and twelve ounces of sugar that was refined and cleared in one pint of water; strain through flannel, cork, seal, and let it lie at least eight weeks.

THE "ONLY WILLIAM," *The Flowing Bowl*, 1892

Dog's-nose

Warm half a pint of ale, and add a wine-glass of gin to it; then add half a pint of cold ale, and serve.

The Family Friend, vol. 4, 1851

Ale Flip

Beat well together in a jug, four eggs with a quarter of a pound of sifted sugar; then add by degrees, stirring all the time, two quarts of old Burton ale, and half a pint of gin; pour backwards and forwards from one jug to another, and when well frothed serve in tumblers. Grate a little nutmeg atop of each portion. This is one of the best "nightcaps" I know—especially after you may have been badger-hunting, or burgling, or serenading anybody on Christmas Eve.

EDWARD SPENCER, *The Flowing Bowl*, 1898

Gin-Sling

(An American Drink)

Put two slices of lemon, and three lumps of loaf-sugar into a tumbler, fill up to the brim with shaves of Wenham Lake ice; add a wineglassful of old gin; stir, and suck through a straw.

NOTE: I am afraid that very genteel persons will be exceedingly shocked at the words "suck through a straw;" but when I tell them that the very act of imbibition through a straw prevents the gluttonous absorption of large and baneful quantities of drink, they will, I make no doubt, accept the vulgar precept for the sake of its protection against sudden inebriety.

CHARLES ELMÉ FRANCATELLI. *The Cook's Guide*, 1884

The Grace-cup and Loving-cup appear to be synonymous terms for a beverage the drinking of which has been from time immemorial a great feature at the corporation dinners in London and other large towns, as also at the feasts of the various trade companies and the Inns of Court, and which is a compound of wine and spices, formerly called "Sack." It is handed round the table before the removal of the cloth, in large silver cups, from which no one is allowed to drink before the guest on either side of him has stood up; the person who drinks then rises and bows to his neighbours. This custom is said to have originated in the precaution to keep the right or dagger hand employed, as it was a frequent practice with the Danes to stab their companions in the back at the time they were drinking. The most notable instance of this was the treachery employed by Elfrida, who stabbed King Edward the Martyr at Corfe Castle whilst thus engaged.

One pint of mountain wine, one of Madeira, and one of Lisbon, one bottle of champagne, one liqueur-glass of pale brandy, three thin slices of lemon, sugar, nutmeg. Ice to taste. (*Cups and Their Customs*, 1869)

Hippocras

A kind of spiced wine of the mediæval age, when one did not yet understand blending the wines, consequently they always were of a certain acidity, which was covered by the addition of honey and spices. A recipe for manufacturing hippocras, which Talleyraut, the head cook of Charles VII, king of France has made, reads as follows: To a quart of wine take one-third of an ounce of very fine and clean cinnamon, one-thirtieth ounce of ginger, twice as much of cloves, as much nutmeg, and six ounces of sugar and honey; grind the spices, put them in a muslin bag, hang this in the wine for ten to twelve hours, and filter several times.

Wherever, nowadays, hippocras is made, it is made in the following manner: Cut eight to ten large, aromatic, well-peeled apples into thin slices; put that in a tureen, add half a pound of sugar, three or four pepper kernels, the rind of a lemon, one-third of an ounce of whole cinnamon, two ounces of peeled and mashed almonds, and four cloves; pour over this two bottles of Rhine wine, cover it well, and let it soak with the other ingredients; filter the wine, and you may use this wine also for a bowl.

THE "ONLY WILLIAM," *The Flowing Bowl*, 1892

A SERVANT TESTING THE WINE

The Ladies' Great Favorite

A large glass,
a squirt of Seltzer,
a spoonful of fine sugar,
fill a wineglass half full with sherry and
    the other half with port wine,
1 dash of brandy;
mix this well.

SELTZOGENE.

Fill your glass with shaved ice; ornament with orange and pineapple, and top it off with ice-cream; serve with a spoon.

THE "ONLY WILLIAM," *The Flowing Bowl,* 1892

Locofoco Drink

This is one of the hot drinks peculiar to America. Whisk the yolks of two fresh eggs for three or four minutes, add a little grated nutmeg, an ounce of honey, and a small glass of curaçao, and beat all together until thoroughly mixed. Add a pint of heated burgundy, and serve in glasses.

Cassell's Dictionary of Cookery [c. 1877]

Possets

To make a Posset with Ale: King William's Posset

Take a quart of cream, and mix with it a pint of ale, then beat the yolks of ten eggs, and the whites of four; when they are well beaten, put them to the cream and ale; sweeten it to your taste, and slice some nutmeg in it; set it over the fire, and keep it stirring all the while; and when it is thick, and before it boils, take it off, and pour it into the basin you serve it in to the table.

PLEDGING HEALTHS—NO. 1.

Drinking from Cow's Horns.

To make the Pope's Posset

Blanch and beat three quarters of a pound of almonds so fine, that they will spread between your fingers like butter, put in water as you beat them, to keep them from oiling; then take a pint of sack or sherry, and sweeten it very well with double-refined sugar, make it boiling hot, and at the same time put half a pint of water to your almonds, and make them boil; then take both off the fire, and mix them very well together with a spoon; serve it in a *China* dish.

E. SMITH, *The Compleat Housewife,* 1739

Claudius Punch

To one pound of Scotch oatmeal mix four quarts of boiling water; whip it in, stirring vigorously; then boil the preparation, working it steadily; add one and a half pounds of seeded Malaga raisins, the peel and juice of four lemons, a pint of good sherry wine and sufficient sugar to sweeten, a little grated nutmeg, ground cloves and cinnamon; also add a quarter of a pound of finely shredded citron, and should it be too thick then put in more boiling water, strain through a fine sieve, let cool and serve.

CHARLES RANHOFFER, *The Epicurean,* 1894

TANKARD FOR SHANDY GAFF.

The Shandy Gaff

A glass of Bass ale and a glass of ginger ale are mixed in a glass together, and served.

THE "ONLY WILLIAM," *The Flowing Bowl,* 1892

120

Sherry Cobler

Fill a tumbler three parts full of pounded ice, to which add two wine-glasses of sherry, a tablespoonful of brandy, two teaspoonfuls of powdered sugar, and two or three small pieces of lemon. Pour the mixture rapidly from one tumbler to another several times, throw in half a dozen strawberries, and drink the mixture through a straw, or stick of maccaroni.

Cups and Their Customs, 1869

To make Almond Shrub

Take three gallons of rum or brandy, three quarts of orange juice, the peels of three lemons, three pounds of loaf sugar. Then take four ounces of bitter almonds, [*Danger!* see page 167 for equivalent] blanch and beat them fine, mix them in a pint of milk, then mix them all well together. Let it stand an hour to curdle. Run it through a flannel bag several times till it is clear, then bottle it for use.

ELIZABETH RAFFALD, *The Experienced English House-Keeper,* 1778

An excellent Syllabub

Fill your Syllabub-pot with Cider (for that is the best for a Syllabub) and good store of Sugar and a little Nutmeg. Stir it well together. Put in as much thick Cream by two or three spoonfuls at a time, as hard as you can, as though you milk it in. Then stir it together exceeding softly once about, and let it stand two hours at least before it is eaten, for the standing makes the Curd.

The Compleat Cook, 1659

JOHN SHAW'S PUNCH HOUSE

A man named John Shaw, who had served in the army as a dragoon, having lost his wife and four or five children, solaced himself by opening a public-house in the Old Shambles, Manchester; in conducting which he was ably supported by a sturdy woman servant of middle age, whose only known name was "Molly." John Shaw, having been much abroad, had acquired a knack of brewing punch, then a favourite beverage; and from this attraction, his house soon began to be frequented by the principal merchants and manufacturers of the town, and to be known as "John Shaw's Punch-house." Sign it had none. As Dr. Aikin says in 1795 that Shaw had then kept the house more than fifty years, we have here an institution dating prior to the memorable '45. Having made a comfortable competence, John Shaw, who was a lover of early hours, and, probably from his military training, a martinet in discipline, instituted the singular rule of closing his house to customers at eight o'clock in the evening. As soon as the clock struck the hour, John walked into the one public room of the house, and in a loud voice and imperative tone, proclaimed "Eight o'clock, gentlemen; eight o'clock." After this no entreaties for more liquor, however urgent or suppliant, could prevail over the inexorable landlord. If the announcement of the hour did not at once produce the desired effect, John had two modes of summary ejectment. He would call to Molly to bring his horsewhip, and crack it in the ears and near the persons of his guests; and should this fail, Molly was ordered to bring her pail, with which she speedily flooded the floor, and drove the guests out wet-shod. On one occasion of a county election, when Colonel Stanley was returned, the gentleman took some friends to John Shaw's to give them a treat. At eight o'clock John came into the room and loudly announced the hour as usual. Colonel Stanley said he hoped Mr. Shaw would not press the matter on that occasion, as it was a special one, but would allow him and his friends to take another bowl of punch. John's characteristic reply was: "Colonel Stanley, you are a law-maker, and should not be a law-breaker; and if you and your friends do not leave the room in five minutes, you will find your shoes full of water." (R. CHAMBERS, ED., *The Book of Days*, vol. I, 1862–4)

To make a very fine Syllibubs

Take a quart and half a pint of cream, a pint of rhenish, half a pint of sack, three lemons, near a pound of double-refined sugar; beat and sift the sugar, and put it to your cream; grate off the yellow rind of your three lemons, and put that in; squeeze the juice of the three lemons into your wine, and put that to your cream, then beat all together with a whisk just half an hour; then take it up all together with a spoon, and fill your glasses: it will keep good nine or ten days, and is best three or four days old. These are called *the everlasting Syllibubs*.

E. SMITH, *The Compleat Housewife*, 1739

Tewahdiddle

A pint of Table Beer, (or Ale, if you intend it for a supplement to your "Night Cap,") a tablespoonful of Brandy, and a teaspoonful of brown Sugar, or clarified Syrup—a little grated Nutmeg or Ginger may be added, and a roll of very thin cut Lemon Peel.

Obs. Before our readers make any remarks on this Composition, we beg of them to taste it: if the materials are good, and their palate vibrates in unison with our own, they will find it one of the pleasantest beverages they ever put to their lips, —and, as *Lord Ruthven* says, "this is a right Gossip's Cup, that far exceeds all the Ale that ever MOTHER BUNCH made in her lifetime." —See his Lordship's *Experiments in Cookery, &c.* 18mo. London, 1654, page 215.

[DR. WILLIAM KITCHINER], *The Cook's Oracle*, 1823

Toddy

The simple admixture of spirits and water is
known either by the name of Toddy, which is a
corruption of an Indian word, Taddi (the sap of
the palm tree), or by the more truly English appellation of Grog, which thus derives its cogno-
men. Before the time of Admiral Vernon, rum
was given to the seamen in its raw state; but he
ordered it to be diluted, previously to delivery,
with a certain quantity of water. This watering
of their favourite liquor so incensed the tars that
they nicknamed the Admiral "Old Grog," in
allusion to a grogram coat which he was in the
habit of wearing.

Cups and Their Customs, 1869

PLEDGING HEALTHS—NO. 2.

To make a Wassel*

Take muskedine or ale, and set it on the fire to
warm. Then boil a quart of cream and two or
three whole cloves. Then have the yolks of three
or four eggs dissolved with a little cream; the
cream being well boiled with the spices, put in
the eggs and stir them well together. Then have
sops or sippets of fine manchet or french bread,
put them in a basin, and pour in the warm wine,
with some sugar and the thick cream on that;
stick it with blanched almonds and cast on
cinamon, ginger, and sugar, or wafers, sugar
plate, or comfits.

ROBERT MAY, *The Accomplisht Cook,* 1678

* The term "Wassail" is derived from the Old English
"waes hael," meaning "be
whole" or "be well" and was
said when proposing the good
health of a person or toasting
him. The reply was either "Waes
hael" or "Drink hael."

123

whether fortunately or otherwise, comes under the heading of "Strange Swallows." It is still consumed in prisons, and other places where sinners and paupers are dieted at the expense of the ratepayer. And hard as are the ways of the transgressor, his daily "quencher" is even harder. "Plain water," wrote a celebrated Mongolian of his day, "has a malignant influence, and ought on no account to be drunk." More especially if it be Thames water. I once saw a drop of this, very much magnified, displayed on a stretched cloth, in a side-show at the Crystal Palace. In that drop of water I counted three boa-constrictors, a few horrors which resembled giant lobsters, and a pair of turtles engaged, apparently, in a duel to the death. Three ladies in the front row of the stalls, at that exhibition, were carried out, swooning. (EDWARD SPENCER, *The Flowing Bowl*, 1898)

Wine for the Gods

Take 2 great Lemons, peel them and cut them in slices, with 2 Pippins pared and sliced like your Lemons, put all this into a dish, with three quarters of a pound of Sugar in powder, a pint of *Burgundy* wine, 6 Cloves, a little Orange-flower-water, cover this up and let it steep 2 or 3 hours, then pass it through a bag as you do Hypocras; and if you will, you may Musk it as you do your Hypocras, and it will be most excellent.

GILES ROSE, *The Officers of the Mouth*, 1682

To make wine of water

Take the grapes of a wild vine and dry them in the sun, then beat them into powder, and put them into water and it will have the taste and colour of wine, and if the grape be white it will have the same colour, if red the like.

Epulario, Or, The Italian Banquet, 1598

Wine-Press.

Hot cross buns!
Hot cross buns!
One a penny, two a penny,
Hot cross buns!
If your daughters do not like them
Give them to your sons;
But if you haven't any of these pretty little elves
You cannot do better than eat them yourselves.

One Seeded Wheat

A FURTHER NOTE ON BUNS

In London, and all over England (not, however, in Scotland), the morning of Good Friday is ushered in with a universal cry of "Hot cross buns!" For a century and a half Chelsea was famous for its buns. Swift mentions the "rare Chelsea buns" in his "Journal to Stella," in 1712. These were made and sold at the Old Chelsea Bun-House, in Jews' Row, a single-story building, with a colonnade projecting over the foot-pavement. It was a great meeting-place on Good Friday mornings, sometimes as many as fifty thousand persons calling for buns, two hundred and forty thousand of which have been sold in a single day.

A rival bun-house arose, and competition became fierce, especially in the reign of George III, when royalty itself deigned to visit Chelsea to partake of these delicacies.

Crying "Hot-Cross-Buns" on "Good Friday"

This and Christmas-day are the only two close holidays now observed throughout London, by the general shutting up of shops, and the opening of all the churches. The dawn is awakened by a cry in the streets of "Hot-cross-buns; one-a-penny buns, two-a-penny buns; one-a-penny, two-a-penny, hot-cross-buns!" This proceeds from some little "peep-o'-day boy," willing to take the "top of the morning" before the rest of his compeers. He carries his covered buns in a basket hanging on one arm, while his other hand is straightened like an open door, at the side of his mouth, to let forth his childish voice, and he "pipes and trebles *out* the sound" to the extremity of his lungs. Scarcely has he departed before others come; "another and another still succeeds," and at last the whole street is in one "common cry of *buns*." Old men and young men, young women and old women, big children and little children, are engaged in this occupation, and "some cry now who never cried before." The bun-venders who eclipse the rest in voice and activity, are young women who drive fruit-barrows—barrows, by the bye, are no more. A couple of these ex-barrow-women trip along, carrying a wicker clothes-basket between them, in which the "hot-cross-buns" are covered, first by a clean flannel or green baise, and outwardly by a clean white cloth, which coverings are slowly and partially removed, for fear of letting the buns cool, when a customer stops to buy, or calls them to the door.

Formerly "hot-cross-buns" were commonly eaten in London by families at breakfast, and some families still retain the usage. They are of the usual form of buns; though they are distinguished from them inwardly by a sweeter taste, and the flavour of all-spice, and outwardly by the mark or sign of the cross.

In the houses of some ignorant people, a Good Friday bun is still kept "for luck," and sometimes there hangs from the ceiling a hard biscuit-like cake of open *cross*-work, baked on a Good Friday, to remain there till displaced on the next Good Friday by one of similar make; and of this the editor of the *Every-Day Book* has heard affirmed, that it preserves the house from fire; "no fire ever happened in a house that had one." This undoubtedly is a relic of the old superstition.

WILLIAM HONE, *The Every-Day Book,* vol. I, 1826

Cross Buns

Rub half a pound of cooking butter into two pounds of flour until perfectly smooth; then add half a pound of castor sugar, a quarter of an ounce of ground cinnamon, and if liked, the same amount of mace may also be used; then mix two ounces of German yeast with a pint of tepid milk and two whole eggs which have been beaten up with a fork; add this to the other ingredients and knead all together into a light dough; put into a basin, cover over with a clean cloth, and place it in the screen before the fire or in some other warm place to rise for about two hours; then mix in, if liked, a quarter of a pound of washed and well dried currants; roll the mixture lightly round with the finger till in the shape of the buns; put them on a buttered tin and mark the tops in the form of a cross; put them into the screen again to rise for about ten to fifteen minutes, then brush over the tops with warm

The history of the cross bun goes back to the time of Cecrops, and to the *liba* offered to Astarte, and thence can be traced upward through the Jewish passover cakes, and the eucharistic bread, or cross-marked wafers, mentioned in St. Chrysostom's Liturgy. So that the Good Friday bun has antiquity and tradition to recommend it; and, indeed, its very name of *bun* is but the oblique *boun*, from *bous*, the sacred ox, the semblance of whose horns was stamped upon the cake. There, too, they also did duty for the horns of Astarte, in which word some philologists affect to trace a connection with Easter. The substitution by the Greeks of the cross-mark in place of the horn-mark would seem to have chiefly been for the easier division of the round bun into four equal parts. (WILLIAM S. WALSH, *Curiosities of Popular Customs,* 1897)

Winter Wheat

Egyptian or many spiked
Wheat

milk, and bake in a quick oven for fifteen to twenty minutes.

The quantity given above will make twenty-four to twenty-eight good size buns.

Mrs. A. B. Marshall's Cookery Book [c. 1888]

* When the buns were baked to a light brown, Marion Harland (*Common Sense in the Household*, 1877) brushed them over with an egg white beaten beyond the "stiff" stage with white sugar. She called this an easy recipe and said, "These are the hot cross buns of the 'London cries.' "

Hot Cross Buns

Three cupfuls of milk, 1 cup of soft yeast, or 1 cake of compressed yeast, dissolved in 1 cup of warm water. Flour to make a thick batter. Set as a sponge over night. In the morning, add half cupful of melted butter, 1 cupful sugar, half nutmeg, grated, 1 saltspoonful salt. Add sufficient flour to make a soft dough. Form into balls, flatten out with the hand, and mark deeply in the form of a cross with the back of a knife. Lay on buttered tins, and set to rise, and bake when light. Some cooks add a teaspoonful of coriander seeds.*

MAUD C. COOKE, *Twentieth Century Cook Book*, 1897

GOOD FRIDAY

The bun so fashionable, called the *Sally Lunn*, originated with a young woman of that name in Bath, about thirty years ago. She first cried them, in a basket with a white cloth over it, morning and evening. Dalmer, a respectable baker and musician, noticed her, bought her business, and made a song, and set it to music in behalf of "Sally Lunn." This composition became the street favourite, barrows were

Sally Lunn Cake

This is a favorite tea cake, and so universally liked that it is well to make a liberal quantity of the mixture, and bake it in two loaves. Sift into a large pan three pounds of fine flour. Warm in a quart of milk half a pound of fresh butter, and add a small tea-spoonful of salt, six eggs well beaten, and add, gradually, two wine glasses of excellent fresh yeast. Mix the flour well into the pan, (a little at a time) and beat the whole very hard. Divide this quantity into two equal portions, and set it to rise in two pans. Cover it with thick cloths, and set it on the hearth to rise.

128

When quite light, grease two loaf-pans with the same butter used for the cakes, and bake it in a moderate oven, keeping up the heat steadily to the last. It should be thoroughly done all through. Send it to table hot, cut in slices, but the slices left standing as in a pound cake at a party.

The Sally Lunn mixture may be baked on a griddle, as muffins in muffin rings, and split and buttered at table.

In mixing this cake, add neither sugar nor spice. They do not improve, but spoil it, as would be found on trial. It is the best of plain tea cakes, if properly made and baked.

Miss Leslie's New Cookery Book, 1857

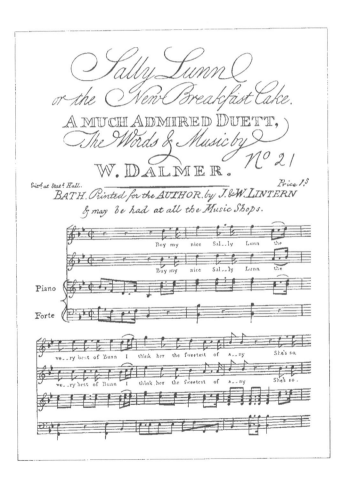

made to distribute the nice cakes, Dalmer profited thereby, and retired; and, to this day, the *Sally Lunn* cake, not unlike the hotcross bun in flavour, claims preeminence in all the cities in England. (WILLIAM HONE, *The Every-Day Book,* vol. I, 1826)

SALLY LUNN

is an honoured name from the Land's End to John o' Groat's. But why should the reader be called upon to meditate upon her virtues in these pages? The reason is that her name has been mixed up with a little culinary scandal; and it is necessary to vindicate her fair fame. The greatest cook of modern times, Carême, came over to England to minister to the palate of the Prince Regent. He did not stay long, but he stayed long enough to appreciate the charms of Sally Lunn and her ever memorable cake. He was a great cook, but a fearful coxcomb—and immeasurable egotist. If ever he made the slightest change in a dish, he vaunted the variation as an original idea, and thenceforward set up as the sovereign creator of the dainty. So it was that he dressed up Sally Lunn a little, and presented her to the Parisian world as his own—his Solilemne. The fact might well be forgotten, but there are stupid asses who will not let us forget it. They come over to England; they send up, among the sweets of a dinner, Sally and her tea-cake, rigged out in the height of French fashion; and like an English dancer or singer who insists on Mademoiselle to her name, the good honest Sally that we know is announced as the incomparable Solilemne. ([E. S. DALLAS], *Kettner's Book Of The Table*, 1877)

Sugar Box.

FRESH BUTTER.

CREAM-SKIMMER.

HENS' EGGS.

Sallylunns

(*Carême's recipe*)

Sift twelve ounces of flour, separate a fourth part, in which make a hollow, put in it nearly half an ounce of yeast and a little lukewarm cream; mix the flour gradually with this, and put it into a small stewpan to rise (it should be very soft). When double its first size, form the remaining flour in the requisite manner, and put in the center a quarter of an ounce of salt, one ounce of pounded sugar, four yolks of eggs, five ounces of butter made warm only, and a gill of lukewarm cream; stir this mixture, mingling the flour with the liquid until of a soft consistence, and beat the paste for some minutes with the palm of the hand; then, if perfect, add the leaven, and work it yet some minutes to render it smooth and elastic; put it into a plain mould six inches wide and five inches high, well buttered, and set it in a proper place to ferment; when double its primitive volume, wash the top with egg, and place it in a quick oven for an hour; when serving, divide it horizontally about the centre, turn the top upside down, and the cake should present the appearance of a honeycomb; throw on it a pinch of salt, and butter it with five ounces of the best butter, putting equal quantities on each; put the top on again, and serve hot.

Cassell's Dictionary of Cookery [c. 1877]

130

Humpty Dumpty sat on a wall,
Humpty Dumpty had a great fall.
All the king's horses,
And all the king's men,
Couldn't put Humpty together again.

Eggs

Eggs have been as violently eulogized as they have been condemned, and both in extremes. In some parts of Africa, where they are very scarce, and the Priests are very fond of them, it has been revealed to the people, that it is sacrilege for any but clerical gentlemen to eat eggs! The lay scruple, if I may so speak, is quieted by the assurance, that, though the sacred hens produce only for the servants at the altar, the latter never address themselves to the food in question,

ACCORDING TO Lina Eckenstein (*Comparative Studies in Nursery Rhymes*, London, 1911), "Among other rhymes which date some way back in history are those which may fitly be called riddle-rhymes. Some of these have close parallels in the nursery lore of other countries. The most interesting example of this class is the rhyme on Humpty-Dumpty which deals with the egg. The egg from the earliest times formed an enigma in itself, and was looked upon as representing the origin of life. Aristophanes knew of the great bird that laid the world-egg. According to *Kalevala*, the Finnish epic, the world-egg fell and broke. Its upper part became the vault of heaven, its lower part the earth. The yolk formed the sun, the white the moon, and the fragments of the shell became the stars in heaven.''

Eckenstein includes variations of Humpty-Dumpty from other languages. Thus, children in other parts of the world also sing of Hümpelken-Pümpelken, Rüntzelken-Püntzelken, Wirgele-Wargele, Gigele-Gagele, Lille-Trille, Annebadadeli and Boule, boule.

without the whole body of the laity profiting thereby! I suppose that Dissenters naturally abound in this part of Africa. There is nothing so unsatisfactory as vicarious feeding. Feeding is a duty which every man is disposed to perform for himself, whether it be expected of him or not. All the eggs in Africa, passing the œsophagus of a Priest, could hardly nourish a layman, even though the eggs were as gigantic as those which an old author says are presented by ladies in the moon to their profoundly delighted husbands, and from which spring young babies, six feet high, and men at all points.

If the matrons in the moon were thus remarkable in this respect, the Egyptian shepherds on earth were not less so in another: they had a singular method of cooking eggs, without the aid of fire. They laid them in a sling, and then applied so violent a rotatory motion thereto, that they were heated and cooked by the very friction of the air through which they passed!

Diviners and dreamers dealt largely in eggs. Livia was told, just before the birth of Tiberius, to hatch one in her bosom, and that the sex of the chick would foretell that of the expected little stranger. In Rome and Greece eggs were among the introductory portions of every banquet. But Rome knew only of twenty different manners of cooking them. What an advance in civilization has been made in Paris, which, according to Mr. Robert Fudge, boasts of six hundred and eighty-five ways to dress eggs!

DR. DORAN, *Table Traits,* 1854

Egyptian Slingers

The Virtues of Eggs

When we reflect that the American hen lays somewhere in the neighborhood of fourteen billion eggs in a year, and that in addition to this we import a good many million dozens of eggs, the importance of the egg department of a cook book is obvious. How many ways there are of cooking eggs we cannot guess. How many there might be is a still more formidable problem. But an egg is the compactest, most convenient, most readily cooked little parcel of nutrition that the world has ever known. It concentrates within its cleanly shell the very essence of food, and in such shape that it may readily be used by itself, or in combinations without number. There are few made dishes which it does not sometimes reinforce or supplement. Is there a lean sauce? an egg enriches it; a meagre cake? an egg helps it out; a barren breakfast table? an egg supplies the want; a nourishment for an invalid called for? an egg does the duty. The egg is the universal resource for whatever is lacking.

Hood's Practical Cook's Book, 1897

On Cooking Eggs

I wish to be of much use to Students, for they most need nourishing meats. But touching the choice of Eggs, first I say that Hen Eggs, as they be most used, so they be best. Yet Eggs of Pheasants and Partridges be not unwholesome; but Eggs of Ducks, Geese, Turkeys and other fowl should be eschewed. And of Hen Eggs the choice rests on three points, that they be white, long, and new. Eggs long and white be nutritive, much better than the round.

COLUMBUS

COLUMBUS

To him the modern table owes more than to any other that can be named. The discovery of America has enriched our tables with the turkey, the canvasbacked duck, the potato, the tomato, cocoa, vanilla, the Jerusalem artichoke, the sugar-cane, red pepper, and a host of good things. Yet the master-cooks of Europe, who lavish their honours on nobodies and confuse their cookery books with a mob of ridiculous names, have not thought it worth their while to consecrate a single dish to his memory—not even the humble egg which he taught his friends to set on end. ([E. S. DALLAS], *Kettner's Book Of The Table,* 1877)

133

TO MAKE AN EGG TO STAND UPON AN END WITHOUT ANY HELP AT ALL

There is an old tale of a good workman who made an egg to stand in salt upon an end, but here the same is more artly performed, and yet without any such supportation. Hold an egg in your right hand, and with your fist give three or four good strong blows upon your left arm, or use any other devise by agitation or shaking, until you have broken the yolk, and so made the white to mingle confusedly with it, and then it will presently stand upon the broad end on an even table. (HUGH PLATTE, *The Jewell House of Art and Nature,* 1594)

EGG-STAND FOR THE BREAKFAST-TABLE

TO MAKE CLEAN THY SHELL OF AN EGG

To make clean thy shell of an egg with thy fingers is a ridiculous and a thing that men laugh at: & to do it putting thy tongue into it, is yet more ridiculous. It is done more properly with thy knife. ([THOMAS PAYNELL], *The Civilitie of Childehode,* 1560)

Now as concerning the dressing of eggs, there is great difference. For either they be boiled, roasted or fried. And they be boiled two ways, either in the Shells, or else the shells being broken, the eggs are put into boiling water: the first is called seething of Eggs, the second potching of Eggs. Both ways are good, but eggs potched are best, and most wholesome. Yet eggs boiled in the shells are better than roasted, because the moistness of the water tempers the heat of the fire which dries up the substance of the Eggs overmuch. And fried Eggs be worst of all, for they engender ill humours, annoy the stomach, and cause corrupt fumes to rise in the head. Wherefore collops and Eggs, which is an usual dish toward shrovetide, can in no wise be wholesome meat, yet it is the less unwholesome if the Eggs be not fried hard. For in the regiment of health, eggs should in no wise be eaten hard, but being in a mean between rare and hard, which Galen calls *Ova tremula*; yet rare eggs, named *Ova sorbilia*, that is to say, little more than thoroughly hot, are good to clear the throat and breast, and they do ease the greases of the bladder and kidneys made with gravel, so that they be taken before any other meat. And if a man would break his fast with a light and nourishing meat, then I say there is nothing better than a couple of Eggs potched, or the yolks of two Eggs sodden rare and put into one shell, seasoned with a little Pepper, Butter and Salt, and supped off warm, drinking after it a good draught of Claret wine. This I know to be very comfortable for weak stomachs, and is often used by the wisest men in England. And this rule is generally to be observed, to drink a good draught of Wine, Ale or beer, after we have eaten an egg, as it is taught in *Schola Sal.*

THOMAS COGAN, *The Haven of Health,* 1605

To make a great compound Egg, as big as twenty Eggs

Take twenty eggs, part the whites from the yolks, and strain the whites by themselves, and the yolks by themselves; then have two bladders, boil the yolks in one bladder, fast bound up as round as a ball. Being boiled hard, put it in another bladder, and the whites round about it, bind it up round like the former, and being boil'd it will be a perfect egg. This serves for grand sallets.

Or you may add to these yolks of eggs, musk, and ambergriece, candied pistaches, grated bisket-bread, and sugar, and to the whites almond paste, musk, juice of oranges, and beaten ginger, and serve it with butter, almond milk, sugar, and juice of oranges.

Robert May, *The Accomplisht Cook,* 1678

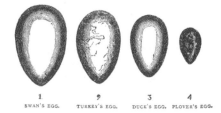

COMPARATIVE SIZES OF EGGS.

1 SWAN'S EGG. 2 TURKEY'S EGG. 3 DUCK'S EGG. 4 PLOVER'S EGG.

Blancmange Eggs

Make a small hole at the end of four or five large eggs, and let out all the egg carefully; wash the shell, drain, and fill them with blancmange, place them in a deep dish filled with rice or barley to keep them steady, and when quite cold, gently break and peel off the shell. Cut the peel of a lemon into delicately fine shreds, lay them into a glass dish, and put in the eggs; or serve them in a glass dish with a pink cream round them.

[Mrs. N. K. M. Lee], *The Cook's Own Book, By A Boston Housekeeper,* 1835

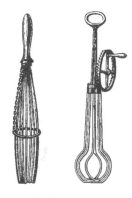

Egg Whisks

Marmalade of Eggs

Chop ½ lb. of citron, put it in a basin with 1 teacupful of orange marmalade, ¼ lb. of sweet almonds, blanched and pounded with a few drops of rose-water, pour in 2 wineglassfuls of brandy, and stir the mixture until quite smooth. Beat the yolks of ten Eggs with the whites of four, stir them into the mixture, sweeten with caster sugar, pour it into a saucepan, and stir it over a moderate fire with a wooden spoon until thick, but without letting it boil, or the Eggs will curdle. Turn the marmalade into a dome-shaped mould, and stand it in a cool place or on ice until quite cold. When about to serve, dip the mould in tepid water, wipe it, then turn the contents on to a fancy dish, and garnish with bunches of fresh or preserved fruits.

THEODORE FRANCIS GARRETT, ED., *The Encyclopædia of Practical Cookery*, 1892–4

DOME MOLD

Marmalade of Eggs, the Jews' Way

[from Hannah Glasse, 1778]

Take the Yolks of twenty-four Eggs, beat them for an Hour; clarify one Pound of the best moist Sugar, four Spoonfuls of Orange Flower Water, one Ounce of blanched and pounded Almonds; stir all together over a very slow charcoal Fire, keeping stirring it all the while one Way till it comes to a Consistence; then put it into Coffee Cups, and throw a little beaten Cinnamon on the Top of the Cups.

MARGARET HUNTINGTON HOOKER, *Yᵉ Gentlewoman's Housewifery*, 1896

Egg Paste, Called in Modern Cookery Nouilles

This is formed by making a paste of flour and beaten eggs, without either butter or water; it must be rolled out extremely thin and left to dry; it may then be cut into narrow strips or stamped with paste cutters. It is more fashionable in soups than vermicelli.*

The Jewish Manual, 1846

* Louis Eustache Ude (*The French Cook,* 1829) uses only the yolks and adds a little butter and water. While still pliable, the dough is often well floured and rolled into a scroll for easier cutting, then the excess flour is removed.

To make an Amulet

Put a quarter of a pound of butter into a frying pan, break six eggs and beat them a little, strain them through a hair sieve, put them in when your butter is hot, and strew in a little shred parsley and boiled ham scraped fine, with nutmeg, pepper and salt, fry it brown on the under-side, lay it on your dish but don't turn it, hold a hot salamander half a minute over it to take off the raw looks of the eggs; stick curled parsley in it, and serve it up.

N.B. you may put in clary and chives or onions if you like.

Elizabeth Raffald, *The Experienced English House-Keeper,* 1778

Egg Omelette for One Person

Two eggs, one and a half tablespoons of fresh milk, and a little salt; beat the eggs and milk together; take a small steel frying-pan, used only for this purpose, and put in a piece of butter the size of a nutmeg; let it warm, but not get very

OMELETS

It is a strange fact, but not the less true, that to get a well-made omelet in a private house in this country is the exception and not the rule. A few general remarks on making omelets will, we hope, not be out of place in writing a book on an exceptional style of cookery, in which omelets should play a most important part.

First of all, we require an omelet-pan. The best omelet-pan of all is a copper one, tinned inside. It is very essential that the frying-pan be absolutely clean, and it will be found almost essential to reserve the omelet-pan for omelets only.

The great question is, how much butter should be allowed for, say, six eggs? On this point the greatest authorities differ. We will first quote our authorities, and then attempt to give an explanation that reconciles the difference. A plain omelet may be roughly described as settings of eggs well beaten up by stirring them up in hot butter. One of the oldest cookery books we can call to mind is entitled "The Experienced English Housekeeper," by Elizabeth Raffald. The book, which was published in 1775, is dedicated to the Hon. Lady Elizabeth Warburton, whom the authoress formerly served as housekeeper. The recipe is entitled "To make an amulet." The book states, "Put a quarter of a pound of butter into a frying pan, break six eggs." Francatelli also gives four ounces of butter to six eggs.

On the other hand, Soyer, the great cook, gives two ounces of butter to six eggs; so also does the equally great Louis Eustache Ude, cook to Louis XVI.

We may add that "Cassell's Dictionary of Cookery" recommended two ounces of butter to six eggs, whilst "Cassell's Shilling Cookery" recommends four eggs.

The probable reason why two such undoubtedly great authorities as Soyer and Francatelli should differ is that in making one kind of omelet you would use less butter than in making another. Francatelli wrote for what may be described as that "high class cooking suited for Pall Mall clubs," where no one better than himself knew how best to raise the jaded appetite

hot: pour in the above mixture, shake the pan so that it will not burn; do not turn it, but roll it up while cooking, by placing your knife under the edges; have ready a hot plate, and just before you think it is done, turn it over on to the plate. This recipe was given to me by one of the best cooks of California, and his Omelettes are delicious.

LADIES OF CALIFORNIA, *California Recipe Book*, 1873

Apple Omelette (Easy)

6 large pippins.	5 or 6 tablespoonfuls sugar.
1 tablespoonful butter.	1 teaspoonful rosewater.
8 eggs.	
Nutmeg to taste.	

Stew the apples, when you have pared and cored them, as for apple-sauce. Beat them very smooth while hot, adding the butter, sugar, and nutmeg. When perfectly cold, put with the eggs, which should be whipped light, yolks and whites separately. Put in the yolks first, then the rosewater, lastly the whites, and pour into a deep bake-dish, which has been warmed and buttered. Eat warm —not hot—for tea, with Graham bread. It is better for children—I say nothing of their elders —than cake and preserves.

MARION HARLAND, *Common Sense in the Household,* 1877

Bread Omelet

Break four eggs into a basin and carefully remove the treadles;* have ready a tablespoonful of grated and sifted bread; soak it in either milk, water, cream, white wine, gravy, lemon-juice, brandy or rum, according as the omelet is intended to be sweet or savory. Well beat the eggs together with a little nutmeg, pepper and salt; add the bread, and, beating constantly (or the omelet will be crumbly), get ready a frying-pan, buttered and made thoroughly hot; put in the omelet; do it on one side only; turn it upon a dish, and fold it double to prevent the steam from condensing. Stale sponge-cake, grated biscuit, or pound cake, may replace the bread for a sweet omelet, when pounded loaf sugar should be sifted over it, and the dish decorated with lumps of currant jelly. This makes a nice dessert.

Mrs. F. L. Gillette and Hugo Ziemann, *The White-House Cook-Book,* 1894

Eggs or Quelque shose

Break forty eggs, and beat them together with some salt. Fry them at four times, but of one side. Before you take them out of the pan, make a composition or compound of hard eggs, and sweet herbs minced, some boiled currants, beaten cinnamon, almond-paste, sugar, and juice of orange. Strew all over these omlets, roll them up like a wafer, put them in a dish with some white-wine, sugar, and juice of lemon; then warm and ice them in an oven, with beaten butter and fine sugar.

Robert May, *The Accomplisht Cook,* 1678

of a wealthy epicure. Soyer's book was written for the people.

In Holland, Belgium, and Germany, and in country villages in France, the omelet is made, as a rule, with six eggs to two ounces of butter. In the higher-class restaurants in Paris, like Bignon's, or the Cafe Anglais, the omelet is lighter, and probably about four ounces of butter would be used to six eggs.

This probably explains the different directions given in various cookery books for making omelets. (A. G. Payne, B.A., *Cassell's Vegetarian Cookery,* 1891)

* Treadles = the two opaque threads or "eyes" of an egg. According to the *Oxford English Dictionary*, the treadle was "so called, because it was formerly thought to be the Sperm of the Cock," and the word "tread," at one time, meant copulation.

Egg Poacher

Macédoine, or à la Washington

Make four omelets of four eggs each, one with apples, one with asparagus or sorrel (according to the season), a third with *fines herbes,* and the fourth *au naturel;* you serve them on the same dish, one lapping over the other. It makes a fine as well as a good dish.

This omelet, or rather these omelets, were a favorite dish with the Father of his Country; they were very often served on his table when he had a grand dinner. It is also served with the four following omelets: *au naturel,* with salt pork, *fines herbes,* and with cheese.

Pierre Blot, *Hand-Book of Practical Cookery,* 1868

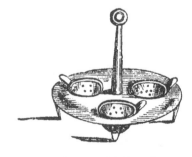

TIN EGG-POACHER

Pochee

(Poached eggs with ginger sauce)

Take eggs and break them in scalding hot water, and when they be boiled enough, take them up. And take the yolks of eggs and raw milk, and swing them together, and put thereto powder ginger, saffron, and salt; set it over the fire, and let it not boil. And take the boiled eggs and cast the liquor on, and serve it forth.

The Forme of Cury [c. 1390]

Poached Eggs in Matelote

Put a bottle of claret wine in a stewpan and set it on a good fire; add to it two sprigs of parsley, one of thyme, a clove of garlic, a middling-sized onion, a clove, a bay-leaf, salt, and pepper; boil fifteen minutes; then take all the seasonings out and have your wine boiling gently; break one egg in by letting it fall gently in order to have it entire, and then take it out immediately with a skimmer, and place it on a dish; do the same with eight eggs; keep them in a warm (but not hot) place. After which put in the wine, without taking it from the fire, four ounces of butter kneaded with a tablespoonful of flour; boil till reduced to a proper thickness, pour it on the eggs, and serve.

Pierre Blot, *Hand-Book of Practical Cookery,* 1868

Towres

Take & make a good thick batter of yolks of Eggs, & marrow as needed, powdered pepper, Mace, cloves, Saffron, Sugar, & Salt; & if you wish, a little cooked Pork or veal chopped. Then take the whites of the Eggs, & strain them into a bowl; then put a little Saffron & Salt to the whites. Set a pan with grease over the fire & beware that the grease is not too hot. Then put a little of the whites in the pan, & let it flow all around as in making a pancake. Then when it is somewhat stiff, lay a small amount of the Eggs, that is to say, of the yolks, in the middle, & loosen the cake all around, & close it four-square, & fry it up, & serve it forth for Suppers in Summer.

Harleian MS. 279 [c. 1430]

OF EGGS

In speaking of eggs in cookery, hens' eggs are understood, because they are the only ones to be had all the year round. Ducks' eggs are common enough in early summer; they are larger, but less delicate for eating than hens'. At that season turkey and goose eggs are too valuable for hatching to be used as food. The former, especially, can be procured in autumn, when there is no chance of rearing the chicks obtained from them. Both are excellent. The only objection to a goose's egg is its inconvenient size. During a limited period, and in a few localities—as in certain parts of Yorkshire and Norfolk—the eggs of a few species of seagulls are taken and sold. They have a peculiar flavour, which to many persons is very agreeable. But they must be regarded as an occasional luxury rather than as a common article of diet. They are the *game* of eggs. The supply, which is much restricted, has greatly fallen off of late years, and will speedily be reduced to nothing unless stringent measures are taken for the preservation of the parent birds. (*Cassell's Household Guide*, vol. II [c. 1885])

Soufflé

Soufflés require the greatest care in their preparation and baking; their lightness mainly depends on the proper whisking of the eggs, but also much on the oven being the right heat. Experience alone can determine this. They should be served the moment they come out of the oven, or they will fall and become heavy. They are better under than over done. A really good soufflé cannot be made without practice and experience. If it fails, there is one consolation, that a soufflé "manqué" generally makes a very good pudding. They should be baked in a proper soufflé-dish, which is double, the inside being put in the oven, and then placed in the finer one when sent to table.

LADY HARRIET ST. CLAIR (LATE COUNTESS MÜNSTER), *Dainty Dishes* [1884]

ORNAMENTAL SOUFFLÉ DISH

Cheese Soufflés

Put two tablespoonfuls of butter in a saucepan and one heaping tablespoonful of flour; when smooth, add one teacupful of milk, one-half teaspoonful of salt and a little cayenne pepper, and cook for two minutes; then add the well-beaten yolks of three eggs and one breakfast cupful of grated cheese, and set it one side to cool. After it is cold, add the whites, beaten to a stiff froth, turn into a buttered dish, and bake for about thirty minutes, then serve immediately.

The Cook Book by "Oscar" of the Waldorf [c. 1896]

PLAIN SOUFFLÉ DISH

Soufflé of Sour Cream

A pint and a half of thick sour cream, eight eggs, four tablespoonfuls of flour, two of sugar, a little vanilla and cinnamon; beat the cream and eggs well together, add by degrees the other ingredients, and lastly the whites of the eggs whipt to a froth; bake three-quarters of an hour.

Lady Harriet St. Clair (Late Countess Münster), *Dainty Dishes* [c. 1884]

Soufflé Espagnole

Boil four ounces of butter and three ounces of bread-crumbs in a stewpan, stirring all the time until the bread-crumbs are slightly coloured, stir in two ounces of sugar and a pint of boiling milk, and let the whole boil until the mixture becomes rather thick; take the mixture off the fire and whilst it is getting cool whip up to a froth the whites of six eggs, on which put two or three drops of vinegar; mix the yolks of the eggs with the mixture and add the whip, turning it lightly over until well mixed; butter and sugar a mould, fill it to within an inch of the top with the mixture, place the mould in a stewpan of hot water with a little paper at the bottom to prevent it slipping, and put in an oven not too hot, and bake for three-quarters of an hour; turn out of the mould and cover with half a pint of Whip Sauce, flavoured with vanilla.

SOUFFLÉ

These dishes, being the last of the Dinner, require the greatest care and taste in executing, as, by the time they come on the table, the appetites of those around it are supposed to be satisfied; the eye and the palate require to be pleased in order to sustain the enjoyments of the table; this is the period of dinner when another of the senses may be gratified by the introduction of music (and which is continually practised on the Continent), and all ought to be of a light and inviting character.

Formerly it was the custom never to give a dinner without a soufflé as the last dish, or, professionally speaking, remove. I do not dislike them, but they require the greatest care and nicety, and are rather difficult to perform in our old-fashioned kitchens, but easy in my new stove. (Alexis Soyer, *The Modern Housewife*, 1851)

143

This Mary was a Jewess who lived in the fourth century of our era, and was devoted to alchemy. She required a bath that would retain heat long at an equable temperature for the metals and vessels upon which she made her experiments. To this end she heated sand and plunged her vessels into it. The modern Mary-bath is an imitation in hot water, which is not so good as sand, since it has no special aptitude for retaining heat, but has the advantage of being easily kept hot by connection with the boiler—and kept thus hot at a temperature which can never exceed 212 degrees Fahrenheit. Transferred with this change of sand into water from the laboratory to the kitchen, the Mary-bath is exceedingly useful as a means of keeping things hot with no danger of their being too hot. Practically, however, this heat is a good way below the boiling point; and it is a mistake to suppose that the same bain marie will at once do for cooking and for keeping things hot. In the language of the French kitchen, to cook *au bain marie* means simply to cook in a double saucepan, the water in the outer saucepan being kept continuously at boiling point. ([E. S. DALLAS], *Kettner's Book Of The Table,* 1877)

Whip Sauce for Puddings

Put in a saucepan the yolks of three eggs, stir with whisk, add a gill of cream, half a glass of sherry, a dessert-spoonful of sugar, and flavouring essence of whatever is required (vanilla, chocolate, coffee, or caramel). Put the saucepan in a bain-marie* or in a larger one of boiling water, and keep turning the whisk until it rises, when pour over the pudding and serve.

MAJOR L. . . . , *The Pytchley Book of Refined Cookery,* 1889

Why did the soufflé rise?

Why did the soufflé rise? Because of the air-bubbles. It is easy to whisk the whites of eggs into a foam, but not the yolks. By separating the whites, therefore, and beating them up separately, we increased our number of air-bubbles to an enormous extent. These bubbles expand with the heat, hence the lightness of the soufflé. On the other hand, as the soufflé cools, the bubbles contract, the soufflé goes down, and a cold soufflé would be as heavy as a hot one is light.

Now the *principle* is the thing to grasp. For instance, in making a cake, you want, of course, to make it light; therefore remember the soufflé —i.e., beat the whites up separate from the yolks. This will have the effect of considerably lightening the cake, though, of course, as the process of baking a large cake is slower than that of baking a soufflé, the cake would not rise in anything like the same proportion.

Cassell's Dictionary of Cookery [c. 1877]

If you plant turnips on the twenty-fifth of July,
You will have turnips, wet or dry.

To make a made dish of Turneps

Pare your Turneps as you would pare a Pippin, then cut them in square pieces, an inch and a half long and as thick as a Butchers pricke or skewer. Put them into a pipkin with a pound of butter, and three or four spoonfuls of strong broth, and a quarter of a pint of Vinegar seasoned with a little Pepper, Ginger, Salt and Sugar, and let them stew very easily upon a soft fire for the space of two hours or more, now and then turning them with a spoon, as occasion shall serve, but by all means take heed you break them not. Then dish them up upon Sippets, and serve them to the Table hot.

JOHN MURRELL, *A Delightfull Daily Exercise*, 1621

THE TURNIP, (*brassica rapa*)

The turnip is a biennial plant, indigenous to Britain. If the cultivated plant be in reality a variety of this, of which there is some doubt, its nature has been greatly changed by the labours of man.

It is averred that the Roman method of cultivating must have been superior to that of the moderns, since Pliny relates that some single roots weighed as much as forty pounds, a weight far surpassing any which has been obtained by the most skillful modern agriculturists. Spec-

145

ulations, however, raised upon what might perhaps have been an exaggerated statement of the Roman naturalist, must be purely hypothetical.

The turnip, in some of its varieties, is of very universal culture throughout Europe. In Sweden it is a very favourite vegetable. In Russia, turnips are used as fruit and eaten with avidity by all classes. In the houses of the nobility, the raw turnip cut in slices is handed about on a silver salver, with brandy, as a provocative to the more substantial meal.

The uses of the turnip as a culinary vegetable, are too familiarly known to require that they should be here enumerated. Though in very extensive favour among the moderns, the different modes of preparing it appear poor and insipid compared with those efforts of gastronomic skill by which the ancients made it assume so many inviting forms. It is related that "the king of Bithynia, in some expedition against the Scythians in the winter, and at a great distance from the sea, had a violent longing for a small fish called *aphy*—a pilchard, a herring, or an anchovy. His cook cut a turnip to the perfect imitation of its shape; then, fried in oil, salted, and well powdered with the grains of a dozen black poppies, his majesty's taste was so exquisitely deceived, that he praised the root to

To make a fried meat of Turneps

Roast the Turnips in the embers or else boil them whole, then cut or slice them in pieces as thick as half the shaft of a knife, which done, take cheese and cut it in the same form and quantity, but somewhat thinner. Then take Sugar, Pepper, and other spices mingled together, and put them in a pan under the pieces of cheese, as if you would make a crust under the cheese, and on top of them likewise. And over it you shall lay the pieces of Turnips, covering them over with the spices aforesaid, and plenty of good Butter, and so you shall do with the said cheese and Turnips till the pan be full, letting them cook the space of a quarter of an hour, or more, like a Tart, and this would be one of your last Dishes.

Epulario, Or, The Italian Banquet, 1598

Turnip or Mixed Hash

Turnips twelve ounces; potatoes twelve ounces; flour, oatmeal, or pease meal, etc., two tablespoonfuls; butter two ounces; one large onion, a table-spoonful of salt. Boil the turnips cut into small dice, and the onion cut small, in three pints of water, add the salt and boil one hour; then put in the potatoes also cut in pieces, and after boiling three quarters of an hour longer add the butter. Rub the flour in a quarter of a pint of cold water until quite smooth, pour it into the pan and let the whole boil slowly fifteen minutes longer, or until all the ingredients are quite tender and the liquid part of the hash has the consistency of thin butter sauce. It will be sufficiently boiled in two hours, and should be covered the whole time.

Carrots, Jerusalem artichokes, vegetable marrows, etc., may be used instead of the turnips.

[JOHN SMITH], *The Principles and Practices of Vegetarian Cookery*, 1860

Swedish Turnips with Sweet Potatoes

Pare two good-sized ruta-bagas and cut them into slices. Wash and bake four sweet potatoes. Cook the Swedish turnips in unsalted water below the boiling point until perfectly tender; drain, and press them through a colander. Open the baked sweet potatoes, scoop out the centres, add them to the Swedish turnips, add a tablespoonful of butter, a saltspoonful of salt, a saltspoonful of pepper. Beat the two until very light, heap them into a baking dish, brush the top with milk and bake in a quick oven until a golden brown, about twenty minutes.

Serve with roasted duck, opossum, or baked rabbit.

SARAH TYSON RORER, *Mrs. Rorer's New Cook Book*, 1898

his guest as an excellent fish. This transmutation of vegetables into meat or fish, is a province of the culinary art which we appear to have lost; yet these are *cibi innocentes* (harmless food) compared with the things themselves. The earliest spring-produced leaves of the turnip are sometimes boiled or stewed, and appear on the table under the name of turnip-tops. The Romans likewise applied these tender leaves to the same purpose." (WILLIAM RHIND, *A History of The Vegetable Kingdom* [c. 1842])

According to the *Century Dictionary*, the turnip "sometimes suffers from an affection called *finger-and-toe* or *dactylorhiza*, in which the root divides into branches, apparently a tendency to revert to the wild state."

SWEDE TURNIPS

Pots to mend

Knee high
By the Fourth of July.

AMERICAN INDIAN CORN is generally planted in the United States of America about the middle of May, so as to avoid the mischance of its experiencing frost after it is once out of the ground. The Indians who inhabited the country previously to the formation of any settlement upon its shores by Europeans, having no calendar or other means of calculating the efflux of time, were guided by certain natural indications in their choice of periods for agricultural operations. The time for their sowing of maize was governed by the budding of some particular

Boiled Indian Wheat or Maize

Ingredients: The ears of young and green Indian wheat; to every ½ gallon of water allow 1 heaped tablespoonful of salt.

Mode: This vegetable, which makes one of the most delicious dishes brought to table, is unfortunately very rarely seen in Britain; and we wonder that, in the gardens of the wealthy, it is not invariably cultivated. Our sun, it is true, possesses hardly power sufficient to ripen maize; but, with well-prepared ground, and in a favourable position, it might be sufficiently advanced by the beginning of autumn to serve as a vegetable. The outside sheath being taken off and the waving fibres removed, let the ears be placed in boiling water, where they should remain for about 25 minutes (a longer time may be necessary for larger ears than ordinary); and, when sufficiently boiled and well drained, they may be sent to table whole, and with a piece of toast underneath them. Melted butter should be served with them.

Time: 25 to 35 minutes.

Sufficient: 1 ear for each person. *Seasonable* in autumn.

Note: William Cobbett, the English radical writer and politician, was a great cultivator and admirer of maize, and constantly ate it as a vegetable, boiled. We believe he printed a special recipe for it, but we have been unable to lay our hands on it. Mr. Buchanan, the present president of the United States, was in the habit, when ambassador here, of receiving a supply of Indian corn from America in hermetically-sealed cases; and the publisher of this work remembers, with considerable satisfaction, his introduction to a dish of this vegetable, when in America. He found it to combine the excellence of the young green pea and the finest asparagus; but he felt at first slightly awkward in holding the large ear with one hand, whilst the other had to be employed in cutting off with a knife the delicate green grains.

Mrs. Isabella Beeton, *The Book of Household Management*, 1861

tree, and by the visits of a certain fish to their waters—both which events observation had proved to be such regular indicators of the season, as fully to warrant the faith which was placed on their recurrence. (William Rhind, *A History of The Vegetable Kingdom* [c. 1842])

Maize, Roasted

The following is William Cobbett's account of this process: "Roasted ears," he says, "are certainly the greatest delicacy that ever came in contact with the palate of man. In America, where they burn wood upon the hearth, they contrive to have a bright fire, with a parcel of live

Wm. Cobbett

CORN GRATER

wood coals on the hearth; they lay something of iron across the two hand-irons, which are used in the fireplace, sweep the ashes up clean, and then they take the ears of corn and set them up along in a row, facing the fire, and leaning gently against the bar which they have put across. When one side is brown, you turn the other side towards the fire; or, rather, you turn them round gradually, until the whole be brown; and when the whole of the grains be brown, you lay them in a dish, and put them on the table. These are so many little bags of roasted milk, the sweetest that can be imagined; or, rather, are of the most delightful taste. You leave a little tail of the ear, two inches long, or thereabouts, to turn it and handle it by. You take a thin piece of butter upon a knife, which will cling to the knife on one side, while you gently rub it over the ear from the other side. Thus the ear is buttered; then you take a little salt, according to your fancy, and sprinkle it over the ear; you then take the tail of the ear in one hand, and the point of the ear in the other hand, and bite the grains off the cob; I need hardly say that this must be done with the fore teeth, and that those who have none must be content to live without green ears, for, as to taking the grains off with a knife, they are too deeply implanted to admit of that; and, if you attempt cutting, you will cut cob and all. When you have finished one ear, you lay the cob aside, and go to another. . . . I defy all the arts of French cookery, upon which so many volumes have been written, to produce anything so delightful to the palate as this.''

Cassell's Dictionary of Cookery [c. 1877]

Spider* Corn Cake
(A Plain Receipt)

For this cake there is required a frying-pan with a handle short enough to go into the oven.

Mix together a cupful and two-thirds of corn meal, one-third of a cupful of flour, one-quarter of a cupful of sugar, and a teaspoonful of salt. Beat two eggs till light, and add to them a cupful of sour milk and one of sweet milk in which a small teaspoonful of soda has been dissolved. Pour this mixture upon the dry ingredients, and mix thoroughly.

Have the frying-pan very hot, and after greasing it with two table-spoonfuls of butter, pour the batter into it. Now pour into the mixture another cupful of sweet milk, but do not stir the cake. Place the frying-pan in a hot oven, and bake for half an hour. When the cake is cooked, slip it gently from the pan on to a platter or large plate.

This is one of the most delicious forms of corn bread.

Maria Parloa, *Miss Parloa's Kitchen Companion*, 1887

* Spider = a skillet or frying pan originally with three legs long enough to stand over hot coals.

Corn Dodgers

One cup of granulated corn-meal, three fourths of a cup of boiling water, half a cup of cold sweet milk, one heaping teaspoon sugar, one level teaspoon salt. Mix the salt and sugar with the meal, pour the boiling water over the mixture, and when thoroughly scalded add the cold milk gradually, and stir well. The dough should be sufficiently stiff to retain its shape without spreading, when placed upon the griddle. Put a

Space between rows well filled and not well filled.

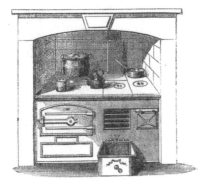

piece of butter about the size of a pea upon the griddle, where the cake is to be placed, and as soon as it melts drop a spoonful of the dough upon it. Fill the griddle in this manner with cakes, and when they are browned on the under side, place a bit of butter upon each of them, turn them over, and gently press as close to the griddle as possible, with a knife or cake paddle. After being turned on the griddle and browned on both sides, the cakes can be transferred to a baking pan, and finished in a hot oven; or if more convenient they can be baked, without the griddle being used, on a baking pan in the oven. Such cakes or dodgers can be baked in thirty minutes, but are sweeter and nicer when baked a longer time. The heat should be moderate so as not to burn the cakes, and if necessary they can be turned several times while baking.

EMMA P. EWING, *The Art of Cookery,* 1896

Indian Dumplings, to Eat with Pork or Goose

Take a quart of Indian meal, a table-spoonful of salt; scald the meal with boiling hot water; let it stand until cold; then wet your hands in cold water; make up balls, the size of a common potato, quite hard; drop them into a saucepan of boiling water; cover them up, and boil them thirty minutes. They are very nice with the gravy of roast goose or pork.

Mrs. Putnam's Receipt Book, 1858

Fried Corn

(Mrs. Kingsbury, Wyandotte)

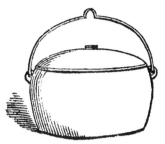

Cut the corn finely from the cob, scraping it when done; put a piece of butter half as large as an egg in the spider, and when hot pour in the corn, and cover up closely. Cook it ten or fifteen minutes, stirring occasionally, but adding no water; the steam and butter will cook it sufficiently. Put in salt and pepper, and when done add one cup of cream. This will taste like roast corn, and is excellent.

The Kansas Home Cook-Book, 1879

Grandmother's Indian Pudding

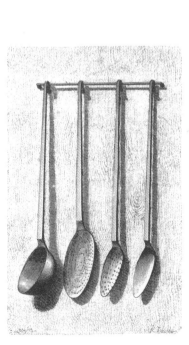

"This is 'the kind that grandmother used to make,' and is the best pudding you ever put in your mouth," says a cook of experience to our Practical Cook. One cup of Indian meal, a piece of butter the size of an egg, one cup of molasses, one egg, one teaspoon of salt and one-half teaspoon each of ginger and cinnamon. Boil one quart of milk and while boiling hot stir in the Indian meal and add the other ingredients. When ready put into a bean-pot and add one pint of cold milk and one-half pint of hot water, without stirring. This is to form the whey. Bake four hours slowly.

Hood's Practical Cook's Book, 1897

German Schpeischlitz

This dish may be made either sweet or savoury. If preferred sweet, the pepper and parsley in the following recipe may be omitted. Put three-quarters of a pint of milk into a saucepan with a quarter of a pound of butter, a tea-spoonful of sugar, and a little pepper and salt. When the milk rises in the pan, stir quickly into it six ounces of maize flour,* and continue stirring over the fire until it forms a smooth compact mass, and leaves the sides of the saucepan with the spoon. Remove it from the fire, and work gradually into it a table-spoonful of chopped parsley, and three fresh eggs. Mould the forcemeat into the form of quenelles with two tea-spoons which have been dipped into hot water, throw the quenelles into boiling milk slightly salted, and poach them until the batter is set. Drain them, cover with fried crumbs, and serve immediately. Send jam to table with sweet schpeischlitz, and grated gruyère or parmesan with savoury schpeischlitz. Sufficient for five or six persons.

* Maize flour = cornstarch.

Cassell's Dictionary of Cookery [c. 1877]

Forefathers' Dinner

Succotash* is the great dish in Plymouth at every celebration of Forefathers' Day, December 22. Tradition says it has been made in that town ever since the Pilgrims raised their first corn and beans, and it is supposed they learned to make it from the Indians.

THE PILGRIMS

Strangers are rather shy of this peculiar mixture; but it is a favorite dish with the natives, and to this day is made by some families many times through the winter season. Although the dish has never been made by the writer, it has been tested by her in that ancient town many times, and the excellence of the following receipt is unquestionable. It is given in the name of *Mrs. Barnabas Churchill*, of Plymouth, a lady who has made it for fifty years after the manner handed down through many generations.

One quart of large white beans (not the pea beans); *six quarts* of *hulled corn*—the smutty white Southern corn; *six* to *eight pounds* of *corned beef,* from the second cut of the rattle rand; *one pound* of *salt pork,* fat and lean; *chicken* weighing from *four* to *six pounds; one large white French turnip; eight* or *ten* medium-sized *potatoes.* Wash the beans, and soak over night in cold water. In the morning put them on in cold soft water. When boiling, change the water, and simmer until soft enough to mash to a pulp and the water is nearly all absorbed. Wash the salt pork and the corned beef, which should be corned only three or four days. Put them on about eight o'clock, in cold water, in a very large kettle, and skim as they begin to boil. Clean, and truss the chicken as for boiling, and put it with the meat about an hour and a quarter before dinner time. Allow a longer time if a fowl be used, and keep plenty of water in the kettle. Two hours before

* Succotash: from the Narraganset "misickquatash," an ear of corn.

dinner time, put the beans, mashed to a pulp, and the hulled corn into another kettle, with some of the fat from the meat in the bottom to keep them from sticking. Take out enough liquor from the meat to cover the corn and beans, and let them simmer where they will not burn. Stir often, and add more liquor if needed. The mixture should be like a thick soup, and the beans should absorb all the liquor, yet it must not be too dry.

Pare, and cut the turnip into inch slices; add it about eleven o'clock, and the potatoes (pared) half an hour later. Take up the chicken as soon as tender, that it may be served whole. Serve the beef and pork together, the chicken, turnip, and potatoes each on separate dishes, and the beans and corn in a tureen. The meat usually salts the mixture sufficiently, and no other seasoning is necessary. Save the water left from the meat, to use in warming the corn and beans the next day, serving the meat cold. This will keep several days in cold weather; and, like many other dishes, it is better the oftener it is warmed over, so there is no objection to making a large quantity. The white Southern corn is considered the only kind suitable for this ancient dinner.

MRS. D. A. LINCOLN, *Boston Cook Book,* 1891

* Mrs. Fisher was said to have been an ex-slave who stated that ''not being able to read or write myself, and my husband also having been without the advantage of an education,'' she dictated this book to a Northern friend—who had undoubtedly heard of the circuit riders, but not of Succotash (Circuit Hash).

Circuit Hash

One dozen tomatoes, one quart of butter beans, one dozen ears of corn cut off from cob, quarter pound of lean and fat pork cut in fine pieces, if pork is not liked, use two tablespoonfuls of butter; put on in a sauce-pan and stew one hour.

NOTE: Five minutes before dinner put in the corn to cook with the rest of stew.

What Mrs. Fisher Knows About Old Southern Cooking,* 1881

156

Ruins of Glastonbury Abbey, as they appeared in 1785.

Little Jack Horner
Sat in the corner,
Eating a Christmas pie;
He put in his thumb,
And pulled out a plum,
And said, What a good boy am I!

A minc't pie

Take a Leg of Mutton, and cut the best of the flesh from the bone, and parboil it well: then put to it three pound of the best Mutton suet, and shred it very small: then spread it abroad, and season it with *Pepper* and *Salt, Cloves* and *Mace*: then put in good store of *Currants*, great *Raisins* and *Prunes* clean washt and pickt, a few *Dates*

BEHIND THE NURSERY RHYME of "Little Jack Horner" is a story of intrigue. It concerns three people: King Henry VIII; Richard Whiting, abbot of Glastonbury Cathedral; and Jack Horner, steward to the wealthy abbot.

King Henry, according to the

story, felt that the churchmen were abusing their power, living like noblemen, dressing in silks and other finery, dining too well at their banquet feasts, and ordering church bells to ring as they rode by. The king was said to have been particularly angered when he heard that the abbot had built a kitchen that could not be burned down. To appease the king, the abbot sent his steward, Jack Horner, with a gift for the king. The gift was a favorite pie, a Christmas mince pie. And, as the story goes, Jack opened the pie on his way to London. He saw that it was not filled with the usual minced meat and fruit, but rather with quite different "plums"; it contained twelve deeds to twelve different manors, or estates. Jack took the deed to the manor of Mells for himself, and left the rest of the pie for the king. The manor of Mells remained in the Horner family.

Another story, however, is that Jack Horner simply bought the manor for £1,831. 9s. 1 3/4d.

In either case, "plum" has come to mean a luscious fruit in the shape of an office under a state government, which many people are on the lookout to secure. The culinary plum, on the other hand, is usually a currant or a raisin.

slic't, and some *Orange* peels slic't: then being all well mixt together, put it into a coffin,* or into divers coffins, and so bake them: and when they are served up open the lids, and strew store of *Sugar* on the top of the meat, and upon the lid. And in this sort, you may also bake Beef or Veal; only the Beef would not be parboiled, and the Veal will ask a double quantity of suet.

[GERVASE MARKHAM], *The English House-wife*, 1631

Henry VIII.

Mince Pies

(Chef de Cuisine, Astor House, N. Y.)

The "Astor House," some years ago, was *famous* for its "mince pies." The chief pastry cook at that time, by request, published the recipe. I find that those who partake of it never fail to speak in laudable terms of the superior excellence of this recipe, when strictly followed.

Four pounds of lean boiled beef, chopped fine, twice as much of chopped green tart apples, one pound of chopped suet, three pounds of raisins, seeded, two pounds of currants picked over, washed and dried, half a pound of citron, cut up fine, one pound of brown sugar, one quart of cooking molasses, two quarts of sweet cider, one pint of boiled cider, one tablespoonful of salt, one tablespoonful of pepper, one tablespoonful of mace, one tablespoonful of allspice, and four tablespoonfuls of cinnamon, two grated nutmegs, one tablespoonful of cloves; mix thoroughly and warm it on the range, until heated through. Remove from the fire and when nearly cool, stir in a pint of good brandy, and one pint of Madeira wine. Put into a crock, cover it tightly, and set it in a cold place where it will not freeze, but keep perfectly cold. Will keep good all winter.

Mrs. F. L. Gillette and Hugo Ziemann, *The White-House Cook-Book,* 1894

GREAT SEAL OF HENRY VIII

Lemon Mince Pies (maigre)

Squeeze out and set aside the juice of six lemons. Boil the rinds till quite tender, changing the water two or three times; then pound in a mortar to paste. When cold, mix this paste with two pounds of clean dry currants, one pound of raisins chopped small, a quarter of an ounce each of cinnamon, mace and nutmeg, two ounces of candied orange, two pounds of sugar, a quarter of a pint of brandy, the lemon-juice, and half a pound of clarified butter poured over, and thoroughly mixed. This is a delicate mincemeat, and will keep well.

Anne Bowman, *The New Cookery Book,* 1869

WRINGING THE WHEY

Little Miss Muffet
Sat on a tuffet,
Eating her curds and whey;
There came a big spider,
Who sat down beside her
And frightened Miss Muffet away.

THIS RHYME may refer to Miss Patience Muffet, daughter of Dr. Thomas Muffet (d. 1604), an entomologist who much admired spiders. Or, it may refer to Mary Stuart (1542–1587), Queen of Scots, and to John Knox as the spider who denounced her. It is interesting

The Use of Buttermilk to make Curds and Whey

The best use of butter milk for the able *House wife*, is charitably to bestow it on the poor neighbours, whose wants do daily cry out for sustenance; and no doubt but she shall find the profit thereof in a divine place, as well as in her earthly business. But if her own wants command her to use it for her own good, then she shall of her butter milk make curds, in this manner: she shall take her butter-milk and put it into a clean vessel, which is much larger than to receive the butter-milk only; and looking unto the quantity thereof, she shall take as it were a third part so much new milk, and set it on the fire, and when it is ready to rise, take it off and let it cool a little; then pour it into the buttermilk, and having stirred it about, let it stand; then with a fine skimmer, when you will use the curds (for the longer it stands the better the curds will eat), take them up into a cullender and let the whey drop well from it; and then eat them either with Cream, Ale, Wine, or Beer. As for the whey, you may keep it also in a sweet stone vessel, for it is that which is called Whigge, and is an excellent cool drink and a wholesome, and may very well be drunk a summer through instead of any other drink, and without doubt will slake the thirst of any labouring man as well, if not better.

[GERVASE MARKHAM], *The English House-wife*, 1631

that because of the mention of the tuffet or footstool, this rhyme carries within it the form of a very old dance—the cushion dance—which is related to ancient choral dances as well as to the more modern cotillion.

In any event, certainly both curds and whey are older than Little Miss Muffet, and older still than the cushion dance. These simple milk products are easily produced through the use of acids such as are found in wine, artichoke blossoms, gizzard lining, sour milk, etc. However, perhaps the simplest way of producing them is to stir a little lemon juice into a glass of hot milk. A separation results. The solid part of the "turned" or "curdled" milk is the curd or cheese; the liquid residue is the whey.

Buttermilk Cheese

Scald the buttermilk; then set it over the fire to boil; skim the top, and put it in a jug to drain; add a little salt, and it is ready for use.

S. ANNIE FROST, *Our New Cook Book*, 1883

MARY STUART.

161

Saucepan, with loose Earthen Lining, for boiling milk, custards, &c., without burning.

Sour Milk Cheese

(sometimes called Dutch, Curd, or Cottage Cheese)

1 quart thick sour* milk.	1 saltspoonful salt.
1 teaspoonful butter.	1 tablespoonful cream.

Place the milk in a pan on the back of the stove, and scald it until the curd has separated from the whey. Spread a strainer cloth over a bowl, pour in the milk, lift the edges of the cloth, and draw them together; drain or wring quite dry. There will be but *half* or *two thirds* of a *cup* of *curd,* but it is worth saving. It is the flesh-forming or nutritive part of the milk. Put it in a small bowl, with butter, salt, and cream; mix it to a smooth paste with a spoon. Take a teaspoonful, and roll in the hand into a smooth ball. It should be quite moist, or the balls will crack. If too soft to handle, put it in a cool place for an hour, and then it will shape easily. Or it may be served without shaping, just broken up lightly with a fork. If scalded too long, the curd becomes very hard and brittle. It is better when freshly made, and is delicious with warm gingerbread. An excellent lunch or tea dish. Season this cheese, with *one tablespoonful* of finely powdered *sage*, if you like the flavor.

Mrs. D. A. Lincoln, *Boston Cook Book,* 1891

* May Perrin Goff (*The Household*, 1881) recommends a proportion of one-half sour milk, one-fourth sweet milk, and one-fourth good buttermilk.

Kitchen Cheese Knife.

Cream-Cheese

Take two quarts of Milk warm from the Cow, Almonds blanched half a pound, beat the Almonds small; add a pint of Cream, and of Rose-water four ounces; half a pound of fine Sugar, and a quarter of an ounce of beaten Cinnamon, and as much Ginger; then put Rennet to the Milk and Cream; and when it is curdled, press out the Whey; and what remains beside, serve up in Cream.

DR. SALMON, *The Family-Dictionary*, 1695

CHEESE HOOP

Cream Cheese

Keep 1 quart of cream for a day or more (according to the state of the weather) till it becomes sour and thick; then wring out a piece of *thick* muslin or thin calico in cold water, and lay it in a small hair sieve, allowing the muslin to hang over the sides; pour in the cream, and stand the sieve in a soup plate to drain. Pour off the whey daily from the soup plate, and when the cream has become solid (which it will do in 3 or 4 days) it is fit for use. Take hold of the muslin to lift the cheese out, and turn it on to a dish; eat salt with it. This is a good way of using cream that has become sour in hot weather.

B. M., *Cookery for the Times*, 1870

Dish of Cheese.

Daryoles

Take curds of the day, & wring out the whey; & take yolks of Eggs not too few, nor not too many, and strain them both together through a strainer, & then bake hard thine cofynne,* & lay thine marrow there-in; & pour thine mixture there-on, bake them, & serve them forth.

HARLEIAN MS. 279 [c. 1430]

* Cofynne = Coffin = crust.

163

To make a made Dish of Curds

Take some very tender curds, wring the whey
from them very well, then put to them two raw
eggs, currants, sweet butter, rose-water, cinnamon, sugar, and mix all together. Then make a
fine paste with flour, yolks of eggs, rose-water,
and other water, sugar, saffron, and butter
wrought up cold. Bake it either in this paste or in
puff-paste. Being baked, ice it with rose-water,
sugar, and butter.

ROBERT MAY, *The Accomplisht Cook,* 1678

Kerry Butter Milk

Put six quarts of butter-milk into a cheese cloth,
hang it in a cool place, and let the whey drip
from it for two or three days; when it is rather
thick, put it into a basin, sweeten it with pounded
loaf sugar, and add a glass of brandy, or of sweet
wine, and as much raspberry jam, or sirup, as
will color and give it an agreeable flavor. Whisk
it well together, and serve it in a glass dish.

[MRS. N. K. M. LEE], *The Cook's Own Book, By A Boston
Housekeeper,* 1835

Mon Amy

To make mon amy, take and boil cows cream and
when it is boiled, set it aside and let it cool. Then
take cow curds and press out the whey. Then
pound them in a mortar and cast them in the pot
to the cream and boil all together. Put thereto

sugar, honey, and May butter. Colour it up with saffron and put in yolks of egg, well beaten and do away the strings. Let the potage be stiff or thick.* Then slice it in dishes and plant therein flowers of violets and serve it.

A Noble Boke Off Cookry [c. 1467]

* Mon Amy is similar in texture to cheesecake but does not necessarily permit a firm slice.

A VIOLET

To make Puffs

Take a pint of Cheese Curds, drain them dry, bruise them small with your hand, and put in two handfuls of flour, a little Sugar, three or four yolks of Eggs, a little Nutmeg, and Salt. Mix those together, and make them in little lumps like Eggs. Fry them in fresh butter. Serve them up with a little fresh butter and Sugar.

Nature Unbowelled, 1655

Boiled yeast milk

(Kokt jästmjölk)

Bring a gallon sweet milk to boiling point and then place aside to cool. Stir into it half that measure of thick sour cream and now let it stand that way over night. Spread a napkin over a coarse strainer which must be placed over a platter. Pour the mixture on the napkin. Thus the whey is separated from the other part. Beat half a gallon thick sour cream to froth, dilute it with as much milk. Into this put lumps of curdled milk from the napkin.

Swedish-English Cookbook, 1897

COTTAGE CHEESE

Says a newspaper correspondent, under date of September, 1897: "At the dinner given by the ladies of the town of Isle la Motte, on the island of that name in Lake Champlain, on the 6th of this month, to the Vermont Fish and Game League, at which dinner President McKinley and Secretary of War Alger were guests, I noticed on every table nice little cottage cheeses, about as large as a big apple, and most delicious, as I made certain as soon as dinner began. I do not see why some enterprising dairyman near every large city does not start the cottage cheese business. It would not be an expensive experiment, and there might be money in it." (*Hood's Practical Cook's Book,* 1897)

Cheese-cakes

Cheese-cakes can be sent to table in two forms, the one some rich kind of custard or cream placed in little round pieces of pastry, or we can have a so-called cheese-cake baked in a pie-dish, the edges only of which are lined with puff-paste. We can also have cheese-cakes very rich and cheese-cakes very plain. The origin of the name cheese-cake is that originally they were made from curds used in making cheese. Probably most people consider that the cheese-cakes made from curds are superior, and in the North of England, and especially in Yorkshire, where curds are exposed for sale in the windows at so much a pound, very delicious cheese-cakes can be made, but considerable difficulty will be experienced if we attempt to make home-made curds from London milk.* Curds are made by taking any quantity of milk and letting it nearly boil, then throw in a little rennet or a glass of sherry. The curds must be well strained.

A. G. PAYNE, B.A., *Cassell's Vegetarian Cookery,* 1891

* In London, the Milk is generally not only *skimmed,* but thinned with *Sky-blue* (water) from the *Iron-tailed Cow,* (the pump).

London Cream, we are told, is sometimes adulterated with Milk, thickened with Potato-starch, and tinged with Turmeric. This accounts for the *Cockneys,* on making an expedition into the country, being *so extremely surprised to find the thickest part of the Cream—at the Top!* ([DR. WILLIAM KITCHINER], *The Cook's Oracle,* 1823)

Richmond Maids of Honour

These delicious little cakes, which every inhabitant of London who pays a visit to the most picturesque part of its environs knows so well, derive their name from a period when cookery was not thought to be a degrading occupation for those honoured with that title. It is stated that they originated with the maids of honour of Queen Elizabeth, who had a palace at Richmond.† I have a little work now before me, called "The Queen's Delight," in which are several receipts

† According to Frederick W. Hackwood in *Good Cheer* (1911), "The cakes are said to have been so named by George II, because they were introduced to the royal table by some of the Queen's maids of honour. In the time of George III, the tables at Windsor and at Kew were regularly supplied with these cheese-cakes. They are now manufactured at

invented by the wives of the first nobles of the land, which I think is an excellent example for those housewives who honour this book by their perusal, to imitate. They are made as follows:—

Sift half a pound of dry curd, mix it well with six ounces of good butter, break the yolks of four eggs into another basin, and a glass of brandy; add to it six ounces of powdered lump-sugar, and beat well together one very floury baked potato cold, one ounce of sweet almonds, one ounce of bitter ditto* pounded, the grated rind of three lemons, the juice of one, and half a nutmeg grated, mix these well together and add to the curds and butter; stir well up; line some tartlet pans, previously buttered, with some puff paste, and place some of the above mixture in, and bake quick.

Alexis Soyer, *The Modern Housewife,* 1851

almost all the confectioners' shops in the town, but it is unknown where the original patent or recipe for their composition came from. A sensation was once created by a report that a thousand pounds had been given for this patent.

"Whatever happened a century or so ago, the patent is now thrown open to all the *cuisiners* of the town and, as the jokers there say, 'men of reputation sell maids of honour for a penny.' "

* Bitter ditto = bitter almonds. *Danger!* The pulp of bitter almonds is poisonous! Use instead one drop of bitter almond extract (which is not poisonous) for each bitter almond, or about 20 drops (⅓ teaspoon) per ounce required. Use an additional ounce of sweet almonds to replace the bitter almond pulp not used.

Orange Cheesecake Mixture

Strain the juice of four Seville oranges and two lemons into two quarts of milk, and put it into a slack oven till a solid curd is formed; when cold, strain off whey. Pound the curd with three-quarters of a pound of fine new honey; add the grated rind of three of the oranges, the beaten yolks of eight eggs, the sixth part of a nutmeg, grated, six ounces of fresh butter, beaten to cream, and a wineglassful of brandy; beat the mixture till it becomes the consistency of a thick cream; put it into a jar, tie it down, and keep it in a cool place.

Cre-Fydd's Family Fare, 1871

PATTY-PANS

When you have made your Cheese, you shall then have care of the Whey, whose general use differs not from that of butter-milk, for either you shall preserve it to bestow on the poor, because it is a good drink for the labouring man, or keep it to make curds out of it, or lastly to nourish and bring up your swine. ([GERVASE MARKHAM], *The English House-wife,* 1631)

Whey

Make a pint of Milk boil; put to it a glass or two of white Wine; put it on the fire till it just boils again; then set it on one side till the Curd has settled; pour off the clear Whey, and sweeten it as you like.

Cyder is often substituted for Wine, or half the quantity of Vinegar that we have ordered Wine.

Obs. When there is no fire in a sick room, this may be put hot into a bottle; and put between the Bed and Mattress; it will keep warm several hours.

[DR. WILLIAM KITCHINER], *The Cook's Oracle,* 1823

Scorbutic Whey

This whey is made by boiling half a pint of scorbutic juices in a quart of cow's milk. More benefit, however, is to be expected from eating the plants than from their expressed juices. The scorbutic plants are bitter oranges, brooklime, garden scurvy-grass, and water-cresses. A number of other wheys may be prepared nearly in the same manner, as orange whey, cream of tartar whey, &c. These are cooling pleasant drinks in fevers, and may be rendered cordial, when necessary, by the addition of wine.

The Book of the Household [c. 1857]

WATER-CRESS

None in August should over the land,
In December none over the sea.

Travelling in Old New England, 1634

To enter into a serious discourse concerning the natural condition of these *Indians*, might procure admiration from the people of any civilized Nations, in regard of their civility and good natures. If a Tree may be judged by his fruit, and dispositions calculated by exteriour, then may it be concluded, that these *Indians* are of affable, courteous, and well disposed natures, ready to communicate their best of their wealth to the mutual good of one another; and the less abundance they have, to manifest their entire friendship, so much is their love, that they are as

BECAUSE TRAVELERS were aware of the hazards of journeying overland in the heat of summer, or venturing on the seas in the stormy winter weather, they tried to plan a safe trip according to their almanacs. But even though they may have reduced some of the hazards by traveling in the "safe" months, and even though they provided themselves with portable foods (see "Bobby Shafto's Gone to Sea," page 34), they still had to rely on the friendliness of the people who lived in the lands they were visiting.

AN ENGLISH PILGRIM

willing to part with their Mite in poverty, as treasure in plenty. As he that kills a Deer, sends for his friends, and eats it merrily, so he that receives but a piece of bread from an *English* hand, parts it equally between himself and his comrades and eats it lovingly. In a word, a friend can command his friend, his house, and whatsoever is his (saving his Wife) and have it freely. And as they are love-linked thus in common courtesy, so are they no way sooner dis-jointed than by ingratitude, accounting an ungrateful person a double robber of a man, not only of his courtesy, but of his thanks which he might receive of another for the same offered, or received kindness. Such is their love to one another, that they cannot endure to see their Country-men wronged, but will stand stiffly in their defence, plead strongly in their behalf, and justify one another's integrities in any warrantable action.

WILLIAM WOOD, *New Englands Prospect,* 1634

Traveling in Old Crete, 1640

. . . departing all alone, scarcely was I advanced twelve miles in my way, when I was beset on the skirt of a Rocky Mountaine, with three *Greeke* murthering *Renegadoes,* and an *Italian Bandido,* who laying hands on me, beat me most cruelly, robbed me of all my clothes, and stripped me naked, threatening me with many grievous speeches.

At last the respective *Italian,* perceiving I was a stranger, and could not speak the *Cretan* tongue, began to ask me in his own language where was my money? to whom I soberly answered, I had no more than he saw, but he not giving credit to these words, searched all my

170

Clothes, yet found nothing, except my linen, and Letters of recommendations, I had from diverse Princes of Christendome, especially the *Duke* of *Venice*, whose subjects they were, if they had been lawful Subjects: which when he saw, did move him to compassion, and earnestly entreated the other three thieves to grant me mercy, and to save my life. A long deliberation being ended, they restored back again my pilgrims Clothes, and Letters, but my blue Gown they kept: such also was their thievish Courtesy towards me, that for my better safeguard on the way, they gave me a stamped piece of clay, as a token to show any of their companions, if I encountered with any of them; for they were about twenty Rascals of a confederate band, that lay in this desert passage.

Leaving them with many counterfeit thanks, I travelled that day seven and thirty Miles, and at night attained to the unhappy Village of *Picke-horno*: where I could have neither meat, drink, lodging, nor any refreshment to my wearied body. These desperate *Candiors* thronged about me, gazing (as though astonished) to see me both want company, and their Language, and by their cruel looks, they seemed to be a barbarous uncivil people: For all these High-landers of *Candy*, are tyranical, blood-thirsty, and deceitful. The consideration of this, and the appearance of my death, signalled to me secretly by a pitiful woman, made me to shun their villany in stealing forth from them in the dark night, *&* privately sought for a secure place of repose in a Cave by the Sea side, where I lay till Morning with a fearful heart, a crazed body, a thirsty stomach, and a hungry belly.

BANDIT

WILLIAM LITHGOW, *The totall Discourse, Of the rare Adventures, and painefull Peregrinations of long nineteene yeares Travailes . . .* , 1640

Death and Funeral of a Squaw
in London, 1835

Examples of the Red Men of North America—
so absurdly called Indians—have at various times
visited England. The readers of the *Spectator*
will remember Addison's interesting account of
four kings of the nations lying between New York
and Canada, who came to London in 1710, and
were introduced to Queen Anne. So lately as 1835,
a party of the Michigan tribe, including the chief,
Muk Coonee (the Little Boar), appeared amongst
us, the object being a negotiation for the sale of
certain lands. Arrangements were made for their
being presented to King William on the 18th of
January; but the chief found on that day a very
different affair on his hands. His squaw, the
Diving Mouse, of only twenty-six years, sickened
and on that day died, at the lodging which the
party occupied in the Waterloo Road.

When this lady of the wild felt a mortal sickness upon her, she refused all medicine, saying if
the Great Spirit intended that she should then
die, he would be angry at any attempt on her
part to avert the doom. The only thing she would
allow to be done for her was the administration
of the rite of baptism, and this was only sub-
mitted to because she was told there might consequently be more ceremony at her funeral. Loud
were the wailings of the chief and his friends
round the couch of the dead squaw.

The chief, with much dignity, addressed to the
persons assembled a few words, which were
translated by his French interpreter, M. Dunord.
"For three years prior to my visit to this
country," he said, "I rested on the bosom of my
wife in love and happiness. She was everything
to me; and such was my fear that illness or
accident might part us in England, that I wished

her to remain behind in our settlements. This she would not consent to, saying, 'That I was all the world to her, and in life or death she would remain with me!' We came, and I have lost her. She who was all my earthly happiness is now under the earth; but the Great Spirit has placed her there, and my bosom is calm. I am not, I never was, a man of tears; but her loss made me shed many.''

R. CHAMBERS, ED., *The Book of Days,* vol. 1, 1862–4

Indians in London

Onion's skin very thin,
Mild winter coming in.
Onion's skin thick and tough,
Coming winter cold and rough.

ONIONS

The best are such as are brought us out of *Spain,* and some that have weighed eight Pounds. Choose therefore the large, sound, white, and thin Skinned. Being eaten crude and alone with Oil, Vinegar, and Pepper, we use them in Salad, not so hot as Garlic, nor at all so rank. In *Italy* they frequently make a *Salad* of *Scallions, Chives,* and

The Onion

Though the history of the onion can be but imperfectly traced in Europe, there is no doubt as to its great antiquity in Africa, since there is evidence to show that this bulb was known and much esteemed in Egypt 2000 years before Christ. It still forms a favourite addition to the food of the Egyptians. Hasselquist, in a panegyric on the exquisite flavour of the Egyptian onion, remarks, that it is no wonder the Israelites, after they had quitted their place of bondage, should have regretted the loss of this delicacy; for whoever has tasted of the onions of Egypt, must acknowledge that none can be better in any part of the universe. "There," says he, "they are mild and pleasant to the palate; in other countries they are strong and nauseous. There they are soft and yielding; but in countries to the north they are hard, and their coats so compact, as to render them less easy of digestion." The Egyptians divide them into four parts, and eat them roasted together with pieces of meat; which preparation they consider so delicious, that they devoutly wish it may form one of the viands of Paradise. A soup made of these onions was pronounced by the learned traveller to be certainly one of the best dishes of which he ever partook.

WILLIAM RHIND, *A History of The Vegetable Kingdom* [c. 1842]

To boil Onions

Take a good many onions and cut them in four quarters, set them on the fire in as much water as you think will boil them tender. And when they be clean skimmed, put in a good many of small raisons, half a spoonful of grosse pepper, a good piece of Sugar, and a little Salt, and when the Onions be through boiling, beat the yolk of an Egg with Verjuice, and put into your pot and so serve it upon soppes. If you like, poach Eggs and lay upon them.

[THOMAS DAWSON], *The Second part of the good Hus-wives Jewell*, 1597

Chibbols only seasoned with *Oil* and *Pepper;* and an honest laborious Country-man, with good *Bread*, Salt, and a little *Parsley*, will make a contented Meal with a roasted Onion. How this noble *Bulb* was deified in Egypt we are told, and that whilst they were building the *Pyramids*, there was spent in this Root *Ninety Tun* of *Gold* among the Workmen. ([JOHN EVELYN], *Acetaria. A Discourse of Sallets,* 1699)

Chibbol = an onion similar in appearance to the leek.

Egyptian Sphinx and Pyramid.

Spanish Onions à la Grecque

Peel off the very outer skins and cut off the pointed ends; put the onions in a deep dish, and put a piece of butter and a little salt and pepper on the place where the point has been cut off, cover with a plate or dish, and let them bake for not less than three hours. They will throw out a delicious gravy.

DAVID CHIDLOW ET AL., *The American Pure Food Cook Book,* 1899

POTATO ONION

* Thomas Austin, editor of the Harleian manuscripts, commented in 1888: "Hanoney—Apparently *Oignoné,* a dish with many onions in it, as this dish has."

Hanoney*

Take and draw the White and the yolks of the Eggs through a strainer; then take Onions, and shred them small; then take fair Butter or grease, & scarcely cover the pan there-with, and fry the Onions, & then cast the Eggs in the pan, & break the Eggs & the Onions together; and then let them fry together a little while; then take them up, and serve forth all mixed together on a fair dish.

HARLEIAN MS. 279 [c. 1430]

TOP ONIONS

Onion Porridge

Take a Spanish onion as big as you can procure, peel and split it into quarters, and put these into a small stewpan with a pint of water, a pat of butter, and a little salt; boil gently for half an hour; add a pinch of pepper, and eat the porridge just before retiring to bed. This is also an excellent remedy for colds, and was imparted to me by a jolly, warm-hearted Yorkshire farmer.

CHARLES ELMÉ FRANCATELLI, *The Cook's Guide*, 1884

Stewpan

Onions, to ragoût

Peel a pint of onions, as young as they can be procured, then peel four large ones and cut them very small; put some good dripping or butter into a stewpan, and when melted, add the onions, and fry until a light brown; then thicken with flour, and give them a shake until thick. Add a quarter of a pint of gravy, a little powdered pepper, salt, and a teaspoonful of mustard; stir all together, and when tolerably thick, pour into the dish and garnish with fried crumbs of bread.

The Family Friend, vol 3, 1851

Brown Onion Soup

Peel and shred twelve middle-sized onions into a stewpan, with half a pound of butter, a teaspoonful of pounded sugar, and a tablespoonful of flour, which must be dredged over the whole. Stir with a wooden spoon, and let them brown for twenty minutes. Then pour over two quarts of strong beef stock, and simmer for an hour; strain the soup, and rub the onions through a tamis; beat the yolks of two eggs with a glass of brandy, and mix well with the soup a minute or two before you serve it.

ANNE BOWMAN, *The New Cookery Book*, 1869

"If Leekes you like, but do their smell dis-leeke,
Eat Onyons, and you shall not smell the Leeke;
If you of Onyons would the scent expell,
Eat Garlicke, that shall drowne the Onyons' smell."
See page 59 of the Philosopher's Banquet, London, 1633.
([DR. WILLIAM KITCHINER], *The Cook's Oracle*, 1823)

Onion Vinegar

6 large onions.	1 tablespoonful white
1 tablespoonful salt.	sugar.
	1 quart best vinegar.

Salière

Mince the onions, strew on the salt, and let them stand five or six hours. Scald the vinegar in which the sugar has been dissolved, pour over the onions; put in a jar, tie down the cover, and steep a fortnight. Strain and bottle.

MARION HARLAND, *Common Sense in the Household*, 1877

Peter, Peter, pumpkin eater,
Had a wife and couldn't keep her;
He put her in a pumpkin shell
And there he kept her very well.

Peter, Peter, pumpkin eater,
Had another, and didn't love her;
Peter learned to read and spell,
And then he loved her very well.

Gourds (cucurbita)

Of the gourd there are many varieties, some of them of beautiful form and colour, and others of an immense size. One sort, the *pumpkin* (*cucurbita pepo*), is occasionally eaten, but always in a baked state, and combined with other substances of higher flavour. In warm situations, and when highly manured, it grows luxuriantly in the open air; and villagers sometimes grow it,

PUMPKINS

Pumpkins possess one peculiar quality—that of absorbing and retaining the flavor of whatever they are cooked with. If stewed with apples they taste exactly like them in puddings and tarts, and they may be used to advantage in most savory cookery. An anonymous writer in the early settlement of America wrote home to England as follows:

"If fresh meat be wanting to fill
  up our dish,
We have carrots, and pumpkins,
  and turnips and fish,
We have pumpkins at morning,
  and pumpkins at noon,
And if it were not for pumpkins
  we should be undone."

    (*Smiley's Cook Book*, 1896)

and, when ripe, convert it into a sort of pie, by cutting a hole in the side, extracting the seeds and filaments, stuffing the cavity with apples and spices, and baking the whole. The pumpkin seems to have been earlier introduced into general culture than either the cucumber or the melon: the pumpkin is, in fact, the melon of the old English writers, the true melon being then styled the musk melon. The pumpkin or gourd enters more into the cookery of the southern nations on the continent, than into those of Britain.

WILLIAM RHIND, *A History of The Vegetable Kingdom* [c. 1842]

Colonial Table

The ancient New-England standing Dish

The Housewives manner is to slice [pumpkins] when ripe, and cut them into dice, and so fill a pot with them of two or three Gallons, and stew them upon a gentle fire a whole day, and as they sink, they fill again with fresh Pumpkins, not putting any liquor to them; and when it is stewed enough, it will look like baked Apples; this they Dish, putting Butter to it, and a little Vinegar (with some Spice, as Ginger, &c.), which makes it tart like an Apple, and so serve it up to be eaten with Fish or Flesh. It provokes Urin extremely and is very windy.

JOHN JOSSELYN, GENT., *New-Englands Rarities*, 1672

Pumpkin Butter

3 pints of mashed pumpkin.	Flavor with ginger root, nutmeg and lemon peel.
1 pound of sugar.	
4 tablespoonfuls of butter.	

Either bake or steam the pumpkin. Rub thoroughly through a sieve, mix with the sugar, butter, flavor, and let simmer on the back of the stove one hour. It becomes thick and can be kept in jars in a dark place. Use the same as fruit jelly or marmalade.

MAUD C. COOKE, *Three Meals A Day*, 189—

STEAMER

To Dry Pumpkins for Pies

Pare the pumpkin, cut into thin strips and again into slices. Spread out in a thin layer and dry in the hot sun or in a moderate oven. In the winter when wanted for use soak over night in cold water. Cook in the same water until tender and use the same as fresh pumpkin.

MRS. S. T. RORER, *How to Cook Vegetables*, 1892

Pumpkin Fried in Small Sticks

(Potiron en Bâtonnets Frits)

Peel and remove the inside part of a pumpkin or marrow squash so that only the meat remains; cut two pounds of this into small sticks an inch and a half long, and three-eighths of an inch across; lay them in a vessel, strew salt over and let macerate for fifteen minutes, then drain, wipe and dip quickly in flour; plunge a few at a time into very hot fat; when cooked, drain, salt and dress on a napkin.

CHARLES RANHOFFER, *The Epicurean*, 1894

The Handy Fryer

Nutmeg Grater

Pumpion-Pye

Take a pound of Pumpion, and slice it; a handful of Thyme, a little Rosemary, sweet Marjoram stripped off the stalks, chop them small; then take Cinnamon, Nutmeg, Pepper, and a few Cloves, all beaten; also ten Eggs, and beat them all together, with as much Sugar as you shall think sufficient. Then fry them like a pancake, and being fried, let them stand till they are cold. Then fill you Pye after this manner: Take Apples sliced thin round ways, and lay a layer of the pancake, and another of the Apples, with Currants between the layers. Be sure you put in a good amount of sweet Butter before you close it. When the Pye is baked, take six yolks of Eggs, some White-wine or verjuice, and make a caudle* thereof, but not too thick; cut up the lid and put it in, and stir them well together, and so serve it up.

* Caudle = a sauce.

Hannah Woolley, *The Gentlewomans Companion*, 1673

Pumpkin and Squash Pie

The usual way of dressing pumpkins in England in a pie is to cut them into slices, mixed with apples, and bake them with a top crust like ordinary pies. A quite different process is pursued in America, and the editor can testify to the immense superiority of the Yankee method. In this country, the pumpkin is grown for show rather than for use; nevertheless, when properly dressed, it is a very delicate vegetable, and a universal favourite with our North American brethren.

The following is the American method of mak-

ing a pumpkin pie: Take out the seeds, and pare
the pumpkin or squash; but in taking out the
seeds do not scrape the inside of the pumpkin;
the part nearest the seed is the sweetest; then
stew the pumpkin, and strain it through a sieve
or colander. To a quart of milk for a family pie,
three eggs are sufficient. Stir in the stewed pumpkin with your milk and beaten-up eggs till it is
as thick as you can stir round rapidly and easily.
If the pie is wanted richer make it thinner, and
add another egg or two; but even one egg to a
quart of milk makes "very decent pies." Sweeten
with molasses or sugar; add two tea-spoonfuls of
salt, two tablespoonfuls of sifted cinnamon, and
one of powdered ginger; but allspice may be used,
or any other spice that may be preferred. The
peel of a lemon grated in gives it a pleasant
flavour. The more eggs, says our American
authority, the better the pie. Some put one egg
to a gill of milk. Bake about an hour in deep
plates, or shallow dishes, without an upper crust,
in a warm oven.

The Guide to Service, 1842

Gourd grown on
a stake

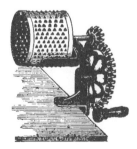

Labor-saving Grater

Grated Pumpkin Pie

Take out the seeds carefully without scraping the
solid part of the fruit; grate the fruit close down
to the outside skin; sweeten the pulp; mix with
milk and cream, flavor with grated lemon, citron,
or cocoa, and bake on a single crust.

R. T. Trall, M.D., *The New Hydropathic Cook-Book,* 1869

183

Crust for Pumpkin Pie

(Mrs. S. Speedy)

Take your pie-dish and butter the tin well; then take some dry corn meal and shake it around in the buttered tin; empty it out, leaving only what sticks to the tin. Have your pumpkin ready, the same as for any pie, pour it in your tin; set it in the oven and bake it. You will be surprised to see what a nice crust it will form.

LADIES' AID SOCIETY, *Los Angeles Cookery*, 1881

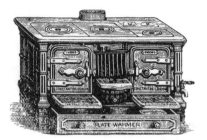

CONSTANTINE'S TREASURE RANGE (No. 84) WITH ROASTER AND OVEN

Yankee Pumpkin Pudding

Take a pint of stewed pumpkin. Mix together a pint of *West India* molasses and a pint of milk, adding two large table-spoonfuls of brown sugar, and two table-spoonfuls of ground ginger. Beat three eggs very light, and stir them, gradually, into the milk and molasses. Then, by degrees, stir in the stewed pumpkin. Put it into a deep dish, and bake it without a crust. This is a good farm-house pudding, and *equally* good for any healthy children.

For a large family, double the quantities of ingredients.

You had best have at hand *more than a quart* of pumpkin, lest when mixed it should not hold out. This pudding is excellent made of winter squash.

Miss Leslie's New Cookery Book, 1857

CRABTREE'S PATENT KITCHENER

Pumpkin and Rice Soup

Wash in cold water the quantity of rice required to make your soup; set it on the fire in cold water, let it boil till nearly done enough, set it aside. Pare your pumpkin, and cut it into bits as big as a walnut; put it in a saucepan with two or three sliced onions, one or two cloves, a leaf each of celery and parsley, a trifle each of pepper, salt, and sugar, and amply sufficient water to make your soup. Boil till you can crush the onions and pumpkin to a mash; mash them well with a large wooden ladle; pour all through a cullender, to strain off the fibrous portions. Then set the strained purée on the fire again; add to it the boiled rice and a good bit of butter, and keep stirring (to mix well, and prevent sticking to the bottom) until the rice is tender. Then serve, and you will have an excellent autumnal soup. There is no reason why, instead of water, you should not use any good meat or poultry-broth (not salt) which you happen to have.

Cassell's Household Guide, vol. 1 [c. 1885]

Polly put the kettle on,
Polly put the kettle on,
Polly put the kettle on,
We'll all have tea.

ON TEA

Different persons require to drink it from different motives, and we must know what these motives are before we can say dogmatically what method of making is the best. All the really valuable qualities, those which refresh and nourish, are to be drawn in the first five minutes after infusion (if the water be *boiling,* which is essential). It is no real economy to extract the whole of the colouring matter

Afternoon Teas

"Afternoon teas," revived in England about twenty years ago, and imported to this country soon afterward, are certainly a most admirable institution. What if the dissipation they afford is of the mildest type? It may be mild, but it is perennial. An afternoon tea is so cheap that anybody can afford to give one, and involves so little trouble and formality that even the most timid or most lazy hostess need not shrink before the very diminutive lions it brings into her path.

Many people who dine late in our large cities have five-o'clock tea served every day, and are almost always at home to friends at that hour. But what a difference is there between the reception you will meet at various houses, even where the invitations are precisely alike and the preparations for receiving guests made on just the same scale!

Some people are so formal in their very natures, that they impart frigidity to all who approach them. Slipping away from the congealing hospitality of this house, you go to another only a few blocks distant, and the sound of merry laughter greets your ear the moment that the door opens to admit you.

The little low five-o'clock tea-tables, with their dainty embroidered cloths, are so pretty and picturesque that it seems a thousand pities not to use them. But they will be found inconvenient, except on very small occasions, not only on account of their diminutive size, but because they are so low. A rather small table of the ordinary height, placed against the wall, may be substituted for the regulation five-o'clock tea-table; at this the hostess is not obliged to sit down every time that she pours out tea.

Afternoon teas, receptions, and kettledrums melt into one another by imperceptible gradations, and the names are often used interchangeably. Strictly speaking, the five-o'clock or afternoon tea is the least formal occasion of the three, the kettledrum coming next in order, while the afternoon reception, or "at home," is the most ceremonious of them all.

Kettledrums are said to have received their name from the fact that they were originally given by the wives of officers at the headquarters of the latter, a drum making an impromptu stand for the tea-equipage.

It is more likely, however, that the name is a and tannin from the leaves; but some, and especially poor persons, who have few luxuries, rather than drink pure water, choose that which is thus coloured and flavoured. The question is simply one of taste.

The Chinese make tea by placing the leaves under a piece of silver perforated or filigree work to keep them from rising, in a porcelain cup which has a cover, and pouring on the boiling water. The Japanese grind the leaves to powder, and stir them in. The Tartars boil the tea leaves in their soup. So much do the methods of using vary according to national taste or custom. The addition of sugar, though not of milk, appears to be wholly a European custom, and we may at this place mention that an excellent and refreshing drink may be composed of weak green tea. (*Cassell's Household Guide*, vol. 2 [c. 1885])

survival or *revival* of the old English "drum," a word which was constantly used in Queen Anne's time and later, to describe fashionable gatherings. Smollet says: "This is a riotous assembly of fashionable people of both sexes at a private house, consisting of some hundreds; not unaptly styled a *drum*, from the noise and emptiness of the entertainment."

The word "kettledrum" is not often used in invitations now, though for a time it was quite the rage to call every afternoon occasion by this name. A *kaffee-klatsch* is the newest name for afternoon tea—or rather coffee drinking. It certainly has an admirably descriptive sound, this title, and conveys the idea of boundless talk, clatter of spoons, and the harmless (?) scratch of gossip better than any of its predecessors.

FLORENCE HOWE HALL, *Social Customs*, 1887

Cranberry Tea

Take ripe cranberries, perfectly sound, mash thoroughly, and pour boiling water over them; let the mixture stand a few minutes, or till cold; then strain off the water, and sweeten to taste. Good tart apples, scraped, and treated in the same way, may be used; and so may dried sour currants, or dried red raspberries.

SUSANNA W. DODDS, A.M., M.D., *Health in the Household*, 1888

OF BLACK TEAS

Bohea, which is a coarse, common leaf and contains a large amount of woody fibre. As it is much roasted, it keeps a long time without becoming musty, and makes a dark infusion. Its name is derived from the Bohea hills, in the black tea district.

Congou, which formed the bulk of the East India Company's importations during their monopoly, is a better and more carefully prepared tea; but, since the trade was thrown open in 1834, it has sunk in repute.

Souchong is the finest of the strong black teas, and is made from younger leaves than the preceding. *Padre Souchong* is Souchong of the finest quality. Some kinds of Souchong, as the *Caper,* are scented by roasting with various flowers.

Pekoe is the finest of black teas. It is made from young buds, picked in April. Very young buds, clothed with down, make *Flowery Pekoe.* Pekoe does not keep well; since, in order to preserve its delicate flavour, it can only be slightly roasted. (*Cassell's Household Guide,* vol. 2 [c. 1885])

Tea with Eggs

The Jesuit that came from *China, Anno* 1664, told Mr. *Waller*, that there they use sometimes in this manner. To near a pint of the infusion, take two yolks of new-laid eggs, and beat them very well with as much fine Sugar as is sufficient for this quantity of liquor; when they are very well incorporated, pour your Tea upon the Eggs and Sugar, and stir them well together. So drink it hot. This is when you come home from attending business abroad, and are very hungry, and yet have not convenience to eat presently a competent meal. This presently discusseth and satisfieth all rawness and indigence of the stomach, flieth suddenly over the whole body, and into the veins, and strengtheneth exceedingly, and preserves one a good while from necessity of eating. Mr. *Waller* findeth all those effects of it thus.

In these parts, he saith, we let the hot water remain too long soaking upon the Tea, which makes it extract into itself the earthy parts of the herb. The water is to remain upon it, no longer than whiles you can say the *Miserere* Psalm very leisurely. Then pour it upon the Sugar, or Sugar and Eggs. Thus you have only the spiritual parts of the Tea, which is much more active, penetrative and friendly to nature. You may for this regard take a little more of the herb; about one drachm of Tea will serve for a pint of water; which makes three ordinary draughts.

The Closet Of the Eminently Learned Sir Kenelme Digby Kt. Opened, 1671

Twankay is a coarse and common description, corresponding to Bohea in black.

Hyson Skin is the lighter and inferior leaves of Hyson, blown from it with a winnowing-fan.

Hyson is, or should be, good green tea, gathered in spring, and carefully dried and rolled.

Young Hyson is an earlier, and therefore a more delicate gathering.

Gunpowder, so called from its granulated appearance, is the finest and most carefully rolled leaves picked from the Hyson. (*Cassell's Household Guide*, vol. 2 [c. 1885])

Tea Kettle

From an early period in the 18th century, the amusements of the inhabitants of Manchester consisted of cards, balls, theatrical performances, and concerts. About 1720 a wealthy lady named Madam Drake, who kept one of the three or four private carriages then existing in the town, refused to conform to the new-fashioned beverages of tea and coffee; so that, whenever she made an afternoon's visit, her friends presented her with that to which she had been accustomed—a tankard of ale and a pipe of tobacco! (R. CHAMBERS, ED., *The Book of Days*, vol. 1, 1862–4)

Thé à la Russe

Place in a tea-pot three heaped tablespoonfuls of English-breakfast tea; pour over a little boiling water, just sufficient to cover the tea, about two tablespoonfuls; let infuse for one minute, then draw the water out, but do not use it. Pour in half a pony of good old Jamaica rum and three pints of boiling water; let infuse for four minutes, and then serve in cup with a decanter of old Jamaica rum separately, thin slices of lemon, and powdered sugar.

This is the old Russian style. Later fashion is to flavor it with a little vanilla flavor and a few drops of lemon juice.

FILIPPINI OF DELMONICO'S, *The Table,* 1891

Coffee

One of the most common drinks is coffee. In my childhood coffee was hardly known in Souabia, and in many a village, it would have been difficult to find a few women capable of preparing it. Now-a-days its use is so general that no house is without it, except perhaps among some country-people who are engaged in very hard labour and justly believe that coffee does not give them sufficient strength.

Six years ago, the daughter of an honourable family came to me, who had been completely given up by the doctors. She was well-made and her parents enjoyed health and strength. The girl told me that she was in the habit of drinking coffee three times a day, but found no longer any relish in solid food. I advised her to take nothing but a spoonful of milk every hour, and three times a day a small portion of bread-soup. Nothing but the fear of a certain early death could induce this passionate coffee-drinker to adopt that diet. After a few days, nature had become accustomed to it, and before many weeks had passed, the girl had recovered her health.

I am fully convinced that coffee is the chief cause of the blood-poverty prevailing among the female sex. What will it lead to, if the evil is not checked in time? Many young mothers told me in tears how infirm and miserable they were and how, in consequence of their inability to perform their domestic duties, they were forsaken or despised by their husbands. Although too much coffee-drinking was not always the cause of the misery, yet it was so very often, and in all cases the distress was invariably connected with an extravagant and irrational way of clothing.

SEBASTIAN KNEIPP, *Thus Shalt Thou Live*, 1897

TEA AND COFFEE

It is true, says Liebig, that thousands have lived without a knowledge of tea and coffee; and daily experience teaches us that, under certain circumstances, they may be dispensed with without disadvantage to the merely animal functions; but it is an error, certainly, to conclude from this that they may be altogether dispensed with in reference to their effects; and it is a question whether, if we had no tea and no coffee, the popular instinct would not seek for and discover the means of replacing them. Science, which accuses us of so much in these respects, will have, in the first place, to ascertain whether it depends on sensual and sinful inclinations merely, that every people of the globe have appropriated some such means of acting on the nervous life, from the shores of the Pacific, where the Indian retires from life for days in order to enjoy the bliss of intoxication with koko, to the Arctic regions, where Kamtschatdales and Koriakes prepare an intoxicating beverage from a poisonous mushroom. We think it, on the contrary, highly probable, not to say certain, that the instinct of man, feeling certain blanks, certain wants of the intensified life of our times, which cannot be satisfied or filled up by mere quantity, has discovered, in these products of vegetable life, the true means of giving to his food the desired and necessary quality. (MRS. ISABELLA BEETON, *The Book of Household Management*, 1861)

COFFEE AND TEA CANISTERS

Tea or Coffee Stand

Burnt Coffee

(In France vulgarly called Gloria)

Make some coffee as strong and as clear as possible, sweeten it in the cup with white sugar almost to syrup, then pour brandy on the top gently over a spoon; set fire to it with a lighted paper, and when the spirit is in part consumed, blow out the flame and drink the gloria quite hot.

ELIZA ACTON, *Modern Cookery*, 1852

Iced Coffee

Make more coffee than usual at breakfast time and stronger. Add one-third as much hot milk as you have coffee and set away. When cold, put upon ice. Serve as dessert, with cracked ice in each tumbler.

MAY PERRIN GOFF, ED., *The Household*, 1881

Mazagran à la General Bugeau

This will be found a superior and pleasantly stimulating summer beverage for ladies, as well as for the sterner sex.

Have six goblets half filled with clean ice, pour in the coffee, evenly divided; add a pony of good cognac to each glass, mix thoroughly with a teaspoon, and serve.

The above is a delicious and healthful after-dinner summer drink, and is enjoyed in nearly all the large cities of Europe, especially by military men, who prefer it to the usual after-dinner demi-tasse, or "gloria," as they call it in Paris.

The name is derived from the village of Mazagran, Province d'Oran, Algeria, famous for a long and heroic siege in 1840, wherein one hundred and twenty-three French soldiers were victorious against twelve thousand Arabs.

FILIPPINI OF DELMONICO'S, *The Table*, 1891

BARLEY

Substitute for Cream in Tea or Coffee

Beat the white of an egg to a froth, put to it a very small lump of butter, and mix well, then turn the coffee to it gradually, so that it may not curdle. If perfectly done it will be an excellent substitute for cream. For tea omit the butter, using only the egg.

Confederate Receipt Book, 1863

Barley Sugar

1 quart barley,   4 or 5 quarts water,
                    Sugar.

Soak the barley 3 minutes in a little lukewarm water, and drain. Put it into a saucepan with the water mentioned above, set over a good fire, and cook till the barley is almost mush; take off from the fire, mash and strain as well as possible. If sufficiently cooked the liquid will become a jelly. Mix the jelly with sugar and fry it. It is better than almost any other kind of candy.*

The Housekeeper Cook Book, 1894

* More water may be needed for boiling. One cup of barley jelly is mixed with about 1½ cups of white sugar and fried or scrambled in ½ cup of butter over a high fire, stirring it well until the mixture almost "balls" or adheres in a ball around the spoon. Remove immediately before it foams.

* Blancmange = formerly a food made of white meats, almonds, cream, sugar, eggs, and so forth; now a sweet dish made without the meat and using isinglass or gelatine. "ffor blankmanger that made he with the beste." (G. CHAUCER, *Canterbury Tales*: Prologue)

† Isinglass = a kind of gelatine, originally made from sturgeon bladders, for which regular gelatine—unwashed—may be substituted ounce for ounce.

Blancmange*

Blanch and pound one ounce of sweet almonds with a glass of sherry, and a table-spoonful of pounded loaf sugar; add it to three-quarters of an ounce of isinglass† dissolved in half a pint of water, and boil it till the flavor of the almonds be extracted, stirring it all the time; strain it through a bit of thin muslin, and mix with it a quart of good cream; stir it till quite cold, and pour it into a shape.

Blancmange, Dutch

Wash one ounce and a half of isinglass, pour a pint and a half of boiling water over it, let it stand for an hour, and then boil it for twenty minutes; strain, and when it is nearly cold, add the beaten yolks of six eggs, a pint of Lisbon wine, the peel of one and juice of two lemons, with a stick of cinnamon, and sweeten with pounded loaf sugar; stir it over the fire till it begins to simmer, but do not allow it to boil; pick out the peel and cinnamon, pour it into a basin, stir it till nearly cold, and put it into a shape.

[MRS. N. K. M. LEE], *The Cook's Own Book, By A Boston Housekeeper*, 1835

Honey Candy
(Miss Belle Riley, Newton, Iowa)

1 cup honey, 1 teaspoon butter; boil until it becomes brittle on being dropped into cold water; pour into a well-greased pan; pull when cooling.

My Favorite Receipt, 1895

To preserve Orenges after the Portugall fashion

Take Oranges & core* them on the side and lay
them in water. Then boil them in fair water till
they be tender, shift them in the boiling to take
away their bitterness. Then take sugar and boil
it to the height of syrup as much as will cover
them, and so put your oranges into it, and that
will make them take sugar. If you have 24 oranges
beat 8 of them till they come to paste with a
pound of fine sugar, then fill every one of the
other oranges with the same, and so boil them
again in your syrup: then there will be marmalade of oranges within your oranges, & it will
cut like an hard egg.

[HUGH PLATT], *Delightes for Ladies,* 1603

" Fair Lemons and Oranges !"

* To core = to remove the inside
pulp.

Orange Marmalade

Quarter some large ripe oranges, and remove
the rind, the seeds, and the strings or filaments,
taking care to save all the juice. Put the pulp,
with the juice, into a porcelain kettle, and mix
with it an equal quantity of strained honey, adding sufficient powdered loaf sugar to render it
very thick and sweet. The honey alone will not
make it sweet enough. Boil it uncovered, and skim
it till very thick, smooth, and clear. Taste it, and
if necessary add more sugar, and boil it longer.
When cold, put it up in tumblers or white-ware
marmalade pots, and cover it securely. This marmalade is exquisite, and very superior to any
other.

Miss Leslie's New Cookery Book, 1857

GRAY AND HIS ELEGY

Sprung of a harsh and unamiable father, but favoured with a mother of opposite character—rising from a youth spent in comparatively humble circumstances—Thomas Gray became, in his mature years, a devoted college-student, a poet, a man of refined taste, and an exemplifier of all the virtues. The only reproach ever intimated against him by his college-associates, was that of fastidiousness.

He had a weakness, in the form of a nervous dread of fire. His chamber in St. Peter's College, Cambridge, being in a second-floor, he thought it very likely that, in case of a conflagration, his exit by the stairs might be cut off. He therefore caused an iron bar to be fixed by arms projecting from the out-

Oxford Pudding

(Thomas Gray's handwritten recipe)

Take grated bread, shred suet, pick'd currants, sugar, of each a quarter of a Pound, mix together; grate in a good deal of lemon-peel & nutmeg. Break in two eggs, stir all together, tie in a fine cloth & boil ½ an hour or more.

WILLIAM VERRAL, *A Complete System of Cookery*, 1759

Genuine Everton Toffee

2 pounds light brown sugar,
Juice of ½ lemon,

1 pound butter,
Dessertspoon vanilla.

Put the sugar and butter into a bright, clean, round-bottom copper basin; melt together over a moderate fire, stirring constantly with a wooden spoon; add the lemon juice and vanilla. Ten minutes' boiling will bring it to the desired degree, the "crack"; pour it upon a buttered marble slab, and, when cool enough, turn in the edges, and cut or mark the batch into small square tables.

The Housekeeper Cook Book, 1894

Tostee

Take wine and honey, and mix it together and skim it clean, and cook it long. Add thereto powder of ginger, pepper, and salt. Toast bread, and lay the mixture thereto. Cut pieces of ginger, and garnish it therewith, and serve it forth.

The Forme of Cury [c. 1390]

Cinamon Toasts

Cut fine thin toasts, then toast them on a gridiron, and lay them in ranks in a dish, put to them fine beaten cinamon mixed with sugar and some claret, warm them over the fire, and serve them hot.

French Toasts

Cut French bread, and toast it in pretty thick toasts on a clean gridiron, and serve them steeped in claret, sack, or any wine, with sugar and juice of orange.

ROBERT MAY, *The Accomplisht Cook*, 1678

Payn Pur-dew*

Take fair yolks of Eggs, & separate them from the white, & draw them through a strainer, & take Salt and caste thereto. Then take fair bread, & cut it in round slices. Then take fair Butter that is clarified, or else fair Fresh grease, & put it in a pot, & make it hot. Then take & wet well thy bread slices in thy yolks, & put them in the pan, and so fry them up. But beware of their cleaving to the pan; & when it is fried, lay them on a dish, & lay Sugar enough thereon, & then serve it forth.

HARLEIAN MS. 279 [c. 1430]

side of his window, designing by a rope tied thereto to descend to the ground, in the event of a fire occurring. This excessive caution, as it appeared to his brother-collegiates, raised a spirit of practical joking in them; and one evening, not long after the fire-escape had been fixed up, a party of them came from a merry-making, and thundered at the door of Gray, with loud cries of ''Fire! fire! fire!'' The nervous poet started from bed, flew to his window, and descended by his rope into the vacant ground below, where of course he was saluted with bursts of laughter by his friends. Gray's delicate nature was so much shocked by this rough affair, that he deserted Peter's College, and took up his residence in Pembroke. The window with the iron apparatus is still shewn, and is faithfully represented.

Among popular English poems, there is none more deservedly distinguished than Gray's *Elegy*. It appeals to a feeling which is all but universal—a tendency to moralise when alone in a churchyard; and thus it is enabled to take hold of the most common-place minds. (R. CHAMBERS, ED., *The Book of Days*, vol. 2, 1862-4)

* Payn pur-dew, or lost bread, has also been called French toast.

Whigs

Put half a pint of warm milk to three quarters of a pound of fine flour, and mix in it two or three spoonsful of light barm.* Cover it up, and set it before the fire an hour, in order to make it rise. Work into the paste four ounces of sugar, and the same quantity of butter. Make it into whigs† with as little flour as possible, and a few seeds, and bake them in a quick oven.

JOHN FARLEY, *The London Art of Cookery*, 1811

* Barm = yeast.

† A whig or wig is a triangular or wedge-shaped bun made with yeast, which may be eaten with butter and marmalade or dunked or "drowned" in ale.

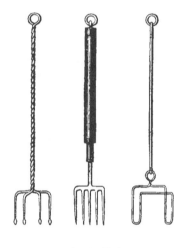

TOASTING FORKS

Sing a song of sixpence,
  A pocket full of rye;
Four and twenty blackbirds,
  Baked in a pie.

When the pie was opened,
  The birds began to sing;
Was not that a dainty dish,
  To set before the king?

The king was in his counting-house,
  Counting out his money;
The queen was in the parlour,
  Eating bread and honey.

The maid was in the garden,
  Hanging out the clothes,
There came a little blackbird,
  And snapped off her nose.

To make Pies that the Birds may be alive in them, and flie out when it is cut up

Make the coffin of a great Pie or pasty, in the bottome whereof make a hole as big as your fist, or bigger if you will. Let the sides of the coffin bee somewhat higher then ordinary Pies, which done, put it full of flower and bake it. Being baked, open the hole in the bottom, and take out the flower. Then having a Pie of the bigness of the hole in the bottom of the coffin aforesaid, you shall put it into the coffin. Put into the said coffin round about the aforesaid Pie as many small live birds as the empty coffin will hold, besides the Pie aforesaid. And this is to be done at such time as you send the Pie to the table, and set before the guests: where uncovering or cutting up the lid of the great Pie, all the Birds will flie out, which is to delight and pleasure shew to the company. And because they shall not bee altogether mocked, you shall cut open the small Pie, and in this way you may make many others, the same you may do with a Tart.

To make the crust of Pie or Tart of Pigeons, Pullets, or Kid

Boning Knife.

French Cook's Knife.

To make the crust of Pigeons, Pullets, or Kid flesh. First boile your meat a little till it be almost enough, then cut it into small peeces, and fry it in good suet. Then in a pan make a crust of thicke paste like a Pie crust, and put the meat in it, covering it with dry Pruines or Cherries. Then take Verjuice with a little whote water and butter, and tenne Egges with parsley and Margerum, and beat them altogether with a knife, and then put them in an earthen pot, and set it upon a fire of coales, stirring it alwases with a spoone. Then poure this broth upon the crust, and set it on the fire, as if it were a Tart, and when you thinke it be baked, send it to the Table, and make the crust sweet or sharpe as your maister fancieth.

Epulario, Or, The Italian Banquet, 1598

WHEAT

Bread

Bread is a vitally important element in our nourishment. Truly, as Frederika Bremer says, "when the bread rises in the oven, the heart of the housewife rises with it," and she might have added that the heart of the housewife sinks in sympathy with the sinking bread.

I would say to housewives, be not daunted by one failure, nor by twenty. Resolve that you *will* have good bread, and never cease striving after this result till you have effected it. If persons without brains can accomplish this, why cannot you? I would recommend that the housekeeper acquire the practice as well as the theory of bread-making. In this way, she will be able to give more exact directions to her cook and to more readily detect and rectify any blemish in the bread. Besides, if circumstances should throw her out of a cook for a short time, she is then prepared for the emergency. In this country fortunes are so rapidly made and lost, the vicissitudes of life are so sudden, that we know not what a day may bring forth. It is not uncommon to see elegant and refined women brought suddenly face to face with emergencies which their practical knowledge of household economy and their brave hearts enable them to firmly meet and overcome.

Flour Sifter.

Marion Cabell Tyree, ed., *Housekeeping in Old Virginia,* 1879

* Kansas Brown Bread omits the butter, substitutes graham flour for rye, and, when done, is browned in the oven for a few minutes.

† Saleratus = baking soda.

‡ This bread was often served warm with baked beans or turkey, or served as a pudding with a sauce made of thick, sour cream, sugar, and nutmeg.

Boston* Brown Bread

Place in a wooden bowl six ounces of flour, six ounces of Indian meal, and six ounces of rye flour; mix well together; then add two ounces of butter and one teaspoonful of saleratus†; mix thoroughly for two minutes; add now half a pint of molasses and one pint of sour milk; mix the whole well together for five minutes. Have a brown-bread mold sufficiently large to hold three quarts, butter the interior well, transfer the preparation into it. Then place the mold in a deep pan five inches high; fill the pan with warm water, place it in a moderate oven to steam for three hours and a half without disturbing it. Take from the oven, lift up the mold from the pan, turn it onto a dish, remove the mold, and it will be ready to serve.‡

FILIPPINI OF DELMONICO'S, *The Table*, 1895

Bread Pan with Cover.

Easy Bread Making

In the first place, take three tablespoons flour, two tablespoons salt, two tablespoons sugar, and scald by pouring on one pint boiling water. Let it stand till cool, then add two yeast cakes or soft yeast of equal quantity and let rise. Take one dozen good sized potatoes, boil and mash, add three quarts hot water, when cool enough put in the above yeast, and let stand over night. Now all that is necessary is to take a quart or more, according to the number of loaves you want, stir it into the flour, knead it into loaves and put it into your tins, let it rise, and bake. No sponging nor fussing. The mixture will keep two weeks. If your family is large and you require more loaves of bread, make up more of the yeast at a time. If you want raised biscuits for tea, just stir a pint or more of the yeast with a little shortening into your flour, make into biscuits, let rise and bake. The contributor of this says it is the nearest to perfect bread that she ever tried.

MRS. FRANCES E. OWENS, *Mrs. Owens' Cook Book*, 1882

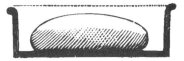

To make French Bread the best way

Take a gallon of fine flour, and a pint of good new ale barm or yeast, and put it to the flour, with the whites of six new laid eggs well beaten in a dish, and mixt with the barm in the middle of the flour, also three spoonfuls of fine salt; then warm some milk and fair water, and put to it, and make it up pretty stiff. Being well wrought and worked up, cover it in a bowl or tray with a warm cloth till your oven be hot;* then make it up either in rolls, or fashion it in little wooden dishes and bake it, being baked in a quick oven, chip† it hot.

ROBERT MAY, *The Accomplisht Cook*, 1678

* Letting bread rise "till your oven be hot" took about two hours in the 1600s. If white flour is used, the amount of liquid is approximately two cups each of milk and water, in addition to the two cups of warm ale and two yeast cakes.

† Chip = chip away the crust.

Rice Bread

Boil 1 lb. rice till tender in water or milk (milk is best) and mash it; then with the hands, rub the rice into 4 lbs. flour, in the same manner that butter is rubbed in, mixing it thoroughly; add 3 teaspoons sugar, 1 tablespoon salt, and 1 cake compressed yeast dissolved in 2 pints lukewarm milk or water, have the dough soft to the touch, knead thoroughly, and let it rise, then knead

again thoroughly, form into loaves, put into greased pans, let rise, and bake in a good oven. Excellent, especially if made with milk.

Smiley's Cook Book, 1896

GLASS, KNIFE, AND BREAD

The glass and the knife being clean must be laid upon the right side, and the bread on the left. Cut bread with a knife, and eat it with reverence. Leave for the delicateness of certain courtiers the manner and use of breaking the bread with the ends of thy fingers, laying thy hand upon it. As concerning thy self, cut it gentlemanly with thy knife, not cutting of the crust round about above and beneath, for that doth savor a delicate person. Our elders in all repasts did eat bread with great reverence as a holy thing: and of that commeth the custom of this time, to kiss the bread, if perchance it be fallen upon the ground. (THOMAS PAYNELL, *The Civilitie of Childehode,* 1560)

White Mountain Bread

Dissolve ½ cake compressed yeast in 1 cupful lukewarm water and milk mixed, add 2 tablespoonfuls sugar and 1 of salt and let it dissolve. Take 1 pint sifted flour and stir the yeast into it, after it is dissolved, have the batter the consistency of waffle batter, more warm water can be added if necessary. Mix well and put aside in a warm place (not hot) to rise, usually 1 or 2 hours.

Now take 1½ quarts sifted flour, add 1 tablespoonful salt, 1 good tablespoonful butter and same quantity lard, mix together and pour in the risen yeast, add ¾ cup milk and water mixed, mix well and set aside to rise all night, say 6 or 7 hours. When *well* risen, pour the dough out on a well-floured biscuit board, knead well for 10 or 15 minutes, and break in 3 equal pieces; braid together like a hair braid, put in a bread pan, cover with another pan and let rise again. Then keep cover over the pan, set in the oven and bake, not too fast. When almost done, remove the cover and brown nicely.

MRS. C. F. MORITZ AND MISS ADÈLE KAHN, *The Twentieth Century Cook Book,* 1898

Some notes about Honey

The Honey of dry open Countries, where there is much wild Thyme, Rosemary, and Flowers, is best. It is of three sorts: Virgin-honey, Life-honey, and Stock-honey. The first is the best. The Life-honey is next. The Virgin-honey is of Bees that swarmed the Spring before, and are taken up in Autumn; and is made best by choosing the whitest Combs of the Hive, and then letting the Honey run out of them lying upon a Sieve without pressing it, or breaking of the Combs. The Life-honey is of the same Combs broken after the Virgin-honey is run from it: the Merchants of Honey used to mingle all the sorts together. The first of a Swarm is called Virgin-honey. That of the next year, after the Swarm was hatched, is Life-honey. And ever after, it is Honey of Old-stocks. Honey that is forced out of the Combs will always taste of Wax.

The Closet Of the Eminently Learned Sir Kenelme Digby Kt. Opened, 1671

French Honey*

White sugar 1 lb.; 6 eggs, leaving out the whites of 2; the juice of 3 or 4 lemons, and the grated rind of 2; and ¼ lb. of butter. Stir over a slow fire until it is about the consistency of honey.

This will be found to come much nearer what it represents, then the Yankee "wooden nutmegs" did, upon trial.

A. W. CHASE, M.D., *Dr. Chase's Recipes*, 1880

TELLING THE BEES

If you would keep your Bees, in the case of a death in the Family, you must acquaint the little Creatures with the fact either by rapping on the Hives and then saying the Name of the Departed, or else by draping the Hives in black and humming in mournful Tune. If you do not do this they will either desert you or die inside of the Hive. (MARGARET HUNTINGTON HOOKER, *Ye Gentlewoman's Housewifery*, 1896)

TELLING THE BEES

* This is also known as lemon butter and is used to fill tarts or to spread on bread.

Sow peas and beans in the wane of the moon;
Who soweth them sooner, he soweth too soon.

The Common Pea

(pisum sativum)

GREEN PEA

Like many of our most familiar domestic vegetables, the period of the introduction into Britain,
or even the native country of this vegetable, is
involved in obscurity. It is probable, however,
that it was introduced into Britain from the
warmer parts of Europe, and may have been
brought to these from Egypt and Syria.

Historical evidence would make it appear that
both the pea and the bean must not only have
been introduced, but extensively cultivated, in
some parts of Scotland, as well as in England, at

a very early period. It is on record, that when the English forces were besieging a castle in Lothian, in the year 1299, their supply of provisions was exhausted, and their only resource was in the peas and beans of the surrounding fields. This circumstance would lead to a belief that the pea was then one of the staple articles of produce for human food.

The more delicate kinds, however, do not appear to have been cultivated in England until a much later period, since Fuller informs us that peas, in the time of queen Elizabeth, were brought from Holland, and were "fit dainties for ladies, they came so far, and cost so dear." In the reign of Henry VIII, too, the pea would appear to be somewhat of a rarity, as in the privy purse expenses of that king is an entry, "paied to a man in rewarde for bringing pescodds to the king's grace, iiijs. viiid."

WILLIAM RHIND, *A History of The Vegetable Kingdom* [c. 1842]

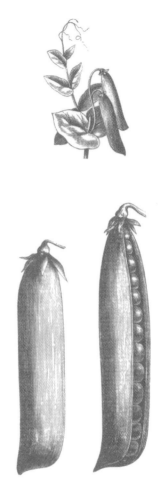

Peas, Green

By far the best and nicest way of cooking green peas when served as a course by themselves is to stew them gently in a little butter without any water at all, like they do in France. The peas are first shelled, and then placed in a stew-pan with a little butter, sufficient to moisten them. As soon as they are tender, which will vary with the size and age of the peas, they can be served just as they are. The flavour of peas cooked this way is so delicious that they are nicest eaten with plain bread. When old peas are cooked this way it is customary to add a little white powdered sugar.

A. G. PAYNE, B.A., *Cassell's Vegetarian Cookery*, 1891

In France asparagus is eaten either with butter or with oil, and people sometimes show strong preference for one or the other. Fontenelle is related to have had a strong liking for asparagus accommodated with oil. His friend, the Abbé Terrason, on the contrary, liked to eat the asparagus with butter. The latter came one day to Fontenelle and invited himself to dinner. Fontenelle, knowing the preference of his guest for buttered asparagus, made, as he said, a sacrifice of half of what he had appointed all for himself; the Abbé was to have his share in butter, the host the remaining half with oil. Shortly before they were going to sit down to dinner, the Abbé grew very ill. Thereupon Fontenelle rose quickly, and, running towards the kitchen, called out: "All the asparagus with oil now —all with oil!" (J. L. W. THUDICHUM, M.D., *Cookery—Its Art And Practice* [c. 1895])

To stew Pease

Take a quart of young peas, wash them and put them into a stew pan with a quarter of a pound of butter, three cabbage [head] lettuces cut small, five or six young onions, with a little thyme, parsley, pepper, and salt, and let them stew all together for a quarter of an hour. Then put to them a pint of gravy, with two or three slices of bacon or ham, and let them stew all together till the peas are enough. Then thicken them up with quarter of a pound of butter rolled in flour.

ELIZABETH RAFFALD, *The Experienced English House-Keeper,* 1778

Asparagus Peas

If the asparagus be properly dressed, it should taste like green peas. Take some young asparagus, which pick with great care; then cut them into small equal pieces, avoiding to put in such parts as are hard or tough. Wash them in several waters, and throw them into boiling water, with a little salt. When the asparagus are nearly done, drain them first on a sieve, and next wipe them quite dry with a towel. Then put them into a stewpan with a small bit of butter, a bunch of parsley, and green onions, and toss them in the stewpan over the fire for ten minutes. Now add a little flour, and a small lump of sugar, and moisten with boiling water. They must boil over a large fire. When well reduced, take out the parsley and green onions, and thicken with the yolks of two eggs beaten with a little cream, and a little salt. Remember that in this entremet sugar must predominate, and that there is to be no sauce. Asparagus are always dressed in this manner, when to be served in the second course.

LOUIS EUSTACHE UDE, *The French Cook*, 1829

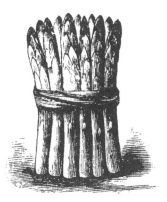

My Lord Lumley's Pease-Potage

Take two quarts of Pease, and put them into an ordinary quantity of water, and when they are almost boiled, take out a pint of the Pease whole, and strain all the rest. A little before you take out the pint of Pease, when they are all boiling together, put in almost an ounce of Coriander-seed beaten very small, one Onion, some Mint, Parsley, Winter-savory, Sweet-marjoram, all minced very small; when you have strained the Pease, put in the whole Pease and the strained again into the pot, and let them boil again, and a little before you take them up, put in half a pound of sweet-butter. You must season them in due time, and in the ordinary proportion with Pepper and Salt.

This is a proportion to make about a gallon of Pease-potage. The quantities are set down by guess. The Coriander-seeds are as much as you can conveniently take in the hollow of your hand. You may put in a great good Onion or two. A pretty deal of Parsley, and if you will, and the season afford them, you may add what you like of other Potage herbs, such as they use for their Potages in *France*. But if you take the savoury herbs dry, you must crumble or beat them to small Powder (as you do the Coriander-seed) and if any part of them be too big to pass through the strainer, after they have given their taste to the quantity, in boiling a sufficient while therein,

SWEET PEA

209

you put them away with the husks of the Pease. The pint of Pease that you reserve whole, is only to show that it is Pease-potage. They must be of the thickness of ordinary Pease-potage. For which these proportions will make about a gallon.

The Closet Of the Eminently Learned Sir Kenelme Digby Kt. Opened, 1671

The Chick Pea

(cicer arietinum)

THE CHICK-PEA

This is a small legume which is occasionally cultivated in the south of Europe, especially in Spain, where it is used as a dyeing ingredient as well as an article of food. It is known there, and on the opposite coast of the Mediterranean, by the name of *garvance* or *garvanzos.* These seeds do not, like most other pulse, become of a soft and pulpy consistence by boiling, and therefore they never constitute a dish by themselves, but are strewed singly as a garnish over certain savoury viands, and form part of the *olla,* a dish composed of bacon, cabbage, pumpkin, and garvanzos, with which a Spanish dinner almost invariably commences. The chick pea, when parched, has been much esteemed among many nations from the earliest periods of history, and in that state it still continues an article of great consumption. According to Bellonius, this pea was the parched pulse which formed the common provision of the Hebrews when they took the field.

In those warm and arid countries where travellers are constrained to carry their scanty provisions with them across vast desert tracts, they gladly supply themselves with small dried substances which require much mastication, and thus stimulate the salivary glands. Under these circumstances parched chick-peas, or *leblebby*, are in great demand, and are so common in the shops as biscuits in those of England. In Grand Cairo and Damascus there are many persons who make it their sole business to fry peas, for the supply of those who traverse the desert.

WILLIAM RHIND, *A History of the Vegetable Kingdom* [c. 1842]

Olla Podrida

(Spanish and Portuguese)

Take half a quart of chick peas previously soaked in water for a few hours, a couple of carrots, chirizos (Spanish red sausages), long pepper, a clove of garlic and an onion, a bunch of parsley, a dozen lettuces, two coleworts,* tomatoes, a slice of gourd, and any other vegetable. These must be cut up and put into the stockpot with about six pounds of brisket of beef, the knuckle end of a leg of mutton, half a pound of smoked streak bacon, a few slices of ham, and a fowl. These should be well covered with water and the liquid carefully skimmed, and only simmered after it has first boiled up. Let it simmer for six hours.

MRS. DE SALIS, *National Viands À La Mode*, 1895

CABBAGE

* Colewort = a young cabbage.

Confederate Army Soup
as Made at General Picketts Head Quarters

One ham bone, one beef bone, one pod red pepper, black-eyed peas. Boil in a mess pot. Splendid soup on a wet day.

MRS. FRANCES E. OWENS, *Mrs. Owens' Cook Book*, 1882

Corn Field or Black Eyed Peas
(Mozis Addums)

Gather your peas about sun-down. The following day, about eleven o'clock, gouge out your peas with your thumb nail, like gouging out a man's eye-ball at a court house. Rinse your peas, parboil them, then fry them with several slices of streaked middling [bacon], encouraging the gravy to seep out and intermarry with your peas. When moderately brown, but not scorched, empty into a dish. Mash them gently with a spoon, mix with raw tomatoes sprinkled with a little brown sugar and the immortal dish is quite ready. Eat a heap. Eat more and more. It is good for your general health of mind and body. It fattens you up, makes you sassy, goes through and through your very soul. But why don't you eat? Eat on. By Jings. Eat. *Stop*! Never, while there is a pea in the dish.

MARION CABELL TYREE, ED., *Housekeeping in Old Virginia.*
1879

Harrowing and Sowing.   (Bayeux Tapestry.)

The Bean

(vicia faba)

The Bean has been cultivated in Britain from very remote antiquity, having been in all probability introduced into this country by the Romans. It is said to have originated in Egypt; perhaps because the Greeks, from whom we have the earliest accounts of it, received it from that country as a cultivated vegetable. Some travellers affirm that the bean is found growing wild in Persia, near the shores of the Caspian; but that part of Asia has been subjected to so many fluctuations, to so many alternations of culture and destruction, that it is not easy to decide whether any plants which may be discovered vegetating spontaneously be really indigenous, or only the remains of a former cultivation. In many parts of Britain, where all other memorials of former habitations and culture have been swept away, certain plants are found growing which a traveller passing hastily over the country would very naturally describe as indigenous, since of their introduction the present inhabitants of the vicinity could most probably give him no account, but which, from history and the nature of the plants themselves, are known to be exotics introduced at a specific time.

WILLIAM RHIND, *A History of The Vegetable Kingdom* [c. 1842]

Baked Pork and Beans

Soak *one quart* of *pea beans* in cold water over night. In the morning put them into fresh cold water, and simmer till soft enough to pierce with

A NOTE ON BEANS

Beans are more than beans, good for food and pleasant to the taste: they are a moral lesson. The priests of Egypt held it a crime even to look at beans—the very sight of them unclean. Lucian introduces a philosopher in hell declaring that it would be difficult to say which were the greater crime—to eat beans, or to eat one's father's head. Pythagoras forbade his disciples to eat beans, because they are formed of the rotten ooze out of which man was created. The Romans ate beans at funerals with awe, from the idea that the souls of the dead were in them. Two thousand years pass by, and here are we now eating beans with the most thorough enjoyment and the most perfect unconcern. Moral—Get rid of prejudice and call nothing unclean. ([E. S. DALLAS], *Kettner's Book Of The Table*, 1877)

Légumier

BROAD BEAN

HARICOT BEANS

a pin, being careful not to let them boil enough to break. If you like, boil *one onion* with them. When soft, turn them into a colander, and pour cold water through them. Place them with the onion in a bean-pot. Pour boiling water over *one quarter* of *a pound* of *salt pork*, part fat and part lean; scrape the rind till white. Cut the rind in half-inch strips; bury the pork in the beans, leaving only the rind exposed. Mix *one teaspoonful* of *salt*—more, if the pork is not very salt—and *one teaspoonful* of *mustard* with *one quarter* of a *cup* of *molasses*. Fill the cup with hot water, and when well mixed pour it over the beans; add enough more water to cover them. Keep them covered with water until the last hour; then lift the pork to the surface and let it crisp. Bake eight hours in a moderate oven. Use more *salt* and *one third* of *a cup* of *butter* if you dislike pork, or use *half a pound* of fat and lean *corned beef*.

The mustard gives the beans a delicious flavor, and also renders them more wholesome. Many add a *teaspoonful* of *soda* to the water in which the beans are boiled to destroy the acid in the skin of the beans. Yellow-eyed beans and Lima beans are also good when baked.

Much of the excellence of baked beans depends upon the bean-pot. It should be earthen, with a narrow mouth and bulging sides. This shape is seldom found outside of New England, and is said to have been modelled after the Assyrian pots. In spite of the slurs against "Boston Baked Beans" it is often remarked that strangers enjoy them as much as natives; and many a New England bean-pot has been carried to the extreme South and West, that people there might have "baked beans" in perfection. They afford a nutritious and cheap food for people who labor in the open air.

MRS. D. A. LINCOLN, *Mrs. Lincoln's Boston Cook Book,* 1891

For to make gronden benes*

Take beans and dry them in a kiln or in an oven, and hull them well, and winnow out the hulls, and wash them clean, and put them to boil in good broth, and eat them with bacon.

The Forme of Cury [c. 1390]

* Gronden benes = Beans stripped of their hulls. This was a dish of the poorer householder.

Bean Porridge

(Mrs. C. M. Poor)

Five pounds of *corned beef*, not too salt, or *four pounds* of *beef* and *one* of *salt pork*; *one pint* of dry *white beans, four tablespoonfuls* of *corn meal, pepper* and *salt* to taste, *one pint* of *hulled corn*. Soak the beans over night. In the morning parboil in fresh water with a pinch of *soda* till soft. Put the corned beef and pork in cold water, skim carefully, and simmer four or five hours, or till tender. Take out, and cut into two-inch pieces, and remove the bone and gristle; also the fat from the liquor. Put the meat and beans into the meat liquor, and simmer very slowly three or four hours, or till most of the beans are broken. Half an hour before serving stir in the meal, first wetting it in cold water to a smooth paste. The meal should thicken the porridge to about the consistency of a thick soup. The meat should be cooked till it falls apart. Season to taste with *salt* and *pepper*. Add the hulled corn, and when hot serve with brown bread. Sometimes the vegetables usually served with a boiled dinner are cooked with the meat, then removed, and the beans cooked as above, in the meat liquor.

"This old-fashioned and very nutritious dish was one of the chief articles of winter food at my grandmother's farm in Northern New Hamp-

BOILING-POT

shire eighty years ago. When cooked, it was poured into bowls or basins holding from a pint to two quarts. A nice tow string was laid in a loop over the edge, and the porridge was placed where it would freeze. By holding the dish in hot water it would cause the porridge to slip out; then it was hung up by the loops in the 'buttery,' and was considered 'best when nine days old.' At early dawn the 'men folks' who went into the forest 'chopping' would take the skillet, or a little three-legged iron kettle, some large slices of 'rye and Indian' bread* in their pockets to keep it from freezing. The porridge was hung, wrapped in a clean towel, upon the sled stakes. Their spoons were made of wood. The hay that lay on the floor of the ox sled was of use to keep their feet warm, and given to the oxen for 'bait' at noon. When it was twelve o'clock 'by the sun,' they kindled a fire by the aid of a 'tinder box,' warmed their porridge, and with their brown bread enjoyed this strong food as no modern epicure can his costly French dishes.''

* Rye and Indian bread = an early form of Boston brown bread.

Mrs. D. A. Lincoln, *Mrs. Lincoln's Boston Cook Book*, 1891

LENTIL PLANT

Lentil Pie

Soak and boil a half pint of lentils. Chop fine a quarter of a pound of Brazilian nuts. Drain the lentils; add the nuts, a level teaspoonful of salt and one grated onion. Rub two tablespoonfuls of peanut butter into a pint of white flour; add cold water to moisten. Knead; roll out in a thin sheet. Put the lentil mixture in a deep pie dish and add a half cup of water. Cover with the crust and bake one hour. Serve hot with English drawn butter.

Sarah Tyson Rorer, *Mrs. Rorer's New Cook Book*, 1898

THE PIPER

The fiddler and his wife,
The piper and his mother,
Ate three half-cakes, three whole cakes,
And three quarters of another.

Brown Stone Front Cake

½ cupful butter creamed with 1 cupful granulated sugar, add 2 whole eggs, ½ cupful warm water with 1 scant teaspoonful soda dissolved in it, then add 2 cupfuls sifted flour and flavor with vanilla. After this is well mixed, mix together 1 cupful bitter chocolate grated, yolk of 1 egg, 1 cupful sugar and ½ cupful warm water. Boil for 2 minutes on a hot fire, stirring all the time; then pour it hot into the cake batter.

Mix well, then bake in 2 layers in a moderate oven, and ice between and on top with the following icing:

How MUCH did each get? According to Peter and Iona Opie in *The Oxford Dictionary of Nursery Rhymes* (1951): "If the fiddler's wife was the piper's mother each received one and three quarters of a cake. It is likely that this solution has been pondered on for more than 350 years."

217

There is no royal road to good fortune in cake-making. What is worth doing at all is worth doing well. There is no disgrace in not having time to mix and bake a cake. You may well be ashamed of yourself if you are too lazy, or careless, or hurried to beat your eggs, cream your butter and sugar, or measure your ingredients.

Yet, sometimes, when you believe you have left no means untried to deserve success, failure is your portion. What then?

If the cake be uneatable, throw it away upon the first beggar-boy who comes for broken meat, and say nothing about it. If streaky or burned, cut out the best parts, make them presentable as possible, and give them to John and the children as a "second-best" treat. Then keep up a brave heart and try again. You *may* not satisfy yourself in a dozen trials. You certainly *will* not, if you never make another attempt. (MARION HARLAND, *Common Sense in the Household,* 1877)

Chocolate Icing

Yolks of 2 eggs, ½ cupful milk, small lump butter, 1½ cupfuls sugar, mix all together and boil 5 minutes, or until it thickens. Remove from fire and add 1 cupful bitter chocolate that has previously been grated and melted over a pan of hot water. Flavor with vanilla and spread on cake.

MRS. C. F. MORITZ AND MISS ADÈLE KAHN, *The Twentieth Century Cook Book,* 1898

Brownies

⅓ cup butter.	1 egg well beaten.
⅓ cup powdered sugar.	⅞ cup bread flour.
⅓ cup Porto Rico molasses.	1 cup pecan meat cut in pieces.

Mix ingredients in order given. Bake in small, shallow fancy cake tins, garnishing top of each cake with one-half pecan.

FANNIE MERRITT FARMER, *The Boston Cooking-School Cook Book,* 1896

Buttermilk Cake

This is the easiest cake in the world to make, and is almost always successful. Melt one cup of butter, stir in three cups of sugar, six well beaten eggs, three cups of sifted flour, and one cup of buttermilk. Sour cream is an excellent substitute for the buttermilk, and, if used, a pinch of soda must be added. Half of this quantity makes a fair sized cake for a small family, and is good with or without frosting.

Hood's Practical Cook's Book, 1897

Chocolate Biscuits

Mix a quarter of a pound of finely-grated chocolate with a quarter of a pound of finely-sifted sugar, and moisten the mixture with sufficient beaten white of egg to make a softish paste. Mould this into small biscuits with a tea-spoon, and place these on a sheet of paper, leaving a little distance between the biscuits. Bake them in a moderate oven, and, when sufficiently cooked, turn the sheets over so that the biscuits may rest on the table, and brush the paper underneath the biscuits with a little water to loosen them. The addition of six ounces of sweet almonds, blanched and pounded, will convert these into chocolate macaroons. Time to bake, twenty minutes. Sufficient for a moderate-sized dish.

Cassell's Dictionary of Cookery [c. 1877]

COCOA TREE

Chocolate Cake

(Easter or Passover Dish)

Beat the yolks of eight eggs and a half a pound of sugar until quite light, add half a pound of almonds which have been blanched and cut fine, like shavings, one-half pound of the finest sweet grated chocolate, half a pound of finest raisins, seeded and chopped, one cup of matzo flour, sifted very fine; add the juice of an orange, a wine-glass full of wine, and the stiff beaten whites added last. A piece of citron shaved very fine adds to this delicious cake. Bake in spring form.

"Aunt Babette's" Cook Book, 1891

COCOA BEAN

PAPER BISCUIT BOX

Diet-Bread* Cake

Beat together five eggs and half a pound of white sugar, then add six ounces of flour well dried and sifted, a little lemon-juice and grated lemon-peel; bake in a moderate oven.

Matso Diet Bread

(Passover)

Simmer one pound of white sugar in a quarter of a pint of water, which pour hot upon eight well-beaten eggs; beat till cold, when add one pound of matso flour, a little grated lemon-peel, and bake in a papered tin, or in small tins; the cake must be removed while hot.

The Jewish Manual, By A Lady, 1846

* The term ''diet'' refers to the wholesomeness of food, not to its caloric value.

TIN BAKING DISH

To make Drop Biscuits

Take eight Eggs and one Pound of double refin'd Sugar, beaten fine, twelve Ounces of fine Flour well dried, beat your Eggs very well, then put in your Sugar and beat it, and then your Flour by Degrees; beat it all very well together without ceasing, your Oven must be as hot as for Half-penny Bread, then flour some Sheets of Tin,† and drop your Biscuits of what Bigness you please, put them in the Oven as fast as you can, and when you see them rise, watch them, if they begin to colour take them out, and put in more; and if the first is not enough, put them in again; if they are right done, they will have a white Ice on them. You may, if you choose it, put in a few Carraways; when they are all baked, put them in the Oven again to dry, then keep them in a very dry Place.

[HANNAH GLASSE], *The Art of Cookery*, 1747

† The pans can also be buttered or buttered and sugared.

220

A Butter Drop

Four yolks, two whites, one pound flour, a quarter of a pound butter, one pound sugar, two spoons rose water, a little mace, baked in tin pans.

AMELIA SIMMONS, AN AMERICAN ORPHAN, *American Cookery,* 1796

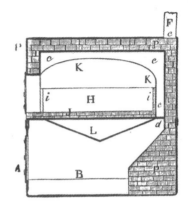

Gimblettes Paste

This kind of paste is made with the yolk of eggs, whereas the whites only are used in making meringues. It is by adherence to these principles of economy, that a good cook distinguishes himself. For eight yolks take two ounces of butter, half a pound of flour, a pinch of salt, one ounce of sugar, and a little milk; work the paste with your hand on the table; add to it a little rasped lemon-peel, or a little orange-flower. Cut the paste into small pieces, which roll up the size of your little finger, and make rings with them: solder them with a little dorure (yolks of eggs well beaten). Next rub a baking sheet over with butter, and lay the gimblettes on it. Mind that they are all of an equal size. Brush them twice over with the dorure, and bake them in an oven that is but very moderately hot. This paste undergoes no change while in the oven; let it get quite dry, for gimblettes require to be made crisp. Sometimes you can twist them to vary the form. This pastry is sometimes given by the French ladies to their little dogs; it is very delicate in flavour, when perfumed with orange-flower, vanilla, lemon, or otherwise.

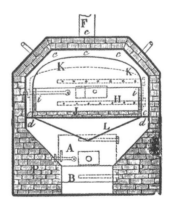

LOUIS EUSTACHE UDE, *The French Cook,* 1829

221

Lafayette Gingerbread

Cut up in a deep pan half a pound of the best fresh butter, with a half pound of excellent brown sugar; and stir it to cream with a spaddle. Add a pint of West India molasses, mixed with half a pint of warm milk; four table-spoonfuls of ginger; a heaped table-spoonful of mixed powdered cinnamon and powdered mace and nutmeg; and a glass of brandy. Sift in a pound and a half of fine flour. Beat six eggs till very light and thick, and mix them, alternately, into the pan of butter, sugar, molasses, &c. At the last, mix in the yellow rind (grated fine) of two large oranges and the juice. Stir the whole very hard. Melt in one cup a very small level tea-spoonful of soda, and in another a small level salt-spoon of tartaric acid. Dissolve them both in lukewarm water, and see that both are quite melted. First stir the soda into the mixture, and then put in the tartaric acid. On no account exceed the quantity of the two alkalis, as if too much is used, they will destroy entirely the flavoring, and communicate a very disagreeable taste instead. Few cakes are the better for any of the alkaline powders, and many sorts are entirely spoiled by them. Even in gingerbread they should be used very sparingly, rather less than more of the prescribed quantity. Having buttered (with the same butter) a large round or oblong pan, put in the mixture, and bake it in a moderate oven till thoroughly done, keeping up a steady heat, but watching that it does not burn. There is no gingerbread superior to this, if well made. Instead of lemon or orange, cut in half a pound of seedless raisins, dredge them well with flour, and stir them, gradually, into the mixture.

This is also called Franklin gingerbread.

Miss Leslie's New Cookery Book, 1857

The Friend of Washington

Ginger Snaps

Take two tea-cups of molasses, one of butter, and one of sugar. Boil the butter and sugar together. Add a table-spoonful of black pepper, two of ginger, a tea-spoonful of saleratus, and flour to roll out. Roll them thin; cut in shapes, and bake quick. These are very nice; and the longer they are kept the better they will be.

AN AMERICAN LADY, *The American Home Cook Book*, 1854

GINGERBREAD VENDOR

Old Hartford Election Cake

(100 years old)

Five pounds of dried and sifted flour.

Two pounds of butter.

Two pounds of sugar.

Three gills of distillery yeast, or twice the quantity of home-brewed.

Four eggs.

A gill of wine and a gill of brandy.

Half an ounce of nutmegs, and two pounds of fruit.

A quart of milk.

Rub the butter very fine into the flour, add half the sugar, then the yeast, then half the milk, hot in winter, and blood warm in summer, then the eggs well beaten, the wine, and the remainder of the milk. Beat it well, and let it stand to rise all night. Beat it well in the morning, adding the brandy, the sugar, and the spice. Let it rise three or four hours, till very light. When you put the wood into the oven, put the cake in buttered pans, and put in the fruit in this way: First dredge it with flour, then put in enough cake to cover the bottom of the pans, then sprinkle some fruit, and do not let any of it rest against the pan, as it burns, and is thus wasted. Then continue to add a layer of fruit and a layer of cake, having no fruit on the top. This saves those that usually burn on the pan, and secures a more equal distribution.

If you wish it richer, add a pound of citron.

Miss Beecher's Domestic Receipt Book, 1856

WOODEN FLOUR TUB

Lebkechen

(Dr. F. A. Genth)

Boil four pounds of honey with an equal amount of sugar, then add one pound of split almonds, one pound of citron, cut small, the grated rinds of four lemons, half an ounce of nutmeg, half an ounce of cloves, three ounces of cinnamon. The mass should be stirred whilst the above substances are added. Then add one tumbler of brandy, and stir into the mixture six pounds of flour. Roll out to a quarter inch thickness, keeping the dough warm; cut into small cakes, bake at once in a hot oven and ice with lemon icing.

PASTEBOARD AND ROLLING PIN

Water Icing

Put two cupfuls of XXXX sugar into a bowl, add the grated yellow rind of an orange, two tablespoonfuls of orange juice and two tablespoonfuls of boiling water. Stir until sufficiently soft to spread nicely. Use at once.

Lemon, vanilla or almond flavoring may be used.

SARAH TYSON RORER, *Mrs. Rorer's New Cook Book,* 1898

Oatmeal Crackers

Wet one pint of fine oatmeal with one gill of water; work with a spoon until it can be made up into a mass; place on a board well covered with dry oatmeal; make as compact as possible and roll out carefully one-sixth of an inch thick and cut into squares. Bake in a very slow oven, or merely scald* and then let them stand until they dry out. These are difficult to make at first, but one soon learns to handle the dough and to watch the oven so that they will not scorch. They are excellent for all the purposes of crackers, and if kept dry, or packed in oatmeal, will last good for months. This is one form of the Scotch "bannock." A rich addition is two heaping tablespoonfuls of ground desiccated cocoanut.

The Housekeeper Cook Book, 1894

OATS

* Scald = place in *very* hot oven and turn off fire.

Parkin

The name of a spiced cake that is manufactured on the 5th of November† in almost every cottage in the neighbourhood of Leeds. It is usual to send slices of Parkin as presents.

Warm 1 lb. of butter and beat it until creamy with ½ lb. of moist sugar, then beat in 1 breakfast-cupful of treacle and the beaten yolks of six eggs, mixing the whole smoothly together with 3 breakfast-cupfuls of fine oatmeal; also mix in 1½ teaspoonfuls each of bicarbonate of soda and cream of tartar, 1 oz. of caraway-seeds, and 2 oz. of thinly-shred candied lemon-peel. Whisk the whites of the six eggs to a stiff froth, and stir it in with the mixture at the last. Butter a shallow

The Autographs of Guido Fawkes
before and after torture.

† The fifth of November is Guy Fawkes Day.

225

baking-dish, turn the Parkin into it, and bake it for about two hours in a moderate oven. Serve when cold.

Or: Put 3½ lb. of oatmeal into a basin and mix in 1 lb. each of flour and butter, ½ lb. of moist sugar, ½ oz. of baking-powder, and make the whole into a stiff dough by working in syrup. Make the dough into rounds, put them on tins, keeping them about 3 in. apart, and bake in a slow oven.

THEODORE FRANCIS GARRETT, ED., *The Encyclopædia of Practical Cookery*, 1892–4

PLATE CARRIER

Scottish Shortbread

(*Excellent*)

With one pound of flour mix well a couple of ounces of sifted sugar, and one of candied orange-rind or citron, sliced small; make these into a paste with from eight to nine ounces of good butter, made sufficiently warm to be liquid; press the paste together with the hands, mould it upon tins into large cakes nearly an inch thick, pinch the edges, and bake the shortbread in a moderate oven for twenty minutes or longer, should it not be quite crisp, but do not allow it to become deeply coloured.

Flour, 1 lb.; sugar, 2 ozs.; candied orange or citron, 1 oz.; butter, 8 to 9 ozs. 20 minutes or more.

ELIZA ACTON, *Modern Cookery*, 1852

Watermelon Cake

½ cup butter.   2 cups flour.
1 cup sugar.   1 teaspoon cream tartar.
½ cup sweet milk.   ½ teaspoon soda.
3 whites of eggs.   Flavor with lemon.

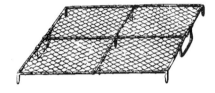

Take a little more than ⅓ of the mixture and to it add 1 teaspoon liquid cochineal and ½ cup raisins. Put the red part in the center and bake. Cover with a frosting colored green with spinach.

Smiley's Cook Book, 1896

White Perfection Cake

(Mrs. C. Jones, Bradford, Vt.)

Three cups sugar, one of butter, one of milk, three of flour, one of corn starch, whites of twelve eggs beaten to a stiff froth, two tea-spoons cream tartar in the flour, and one of soda in half the milk; dissolve the corn starch in the rest of the milk, and add it to the sugar and butter well beaten together, then the milk and soda, and the flour and whites of eggs. This cake is rightly named "Perfection."

Turk's Head Cake Mould

Buckeye Cookery, 1883

227

Yorkshire Secret Cake

Roll rich puff-paste into rounds the size of a breakfast plate and half an inch in thickness; strew thickly over one pound of currants, with a little chopped candied lemon, which have been well steeped in rum or brandy; over this place another round of paste; unite it closely round; cut it into quarters, but leave them close together, and bake immediately. Serve each cake on a plate without separating the quarters, either hot or cold. This is a most delicious tea or breakfast cake.

ANNE BOWMAN, *The New Cookery Book,* 1869

ROSE BRANDY FOR FLAVORING

Gather leaves [petals] from fragrant roses, without bruising; fill a pitcher with them, and cover them with French brandy; next day pour off the brandy, take out the leaves, and fill the pitcher with fresh ones, and return the brandy. Do this until it is strongly impregnated; then bottle it. Keep the pitcher closely covered during the process. It is better than distilled rose-water for cakes, etc. (MARY STUART SMITH, *Virginia Cookery-Book,* 1885)

MAHOGANY FOLDING TRAY

KING OF HEARTS   QUEEN OF HEARTS

The Queen of Hearts
She made some tarts,
All on a summer's day;
The Knave of Hearts
He stole the tarts,
And took them clean away.

The King of Hearts
Called for the tarts,
And beat the Knave full sore;
The Knave of Hearts
Brought back the tarts,
And vow'd he'd steal no more.

CARDS were originally invented in Egypt; though the current opinion of the present day is, that they were invented about a century or two back, and first used for the amusement of a young French prince. That Cards, however, are of the high origin asserted, is easily proved by their numbers, suites, and characters, corresponding strictly with the astronomical signs and calculations of the ancient Egyptians, who are acknowledged to have been better acquainted with the motions of the heavenly bodies than any other nation that ever existed. But to the proof:

The *Colors* are *two,* Red and Black, answering to the *two Equinoxes.*

The *Suites* are *four,* answering to the *four Seasons.* The emblems of these formerly were, and still are in Spain: for the *Heart,* a *Cup,* which is emblematic of *Winter*; for the *Spade* an *Acorn,* the emblem of *Autumn*; for the *Club* a *Trefoil,* the emblem of *Summer*; and for the *Diamond* a *Rose,* which is the emblem of *Spring.*

The *twelve Court Cards* answer to the *twelve Months*; and these were formerly painted with the *Signs of the Zodiac.*

The *fifty-two Cards,* or whole *Pack,* answer to the number of *Weeks* in the *Year.*

The *thirteen Cards* in each

Tartus

Take fair soft cheese that is buttery, and pare it, and grind it in a mortar. Add fair cream and grind it together; mix it with good milk, that it be no thicker than raw cream, and cast thereto a little salt if need be; and if thy cheese be salty, cast thereto never a deal; color it with saffron. Then make a large coffin [crust] of fair paste, & let the edges be raised more than an inch in height. Let the coffin harden in the oven. Then take it out, put lumps of butter in the bottom thereof, and cast the cheese stuff there-to, and cast pieces of butter there-upon, and set it in the oven without a lid, and let bake enough. Then cast sugar thereon, and serve it forth. And if thou wish, let it have a lid; but then thy stuff must be as thick as pounded meat.

HARLEIAN MS. 4016 [c. 1450]

To Make a Tarte of Prunes

Take prunes and set them upon a chafer with a little red wine and put thereto a manshet and let them boil together. Then draw them through a strainer with the yolks of four eggs and season it up with sugar and so bake it.

A Proper newe Booke of Cokerye [c. 1548–72]

To Make a Cover Tarte After the Frenche Fashyan

Take a pint of cream and the yolks of ten eggs, and beat them all together, and put thereto half a dish of sweet butter, and sugar, and boil them till they be thick. Then take them up and cool them in a platter, and make a couple of cakes of fine paste, and lay your stuff in one of them and cover it with the other, and cut the vent above, and so bake it.

A Proper newe Booke of Cokerye [c. 1548–72]

Chocolate Tarts

Rasp a quarter of a pound of chocolate, a stick of cinnamon, add some fresh lemon peel grated, a little salt, and some sugar: take two spoonsful of fine flour, and the yolks of six eggs well beaten, and mixed with some milk. Put all these into a stewpan, and let them be a little over the fire: add a little lemon peel cut small, and let it stand to be cold. Beat up the whites of eggs enough to cover it, and put it in puff paste. When it is baked, sift some sugar over it, and glaze it with a salamander.

JOHN FARLEY, *The London Art of Cookery*, 1811

Doucettes

Take Pork, & hack it small, & Eggs mixed together, & a little Milk, & mix them together with Honey & Pepper, & bake them in a coffin, & serve forth.

HARLEIAN MS. 279 [c. 1430]

Suite answer to the number of *Weeks* in a *Lunar Quarter.*

The aggregate of *Pips,* or *Spots,* calculated in the following manner, amount to *three hundred and sixty-five,* or the number of *Days* in a *Year.*

The number in each Suite is	55
Multiply by four Suites	4
The number of Pips in the Pack	220
Four Knaves, equivalent to, or counting eleven each	44
Four Queens, equivalent to twelve each	48
Four Kings, equivalent to thirteen each	52
Ace of Spades, as chief, counting	1
The number of Pips in the Pack, and of Days in a Year . .	365

(Madame Le Normand, Fortune-Teller To The Emperor Napoleon, *The Unerring Fortune-Teller,* 1866)

NAPOLEON.

French tart with preserves

(Fransk tårta med sylt)

Work together 12 yolks, 4 whole eggs, and 3 pints powdered sugar until it begins to appear white; then pour in an eighth of a pint of melted butter and add fine flour, sufficient enough to allow the dough to be rolled into a thickness of a half dollar. Out of this cut 9 or 10 cakes, round or oblong according to taste. Place these in buttered pans and prick to prevent bubbling. Bake them brown and put up on a platter, placing different kinds of preserves between them. Boil sugar in water until it fastens around the finger after it has been dipped in cold water. Dip a beater in the sugar water and sprinkle the tarts until covered.

Swedish-English Cookbook, 1897

A Flaune of Almayne

First take raisins of currants, or else other fresh raisins, and good ripe pears, or else good apples, and pick out the cores of them, and pare them. And grind them, and the raisins in a clean mortar, and add to them a little sweet cream of milk, and strain them through a clean strainer, and take 10 eggs, or as many more as will suffice, and beat them well together, both the white and the yolk. And draw it through a strainer, and grate fair white bread, and add thereto a good quantity, and more sweet cream. And mix all this together. And take saffron, and powder of ginger, and cinnamon, and add thereto, and a little salt,

and a quantity of fair sweet butter. And make a fair coffin, or two, or as many as needs be, and bake them a little in an oven. And put this batter in them, and let them bake as thou wouldst bake flauns, or custards, and when they be baked enough, strew upon them powder of cinnamon, and of white sugar. And this is a good manner of custard.

The Forme of Cury [c. 1390]

To make Petty Patty

(Mrs. Barnardiston)

Take the breast of a fowl or Turkey, mince it very fine, with the marrow of one bone, a few Crumbs of bread, a little Parsley and thyme, some pepper & salt, & a little onion. Mix all these together with an Egg as for force meat, then bake them in the smallest patty pans you have, in puff paste, & before you send them to Table cut the tops off, and put in a little gravy. To be eaten hot.

The Receipt Book of Mrs. Ann Blencowe, 1694

Fine Puff-Paste

Into one quart of sifted flour, mix two teaspoonfuls of baking-powder, and a teaspoonful of salt; *then sift again.* Measure out one teacupful of butter and one of lard, hard and cold. Take the lard and rub into the flour until a very fine, smooth paste. Then put in just enough *ice-water*, say half a cupful, containing a beaten white of

egg, to mix a very stiff dough. Roll it out into a thin sheet, spread with one-fourth of the butter, sprinkle over with a little flour, then roll up closely in a long roll, like a scroll, double the ends towards the centre, flatten and reroll, then spread again with another quarter of the butter. Repeat this operation until the butter is used up. Put it on an earthen dish, cover it with a cloth and set it in a cold place, in the ice-box in summer; let it remain until *cold*; an hour or more before making out the crust. Tarts made with this paste cannot be cut with a knife when fresh; they go into flakes at the touch.

You may roll this pastry in any direction, from you, towards you, sideways, anyway, it matters not, but you must have nice flour, *ice-water*, and very *little* of it, and strength to roll it, if you would succeed.

This recipe I purchased from a colored cook on one of the Lake Michigan steamers many years ago, and it is, without exception, the finest puff-paste I have ever seen.

Mrs. F. L. Gillette and Hugo Ziemann, *The White-House Cook-Book,* 1894

THE ARCHDUKE OF AUSTRIA CONSULTING A FORTUNE-TELLER.

A Carolina Rice-field

There was an old man of Tobago,
Who lived on rice, gruel, and sago;
Till, much to his bliss,
His physician said this—
To a leg, sir, of mutton you may go.

Rice

There is little reason for doubting that this grain is of Asiatic origin. From the earliest records it has formed the principal, if not the only food of the great mass of the population on the continent and islands of India and throughout the Chinese empire. The Egyptians are supposed to have learned the cultivation of rice under the reign of the Caliphs, at which time many useful plants were brought over the Red sea to Egypt, which now grow spontaneously there and enrich the country.

The introduction of rice as an object of cultivation in America is of very modern occurrence.

DR. ABERNETHY'S BLUE PILL

A patient being asked by the Doctor in his peculiar brusque manner what medicine he had been taking, replied, "Your blue pill, sir," received, to his astonishment and dismay, the following alarming confession of error:

"I thought so, I thought so; it's the worst, the very worst thing in the world, sir! Make your will, sir, make your will; for it will kill you, sir, kill you."

"But," urged the trembling patient, "you yourself prescribed it for me ten years ago."

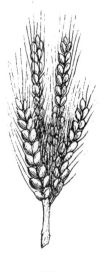

RICE

The author of a work "On the importance of the British Plantations in America," which was published in London during the year 1701, has recorded, as a circumstance then recent, that "a brigantine from the island of Madagascar happened to put in at Carolina, having a little seed-rice left, which the captain gave to a gentleman of the name of Woodward. From part of this he had a very good crop, but was ignorant for some years how to clean it. It was soon dispersed over the province; and by frequent experiments and observations, they found out ways of producing the manufacturing it to so great perfection, that it is thought to exceed any other in value."

The swamps of South Carolina, both those which are occasioned by the periodical visits of the tides, and those which are caused by the inland floodings of the rivers, are well suited for the production of rice.

The rice harvest in the United States usually commences at the end of August, and extends through the entire month of September, or even somewhat later. The reaping is performed with a sickle by male negroes, and these are followed by females, who collect the rice into bundles.

This cultivation is found to be extremely unhealthy to the negroes employed in its prosecution. The alternate flooding and drying of the land in so hot a climate, where natural evaporation proceeds with great rapidity, must necessarily be prejudicial to health. To avoid exposure to this unwholesome atmosphere, the whole white population abandon the low grounds to the care of negro cultivators. The mortality thus occasioned among the labourers in rice districts is so great, that while the general increase of population in the States exceeds by far that realized in the older settled countries of Europe, fresh supplies of negro slaves must continually be brought,

to repair the waste of life, from the more northern slave states of the Union.

Wıllıam Rhınd, *A History of The Vegetable Kingdom*
[c. 1842]

Rice, Andalusian

This dish, which is one very commonly served in
Spain and Portugal, is valued as a tonic during
the heats of summer, and is also recommended
as a preventative of intestinal indisposition: it is
peculiar, but the taste for it is an easily acquired
one. Warm in a saucepan half a pound of best
olive-oil or fresh butter. Throw in half a pound
of picked rice, and one pound or one pound and
a half of veal or poultry flesh, cut into neat
squares. Add half a pint of tomato sauce, or three
or four fresh tomatoes, one or two chopped
onions, a table-spoonful of shred parsley, a pinch
of powdered saffron, and a little pepper, salt, and
cayenne. In Spain a clove of garlic is always
added. Stir these ingredients into the warm oil,
and let them stew gently for ten minutes; pour
over them a pint of stock or water, cover the
saucepan closely, and let its contents simmer
gently until the rice has absorbed the liquor.
Throw the whole into a heated strainer for a
minute to drain off any oil that may be left, and
pile the rice, which will be a bright yellow colour,
upon a hot dish. Hold a red-hot shovel or salamander over the top for a minute or two to brown
the surface, and send the dish to table with cut
lemons, that each guest may squeeze a little juice
over his plate. Time, half to three-quarters of an
hour to simmer the rice. Sufficient for five or six
persons.

Cassell's Dictionary of Cookery [c. 1877]

Saucepan, with Lip, for melted
butter, gravy, &c.

SAFFRON

Rice, Boiled in the Indian Fashion

INDIAN COOKS.

Wash it well in cold water two or three times, then put it *loose* into a saucepan with a large quantity of *boiling* water; boil very fast for twenty minutes. Strain through a colander, and pour over it a teacupful of cold water; shake the colander until all the water is gone, then lightly shake the rice into a hot dish, let it dry for a few minutes before the fire, and serve.

N.B. Many English cooks, after straining the rice, replace it in the saucepan, and either cover it with the lid or a cloth, like potatoes, and set it on the hob to dry; but the method which I give, from Indian experience, will be found the best, as it makes the rice "rocky," which is the great point of "native" cookery. "Sticky rice, beat wife," is a well known Hindustanee maxim.

TABITHA TICKLETOOTH, *The Dinner Question*, 1860

Rice à la Berne

(Swiss)

Blanch half a pound of rice, drain and put it into a stewpan; moisten it with warm milk, and let it cook on a moderate fire, and when tender and dry add sugar enough to sweeten it; then cover it over and let it remain till nearly cold; then mix in a small glass of kirschwasser or maraschino. Have ready a dome-shaped mould which has been well cooled on ice, and put the rice into it in layers alternately with some preserved fruits cut small which have soaked in kirschwasser or maraschino for an hour. When the mould is full cover it first with a round of paper reaching beyond the rims, then with its own lid; butter liberally where the cover joins and put it on ice for an hour, and then turn out in the usual way and serve whipped cream round it.

Mrs. De Salis, *National Viands À La Mode*, 1895

Rice (à l'Italienne)

Wash half a pound of rice in several waters. Throw it into boiling water, and let it boil until tender. Drain and dry it. Wash and drain a moderate-sized cabbage, and shred it finely. Melt a slice of fresh butter in a saucepan, and fry in this four ounces of streaky bacon cut into dice, and add the shred cabbage, a table-spoonful of chopped parsley, and a little pepper and salt. A clove of garlic and a sprig of fennel may be also added, if liked. Cover the saucepan closely, and stew the cabbage as gently as possible for three-quarters of an hour. Put in the boiled rice, stew the whole a quarter of an hour longer, and serve the preparation piled high on a hot dish with grated Parmesan or Cheddar cheese sprinkled over the top.

ITALIAN KITCHEN.

Cassell's Dictionary of Cookery [c. 1877]

Rice

(Milanese Fashion)

Fry the boiled rice in a sautepan with a piece of butter; season with grated Parmesan or other cheese; add any remains of dressed fowl, game, tongue, ham, or truffle, prawns, lobster, or any kind of meat or fish most convenient; any or several of these may be used together, and should be cut for the purpose into shreds or squares; season with a little nutmeg, pepper and salt; serve hot.

(Piedmontese Fashion)

Chop a small onion very fine, and fry it in a sautepan with an ounce of butter; then add half a pound of boiled rice dry, and the pulp of three baked potatoes; season with an ounce of grated Parmesan cheese, and a pinch of cayenne and salt; pile up the rice in a hot dish; strew over the surface some cleansed fillets anchovies or sardines, and send to table quite hot.

(Turkish Fashion)

Fry the boiled rice with a little butter, cayenne, and saffron powder; season with a little salt, and throw in a handful of cleaned Smyrna raisins; serve quite hot.

CHARLES ELMÉ FRANCATELLI, *The Cook's Guide*, 1884

Stuffed Vine-Leaves

Put a few dozen young Vine-leaves in a large bowl, pour boiling water over them, then turn them on to a sieve, and leave till well drained. Peel and finely chop seven or eight large onions; put ½ lb. of butter into a stewpan, place it over the fire till hot, then add the onions, and toss them about until beginning to brown. Wash in plenty of water about 2 lb. of the best rice, and dry it on a cloth: put the rice in with the onions, and stir it over the fire till on the point of browning, then pour in ½ pint of water, and continue stirring until dry. Season the mixture with powdered mint and cinnamon, and salt and pepper; stir it well, then move it from the fire. Spread the Vine leaves out, put a small quantity of the mixture on each, then roll them round lengthwise, pressing gently to prevent them opening. Cover the bottom of a saucepan with some small bones, and lay the Vine leaves on them, putting in now and then one or two sour plums; by doing this the flavour will be improved by the acidity from the plums. Press a plate over the Vine-leaves, moisten to height with water, and boil gently. When all the moisture has evaporated, take out one of the stuffed leaves and see if the rice is tender; if not, add more hot water. Arrange the leaves tastefully on a fancy dish-paper or a folded napkin on a hot dish, and serve them. Lemon juice can be used in place of the plums when they are not in season, but the latter are preferable.

THEODORE FRANCIS GARRETT, ED., *The Encyclopædia of Practical Cookery*, [1892–4]

Almond Gruel

To make almond gruel, take unblanched almonds and crush them, put there to oatmeal and grind them together, and add water. Then boil it and colour it with saffron and serve it.

A Noble Boke Off Cookry [c. 1467]

Barley Gruel

Wash four ounces of pearl barley; boil it into two quarts of water, with a bit of cinnamon, till it is reduced to one quart; strain, and return it to the sauce-pan, with a little sugar and three-quarters of a pint of port wine; make it quite hot, and it is ready to be used as wanted. It is very strengthening.

LADY HARRIET ST. CLAIR (LATE COUNTESS MÜNSTER), *Dainty Dishes* [1884]

PORRINGER

An excellent Gruel

Boil fair Water in a Skillet, and put thereto grated White-bread, good store of Currants, Mace and whole Cinamon; being almost boiled, and indifferent thick, put in a little Sack, some Sugar, and some strained yolks of Eggs. You may put to it some butter.

T. P. J. P. R. C. N. B. AND SEVERAL OTHER APPROVED COOKS OF *London* AND *Westminster, The Compleat Cook*, 1694

Pestle and Mortar

Pork Gruel enriched

Gruel a-forsydde: Take oatmeal and grind it small, and boil it well. Then pull off the skin and take out the bones of pork, and then chop it, and grind it small in a mortar; Then take thine gruel and mix them together, then strain it through a strainer, and put it in a pot and boil it a little, and salt it equally, and color it with saffron, and serve it forth running.

HARLEIAN MS. 279 [c. 1430]

Sago

Sago, which is a starch obtained from the pith of the stem of the sago-palm and other plants, is prepared in grains like tapioca, with similar results. Both sago and tapioca contain a little gluten, and therefore have more food-value than arrowroot.

W. MATTIEU WILLIAMS, *The Chemistry of Cookery*, 1885

Apple Sago Pudding

For a 2-quart pudding dish, take a cup of sago (tapioca if preferred), put it in a pan of cold water, let heat and cook gradually, adding hot water; if required, add a little salt. In the meantime, pare and core apples enough to fill the dish. Fill the holes with sugar and season with nutmeg. Put a little water in the dish and partly bake them, then take the dish out, pour the sago over, return and bake till apples are done. Eat with sugar and cream. Better to be done half an hour before meal time. One of my best puddings.

MRS. FRANCES E. OWENS, *Mrs. Owens' Cook Book*, 1882

Kew Mince, or Haggis Royal

Cut one pound of lean meat from a cold roast leg of mutton. Mix it with half a pound of finely-shred suet, four table-spoonfuls of finely-grated bread-crumbs, one boned anchovy, one tea-spoonful of minced parsley, half a tea-spoonful of chopped lemon-rind, one small tea-spoonful of

Apples are highly useful in families, and ought to be more universally cultivated, excepting in the compactest cities. There is not a single family but might set a tree in some otherwise useless spot, which might serve the two fold use of shade and fruit; on which 12 or 14 kinds of fruit trees might easily be engrafted, and essentially preserve the orchard from the intrusions of boys, &c. which is too common in America. If the boy who thus planted a tree, and guarded and protected it in a useless corner, and carefully engrafted different fruits, was to be indulged free access into orchards, whilst the neglectful boy was prohibited— how many millions of fruit trees would spring into growth—and what a saving to the union. The net saving would in time extinguish the public debt, and enrich our cookery.

AMELIA SIMMONS, AN AMERICAN ORPHAN, *American Cookery*, 1796

SAGO PALM

It is said, there are SEVEN *chances against even the most simple dish being presented to the Mouth in absolute perfection*; for instance A LEG OF MUTTON.

1st. —The Mutton must be *good,*

2d. —Must have been kept a *good* time,

3d. —Must be roasted at a *good* fire,

4th.—By a *good* Cook,

5th.—Who must be in *good* temper,

6th.—With all this felicitous combination you must have *good* luck, and

7th.—*Good* Appetite. The Meat, and the mouths which are to eat it, must be ready for each other, at the same moment.

([DR. WILLIAM KITCHINER], *The Cook's Oracle*, 1823)

salt, and half a tea-spoonful of pepper. When the dry ingredients are thoroughly blended, add a wine-glassful of port or claret, and the yolks of four well-beaten eggs. Put the mixture neatly into the veal caul (or when this cannot be procured, put it into a saucepan), and bake in a quick oven. Serve as hot as possible, with half a pint of good brown gravy in the dish. Time, three-quarters of an hour to bake. Sufficient for four or five persons.

Cassell's Dictionary of Cookery [c. 1877]

Leg of Mutton Stewed

Take the large bone out, leaving the bone at the smaller end as a handle; cut off also the bone below the knuckle, and fix it with skewers; then put it in a stew-pan with a pinch of allspice, four onions, two cloves, two carrots cut in four pieces each, a small bunch of parsley, two bay-leaves, three sprigs of thyme, salt, pepper, two ounces of bacon cut in slices, a quarter of a pint of broth, and water enough just to cover it; set on a good fire, and after one hour of boiling add a liquor-glass of French brandy. Let simmer then for about five hours, in all about six hours; then dish it, strain the sauce on it, and serve.

We would advise those who have never tasted of a leg of mutton cooked as above, to try it.

PIERRE BLOT, *Hand-Book of Practical Cookery*, 1868

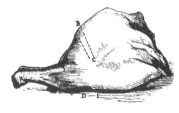

LEG OF MUTTON

Mutton Sausages

A delicate sausage is made from the remains of
an underdone leg of roast mutton, or any other
joint from which slices can be got without fat.
Chop a pound of lean underdone mutton and six
ounces of beef suet separately; then mix them
with four ounces of finely-prepared bread-
crumbs, and put them into a basin with a pint of
oysters bearded and chopped, two anchovies, a
seasoning of thyme, marjoram, and powdered
mace, and some pepper and salt. Moisten with
two beaten eggs, and a little of the anchovy
liquor if required. Make into a firm paste, and
roll into sausages or make into balls, but the
sausage-meat will keep for a few days. Time to
fry, seven or eight minutes.

Cassell's Dictionary of Cookery [c. 1877]

SAUSAGES

KING ARTHUR'S ROUND TABLE.

When Arthur first in Court began
 To wear long hanging sleeves,
He entertained three servingmen
 And all-of them were thieves.

The first he was an Irishman,
 The second was a Scot,
The third he was a Welshman,
 And all were knaves, I wot.

The Irishman loved usquebaugh,
 The Scot loved ale called bluecap,
The Welshman he loved toasted cheese,
 And made his mouth like a mouse-trap.

Usquebaugh burnt the Irishman;
 The Scot was drowned in ale;
The Welshman had like to be choked by a mouse,
 But he pulled it out by the tail.

Usquebaugh

To make this the right *Irish* way, who were the first Inventors that we can hear of: Take two gallons of rectified Spirit,* half a pound of *Spanish* Licorice, a quarter of a pound of Raisins of the Sun, three ounces of Dates sliced, the Tops of Thyme and Balm, of each a pugil;† the Tops or Flowers of Rosemary two ounces, Cinnamon and Mace well bruised, of each an ounce; Annis-seed & Corriander-seeds bruised likewise, of each two ounces; Citron, or Lemon, and Orange-peel finely scraped, of each half an ounce: let these infuse in a warm place forty eight hours, with often shaking together, and somewhat, if it may be, increasing the heat; then let them stand in a cool place for the space of a Week, sweeten it with Sugar Candy, and so draw off the Liquor, and press out the Liquid part that remains in the Ingredients. For a weaker sort, put other Spirits to them, and do as before.

This is not only pleasant to drink, but moderately taken greatly preserves the Lungs against cold Distilations of Rheums, and other Defects that afflict them, and incline them to Consumption. It lengthens the Breath, cheers the Heart, and keeps out ill Airs occasioned by Damps and Fog, &c.

[DR. SALMON], *The Family Dictionary*, 1695

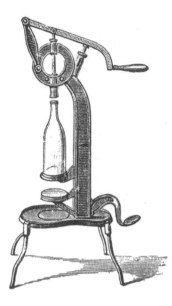

* Rectified spirit = a pure distilled alcohol for which an inexpensive vodka can be substituted.

† Pugil = a pinch, or as much as can be taken up between the thumb and two fingers.

Irish Usquebaugh

This famous cordial, which the French call Scubac, is prepared in various ways. In small quantities this liquor is prepared by Irish housewives as follows:

Infuse one pound of seedless raisins, half an

ounce of grated nutmeg, one-fourth of an ounce of pulverized cloves, as much of cardamom, the peel of a sour orange rubbed off on sugar, half a pound of brown rock-candy; and a little saffron tincture in two quarts of brandy a fortnight; stir daily; filter and bottle.

THE "ONLY WILLIAM," *The Flowing Bowl*, 1892

Gem Apple Corers

Whiskey Apples

American pippins are the best, but any sweet, sound apples may be used. Peel them neatly, scoop out the core with a narrow sharp-pointed knife. To every pound of apples allow three-quarters of a pound of loaf sugar, the thin rind and strained juice of a lemon, two inches of cinnamon, two cloves, half an inch of bruised ginger, half a gill of whisky, and half an inch of stick vanilla. Put the whole into a skillet, place it over a slow heat, and simmer gently for an hour and a half. Turn the apples frequently with a silver spoon, and skim often. If carefully attended to, the apples become quite transparent, and will keep for more than a year; place them in large glazed jars; boil the syrup for five minutes; strain it over the apples, and when cold, tie them down. To be served at dessert.

Cre-Fydd's Family Fare, 1871

ASPARAGUS HOLDER

Savory tosted or melted Cheese

Cut pieces of quick, fat, rich, well tasted Cheese (as the best of *Brye, Cheshire, &c.* or sharp thick Cream-cheese) into a dish of thick beaten melted

Butter, that has served for Asparages, or the like, or Pease, or other boiled Sallet, or ragout of meat, or gravy of Mutton. And if you will, chop some of the Asparages among it, or slices of Gambon of Bacon, or fresh collops, or Onions, or Anchoves, and set all this to melt upon a Chafing-dish of Coals, and stir all well together, to incorporate them. And when all is of an equal consistence, strew some gross white-pepper on it, and eat it with toasts or crusts of white-bread. You may scorch it at the top with a hot fire-shovel.

The Closet Of the Eminently Learned Sir Kenelme Digby Kt. Opened, 1671

Cheese Toaster

Toast and Cheese

Cut a slice of Bread about half an inch thick, pare off the crust, and *toast it very slightly* on both sides, so as just to brown it, without making it hard, or burning it.

Cut a slice of Cheese (good fat mellow Cheshire cheese, or double Gloster, is better than poor, thin single Gloster), a quarter of an inch thick, not so big as the bread by half an inch on each side; pare off the rind, cut out all the specks and rotten parts,* and lay it on the toasted Bread in a cheese-toaster; carefully watch it, that it does not burn, and stir it with a spoon, to prevent a pellicule forming on the surface. Have ready good Mustard, Pepper and Salt.

If you observe the directions here given, the Cheese will eat mellow, and will be uniformly done, and the Bread crisp and soft, and will well deserve its ancient appellation of a "Rare Bit."

[DR. WILLIAM KITCHINER], *The Cook's Oracle,* 1823

MUSTARD

* "*Rotten Cheese* toasted," Kitchiner notes, "is the *ne plus ultra* of *Haut Gout,* and only eatable by the thorough-bred Gourmand, in the most inverted state of his jaded Appetite."

BRILLAT SAVARIN

French Rabbit

Butter an earthen dish, and place in the bottom a layer of buttered bread, then a layer of thinly cut cheese, suitable for a rabbit, and alternate layers of buttered bread and cheese until the dish is full, having cheese on the top. Turn over this two cups of milk into which two eggs have been beaten. Bake twenty minutes. This is less work than to make the ordinary Welsh rabbit, and it may be seasoned with beer, mustard, and Worcestershire, if desired.

Hood's Practical Cook's Book, 1897

Welsh Rare-bit

Brillat Savarin, the famous French *Gourmet,* gives the following recipe taken from the papers of M. Trollet, bailiff in Meudon, in the Canton of Berne: "Take as many eggs as you wish, according to the number of guests, and weigh them; then take a piece of cheese weighing a third of the weight of the eggs, and a slice of butter weighing a sixth; beat the eggs well up in a saucepan, after which put in the butter and cheese, the latter either grated or chopped up very small; place the saucepan on a good fire, and stir it with a flat spoon until the mixture becomes sufficiently thick and soft; add a little salt and a large portion of pepper, and serve it up in a hot dish. Bring out the best wine, and let it go round freely, and wonders will be done."*

Cassell's Dictionary of Cookery [c. 1877]

* This Welsh rabbit is also called fondue, and according to Mary Ronald (*The Century Cookbook,* 1895) Brillat-Savarin "relates an anecdote of the sixteenth century of a M. de Madot, newly appointed Bishop of Belley, who at a feast given in honor of his arrival, mistaking the fondue for cream, ate it with a spoon instead of a fork. This caused so much comment that the next day no two people met who did not say: 'Do you know how the new bishop ate his fondue last night?' 'Yes; he ate it with a spoon. I have it from an eye-witness.' And soon the news spread over the diocese."

The Maccaroni-seller of Naples.

Yankee Doodle came to town,
Riding on a pony,
He stuck a feather in his cap,
And called it macaroni.

Yankee Doodle keep it up,
Yankee Doodle dandy,
Mind the music and the step,
And with the girls be handy.

Father and I went down to camp,
Along with Captain Goodin,
And there we saw the men and boys
As thick as hasty puddin'.

THE ORIGIN of Yankee Doodle is not known. Some say that the name came from an old Dutch folk song. Others say that it came from a Cherokee word, "eankke," meaning a coward or slave—as applied to the Colonists by the British. So many conflicting suggestions had been offered and so great was the interest, that the Library of Congress authorized a full report of the matter in 1909.* But no decision could be reached.

The actual meaning of "macaroni" in this rhyme is that of an over-dressed person, a dandy, or a fop. Thus it is Yankee Doodle, himself, who is the macaroni, and not the feather. Although the analogy to macaroni is only half-understood in the song, the reference to "hasty pudding" is clear, for the test of this thick porridge is that the pudding stick will stand upright in it alone.

For more on macaroni, see Hollow Pipes, page 36.

* "Report on the Star Spangled Banner, Hail Columbia, America, Yankee Doodle," compiled by Oscar George Theodore Sonneck (Washington, D.C.: U.S. Government Printing Office, 1909).

A Macaroni

The year of their ascendant was 1772, and the engraving represents a macaroni of that period; distinguished by an immense knot of artificial hair behind, a very small cocked-hat, an enormous walking-stick with long tassels, and a jacket, waistcoat, and small-clothes cut to fit the person as closely as possible.

The macaronis took the town of London by storm. Nothing was fashionable that was not *à la macaroni*. Even the clergy had their wigs combed, their clothes cut, and their delivery refined *à la macaroni*. The shop-windows were filled with prints of the new tribe; there were engraved portraits of turf macaronis, military macaronis, college macaronis, and other varieties of the great macaroni race.

The periodical literature, such as it was, of the time is very severe on the macaronis. Living in the days of six-bottle men, one grave charge brought against them was that they hated "all drinking, except tea, capillaire, and posset." In a very successful five-act drama of the day, entitled *The Macaroni,* the hero of the piece—the macaroni *par excellence*—is held up to ridicule, principally because he respects female virtue, and swears by such mild and milk-and-water oaths as, "May I be deaf at the opera!" We now know how to appreciate these distinctions.

R. CHAMBERS, ED., *The Book of Days*, vol. II, 1862–4

Neapolitan Macaroni

(Mrs. John Furey, 125 Congress Street, Brooklyn, N.Y.)

1 qt. strong beef broth, 1 onion cut fine, ½ cup chopped parsley, 1 can mushrooms, ½ can tomatoes, ½ teaspoon ground mace, 1 claret-glass sherry wine, 1 teaspoon extract of vanilla, ½ lb. Swiss cheese, grated fine; 1 lb. macaroni. Have your pan hot, with plenty of beef drippings or butter. Fry the onion and parsley; at the same time put in the mushrooms. Let them cook until thoroughly done, then add the tomatoes, cook 20 minutes; then add the broth, which you thicken with 1 tablespoon flour; then the mace, pepper and salt to your taste. When cooked, add the sherry wine and vanilla. Put the macaroni in boiling water, with 2 tablespoons salt, cook 50 minutes or until soft, then drain it; put a layer of macaroni on dish, then gravy, then grated cheese and so on; cheese on top. Send to table with plate of grated cheese.

My Favorite Receipt, 1895

A MACARONI

Macrows*

Take and make a thin sheet of dough, and cut it in pieces, and cast them on boiling water, and boil it well. Take cheese, and grate it, add butter and cast beneath and above, and serve forth.

The Forme of Cury [c. 1390]

* According to the Reverend Warner, who edited *The Forme of Cury* in 1791, Macrows meant "*Maccherone* evidently, as this receipt corresponds nearly with the dish known at present by that name. This dish in the 16th century gave its name to a certain fantastic species of poetry, the leading features of which were burlesque, ridicule, and a redundancy of exotic, or plebeian words and expressions."

To make a deviled meat after the Roman manner

Take white flour, and make a paste of it somewhat thicker than a pancake, and roll it about a staff, then take out the staff. Then cut the paste in pieces of the length of thy little finger, whereby they will be hollow and round. Then boil them in fat broth or in water depending on the season, but the broth or water must boil when you put them in. And if you boil them in water put a little sweet Butter and salt in it, and when they are boiled enough, dish them with Cheese, Butter, and Spices.

Epulario, Or, The Italian Banquet, 1598

CANELLONI FOR STUFFING

To make a Drunken Loaf

Take a French roll hot out of the oven, rasp it, and pour a pint of red wine upon it, and cover it close up for half an hour. Boil one ounce of mackarony in water, till it is soft, and lay it upon a sieve to drain. Then put the size of a walnut of butter into it, and as much thick cream as it will take, then scrape in six ounces of Parmasan cheese, shake it about in your tossing pan, with the mackarony till it be like a fine custard, then pour it hot upon your loaf; brown it with a salamander, and serve it up. It is a pretty dish for supper.

Elizabeth Raffald, *The Experienced English House-Keeper,* 1778

Maccaroni Pudding

One of the most elegant preparations of Maccaroni is the *Timballe de Maccaroni.* Simmer half a pound of Maccaroni in plenty of water, and a tablespoonful of salt, till it is tender; but take care not to have it too soft; though tender it should be firm, and the form entirely preserved, and no part beginning to melt (this caution will serve for the preparation of all Maccaroni). Strain the water from it. Beat up five yolks and the white of two eggs—take half a pint of the best cream, and the breast of a fowl, and some thin slices of Ham. Mince the breast of the fowl with the Ham—add them with from two to three tablespoonsful of finely grated Parmesan Cheese, and season with Pepper and Salt. Mix all these with the Maccaroni, and put into a pudding mould well buttered, and then let it steam in a stewpan of boiling water for about an hour, and serve quite hot, with rich gravy.

Obs. This, we have been informed, is considered by *a Grand Gourmand,* as the most important recipe which was added to the collection of his Cook during a gastronomic tour through Europe: it is not an uncommon mode of preparing Maccaroni on the continent.

[Dr. William Kitchiner], *The Cook's Oracle,* 1823

Round Pudding Mould

Sparghetti

Sparghetti is a peculiar form of macaroni. Ordinary macaroni is made in the form of long tubes, and when macaroni pudding is served in schools, it is often irreverently nicknamed by the boys gas-pipes. Sparghetti is not a tube, but simply macaroni made in the shape of ordinary wax-tapers, which it resembles very much in appearance. In Italy it is often customary to commence dinner with a dish of sparghetti, and should the dinner consist as well of soup, fish, entree, salad, and sweet, the sparghetti would be

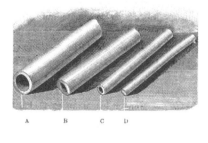

A   B   C   D

STYLES OF MACARONI

served before the soup. Take, say, half a pound of sparghetti, wash it in cold water, and throw it instantly into boiling salted water; boil it till it is tender, about twenty minutes, drain it, put it into a hot vegetable-dish, and mix in two or three tablespoonfuls of grated cheese; toss it about lightly with a couple of forks, till the cheese melts and forms what may be called cobwebs on tossing it about. Add also two tablespoonfuls of tomato conserve (sold by all grocers, in bottles), and serve immediately. This is very cheap, very satisfying, and very nourishing; and it is to be regretted that this popular dish is not more often used by those who are not vegetarians, who would benefit both in pocket and in health were they to lessen their butcher's bill by at any rate commencing dinner, like the Italians, with a dish of sparghetti.

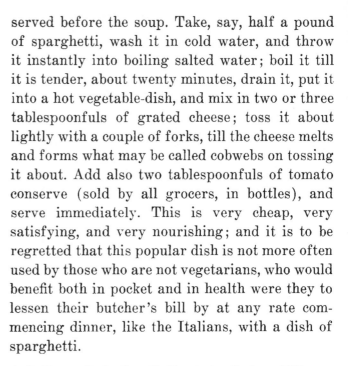

A. G. Payne, B. A., *Cassell's Vegetarian Cookery*, 1891

Count Rumford on Hasty-pudding

In regard to the most advantageous method of using Indian corn as food, I would strongly recommend, particularly when it is employed for feeding the poor, a dish made of it that is in the highest estimation throughout America, and which is really very good and very nourishing. This is called hasty-pudding, and it is made in the following manner: A quantity of water, proportioned to the quantity of hasty-pudding intended to be made, is put over the fire in an open iron pot or kettle, and a proper quantity of salt for seasoning the pudding being previously dissolved in the water, Indian meal is stirred into it by little and little, with a wooden spoon with a long handle, while the water goes on to be heated and made to boil; great care being taken to put in the meal by very small quantities, and by sifting it slowly through the fingers of the left hand, and stirring the water about very briskly at the same time with the wooden spoon with the right hand to mix the meal with the water in such a manner as to prevent lumps being formed. The meal should be added so slowly that, when the water is brought to boil, the mass should not be thicker than water-gruel, and half an hour more at least should be employed to add the additional quantity of meal necessary for bringing the pudding to be of the proper consistence, during which time it should be stirred about continually and kept boiling. The method of determining when the pudding has acquired the proper consistency is this: The wooden spoon used for stirring it being placed in the middle of the kettle, if it falls down more meal may be added, but if the pudding is sufficiently thick and adhesive to support it in a vertical position, it is declared to be proof, and no more meal is added. If the boiling, instead of being continued only half an hour, be prolonged to three-quarters of an hour or an hour, the pudding will be considerable improved by the prolongation.

The hasty-pudding, when done, may be eaten in various ways. It may be put, while hot, by spoonfuls into a bowl of milk, and eaten with the milk with a spoon in lieu of bread; and used in this way it is remarkably palatable. It may likewise be eaten, while hot, with a sauce composed of butter and brown sugar, or butter and molasses, with or without a few drops of vinegar; and however people who have not been accustomed to this American cookery may be prejudiced against it, they will find upon trial that it makes a most excellent dish, and one which never fails to be much liked by those who are accustomed to it.

The universal fondness of Americans for it proves that it must have some merit; for, in a country which produces all the delicacies of the table in the greatest abundance, it is not to be supposed that a whole nation should have a taste so depraved as to give a decided preference to any particular species of food which has not something to recommend it.

The manner in which hasty-pudding is eaten with butter and sugar, or butter and molasses, in America, is as follows: The hasty-pudding being spread out equally upon a plate while hot, an excavation is made in the middle of it with a spoon, into which excavation a piece of butter as large as a nutmeg is put, and upon it a spoonful of brown sugar, or, more commonly, of molasses. The butter, being soon melted by the heat of the pudding, mixes with the sugar or molasses, and forms a sauce, which, being confined to the excavation made for it, occupies the middle of the plate. The pudding is then eaten with a spoon, each spoonful of it being dipped into the sauce before it is carried to the mouth, care being had in taking it up to begin at the outside or near the rim of the plate, and to approach the centre by gradual advances, in order not to demolish too soon the excavation which forms the reservoir for the sauce.—"An Essay on Food," by Count Rumford

Cassell's Dictionary of Cookery [c. 1877]

BIBLIOGRAPHY

ELIZA ACTON. *Modern Cookery, In All Its Branches;
Reduced To A System of Easy Practice, For the Use
of Private Families, In A Series Of Receipts, Which
Have Been Strictly Tested, And Are Given With The
Most Minute Exactness.* Twelfth edition. London:
Longmans, Brown, Green, and Longmans, Paternoster
Row, 1852. 1st edition 1845.

AN AMERICAN LADY. *The American Home Cook Book,
With Several Hundred Excellent Recipes, Selected
and Tried with great care . . . The whole based on
many years of experience.* New York: Dick & Fitzgerald, Publishers, 1854.

ASHMOLE MS. 1429 [c. 1430]. Edited by Thomas
Austin and included in his work: *Two Fifteenth-
Century Cookery-Books.* London: The Early English
Text Society, 1888.

"AUNT BABETTE" (pseud. [Kramer, Mrs. Bertha F.]).
*"Aunt Babette's" Cook Book. Foreign and Domestic.
Receipts for the Household. A valuable collection of
receipts and hints for the housewife, many of which
are not to be found elsewhere.* Cincinnati and Chicago: The Bloch Publishing and Printing Co., 1891
(1st edition, 1889).

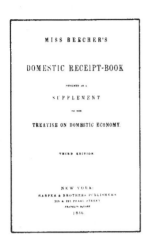

MISS BEECHER. *Miss Beecher's Domestic Receipt-Book, Designed as a Supplement to her Treatise on Domestic Economy.* Third edition. New York: Harper & Brothers, Publishers, 329 & 331 Pearl Street, Franklin Square, 1856. 1st edition, 1846.

CATHERINE E. BEECHER and HARRIET BEECHER STOWE. *The New Housekeeper's Manual: Embracing a new revised edition of The American Woman's Home; or, principles of domestic science. Being a guide to Economical, Healthful, Beautiful, and Christian homes.*

Together with The Handy Cook-Book: a complete condensed guide to wholesome, economical, and delicious cooking. Giving nearly 500 choice and well-tested receipts. By Catherine E. Beecher. New York: J. B. Ford and Company, 1873.

[MRS. ISABELLA BEETON.] *Beeton's Every-Day Cookery and Housekeeping Book . . . Containing new and valuable recipes, including instructions for Foreign and Vegetarian cookery . . .* London: Ward, Lock & Co., Ltd., nd. [c. 1865].

MRS. ISABELLA BEETON. *The Book of Household Management; Comprising Information for the Mistress, Housekeeper, Cook, Kitchen-Maid, Butler, Footman, Coachman, Valet, Upper and Under House-Maids, Lady's-Maid, Maid-of-all-work, Laundry-Maid, Nurse and Nurse-Maid, Monthly, Wet, and Sick Nurses, Etc. Etc. Also, Sanitary, Medical & Legal Memoranda; with a History of the Origin, Properties, and Uses Of All Things Connected With Home Life and Comfort.* London: S. O. Beeton, 1861. Reprinted New York: Farrar, Straus and Giroux, 1969.

[MRS. ANN BLENCOWE.] *The Receipt Book of Mrs. Ann Blencowe,* A.D. 1694. London: The Adelphi. Guy Chapman, 1925.

PIERRE BLOT, Professor of Gastronomy, and Founder of The New York Cooking Academy. *Hand-Book of Practical Cookery, for Ladies and Professional Cooks. Containing the whole science and art of preparing human food.* New York: D. Appleton and Company, 443 & 445 Broadway, 1868.

The Book of the Household; or Family Dictionary of Everything connected with housekeeping, and do-

mestic medicine. With the treatment of children; management of the sick room; the sanitary improvements of the dwelling; the duties of servants; and full information on all other subjects relating to personal and domestic comfort. Compiled by competent persons, under the superintendence of an association of heads of families and men of science. London and New York: The London Printing and Publishing Company, Ltd. [c. 1857].

B. M. *Cookery For The Times. Recipes combining excellence with economy.* London: Bemrose & Sons, 21, Paternoster Row, and Derby, 1870.

Most of the recipes are from the kitchens of old Yorkshire families.

ANNE BOWMAN. *The New Cookery Book: A Complete Manual of English and Foreign Cookery on sound principles of taste and science; comprehending carefully tried receipts for every branch of the art.* London: George Routledge and Sons; The Broadway, Ludgate; New York, 416, Broome Street, 1869.

R. BRADLEY, Professor of Botany in the University of Cambridge, and F.R.S. *The Country Housewife and Lady's Director, in the Management of a House, and the Delights and Profits of a Farm.* Sixth edition. London: Printed for D. Browne, at the Black-Swan without Temple-Bar; and T. Woodman, in Russel-street, Covent-Garden, 1732.

Buckeye Cookery, with hints on practical housekeeping. Revised and enlarged. TWO HUNDREDTH THOUSAND. Minneapolis: Buckeye Publishing Company, 1883. (Copyright, 1880.)

J. S. BUELL. *The Cider Makers' Manual. A practical hand-book, which embodies treatises on the apple; construction of cider mills, cider-presses, seed-washers, and cider-mill machinery in general; cider making, etc., etc.* Buffalo: Haas, Nauert & Klein, 196–202 Main Street, 1879.

Old Doctor Carlin's Recipes being a complete collection of recipes on every known subject, as selected from the MSS. of Old Doctor William Carlin, of Bedford, England, together with additions by the American editor, on various subjects; embracing also a Department for the Household of most thoroughly tried

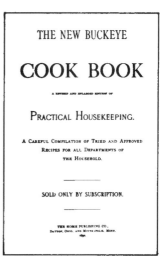

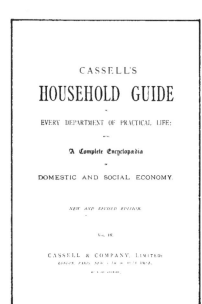

recipes; a treatise on bees; a treatise on poultry, etc.; being the latest and most reliable collection of recipes for the Farm, the Household, the Sick Room, the Kitchen. Toledo, Ohio; The Toledo Blade Co., 1881.

Dr. William Carlin (1780–1870) came from a wealthy family of physicians and he "never took a fee for his services." At the age of seventy, he compiled his recipes.

Cassell's Dictionary of Cookery; Containing about Nine Thousand Recipes. London, Paris & New York: Cassell Petter & Galpin, [c. 1877].

Cassell's Household Guide to Every Department of Practical Life: being A Complete Encyclopaedia of Domestic and Social Economy. New and Revised Edition. Volumes I-IV. London, Paris, New York & Melbourne: Cassell & Company, Limited: c. 1885. First issued, 1869–71.

ROBERT CHAMBERS, ed. *The Book of Days. A Miscellany of Popular Antiquities in connection with The Calendar including Anecdote, Biography, & History, Curiosities of Literature and Oddities of Human Life and Character.* Two volumes. London & Edinburgh: W. & R. Chambers, 1862–4. Reprinted 1883.

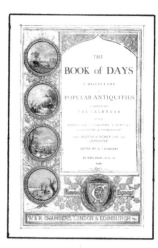

A[LVIN] W[OOD] CHASE, M.D. *Dr. Chase's Recipes—or—Information for Everybody. An invaluable collection of about one thousand practical recipes—for —Merchants, Grocers, Saloon Keepers, Physicians, Druggists, Tanners, Shoemakers, Harnessmakers, Painters, Jewellers, Blacksmiths, Tanners, Gunsmiths, Farriers, Barbers, Bakers, Dyers, Renovators, Farmers, and Families Generally; To which has been added Additional treatment of Pleurisy, Inflamation of the Lungs, and other Inflamatory Diseases; and also, for General Female Debility and Irregularities, all arranged in their Appropriate Departments, Together with an Appendix of 30 pages, Never before published in book form.* Fifth Canadian edition, revised. London, Ontario, Canada: Wm. Bryce, 168 and 215 Dundas Street, 1880.

DAVID CHIDLOW et al. *The American Pure Food Cook Book and Household Economist.* Chicago: Geo. M. Hill Company, 1899.

The Cookery Book of Lady Clark of Tillypronie. Arranged and edited by Catherine Frances Frere. London: Constable & Company, Ltd., 1909.

Lady Clark of Tillypronie died on October 11, 1897, in her 74th year.

THOMAS COGAN. *The Haven of Health, Chiefly made for the comfort of Students, and consequently for all those that have a care of their health, amplified upon fine words of Hippocrates, written Epid. 6. Labour, Meat, Drinke, Sleepe, Venus: By Thomas Cogan, Master of Artes, and Bachelor of Physicke: and now of late corrected and augmented. Hereunto is added a Preservation from the Pestilence: with a short censure of the late sicknesse at Oxford.* London: Printed by Melch. Bradwood for John Norton, 1605.

MRS. MARY COLE,   Cook to the Right Hon. The Earl of Drogheda. *The Lady's Complete Guide; or, Cookery in all its Branches. Containing The most approved Receipts, confirmed by Observation and Practice, in every reputable English Book of Cookery now extant; besides a great Variety of others which have never before been offered to the Public. Also several translated from the Productions of COOKS of Eminence who have published in FRANCE, particularly the DUKE DE NIVERNOIS's, M. COMMO's HISTOIRE DE CUISINE, M. DISANG's MAITRE D'HOTEL, M. VALOIS, and M. DELATOUR, with their respective Names to each Receipt . . . The Third Edition Very Much Improved.* London: Printed for G. Kearsley, No. 46, Fleet Street, 1791.

In her Preface, Mrs. Cole says, ''When I have found the same receipt in three or four different publications, I have *sometimes* quoted all their names, with references to the pages where it is to be found. . . . If all the writers upon Cookery had acknowledged from whence they took their receipts, as I do, they would have acted with more candour by the public. Their vanity to pass for Authors, instead of Compilers, has not added to their reputation.''

The Compleat Cook: Expertly prescribing the most ready wayes, whether Italian, Spanish, or French, For dressing of Flesh, and Fish, ordering of Sauces, or making of Pastry. London: Printed for Nath. Brooke, at the Angel in Cornhill, 1659.

DR. A. W. CHASE

Confederate Receipt Book. A Compilation of Over One Hundred Receipts, Adapted to the Times. Richmond, Va.: West & Johnston, 1863. Reprinted by the University of Georgia Press, Athens, with an introduction by E. Merton Coulter.

ANN COOK, Teacher of the True Art of Cookery. *Professed Cookery . . .* Third edition. London: printed for and sold by the Author, at her Lodgings, in Mr. Moors, Cabinet-maker, Fuller's Rents, Holborn, 1760.

Under the title "Ann Cook and Friend," this book was reprinted by the Oxford University Press, London, 1936, with introductory notes by Regula Burnet.

MAUD C. COOKE. *Three Meals A Day. A Choice Collection of Valuable and Reliable Receipts in All Classes of Cookery and a comprehensive cyclopædia of information for the home including toilet, health and housekeeping departments, cooking receipts, menus, table etiquette, and a Thousand Facts Worth Knowing.* Chicago: The Educational Company, 189–.

————. *Twentieth Century Cook Book containing all the latest approved recipes in every department of cooking; instructions for selecting meats and carving; descriptions of the best kitchen utensils, etc. including hygienic and scientific cooking, rules for dinner giving; use of the chafing dish; menu cards for all special occasions; cooking for invalids; valuable hints for economical housekeeping, etc. the whole forming a standard authority on the culinary art.* Chicago: A. B. Kuhlman & Co., 1897.

This book is also published as *Breakfast, Dinner and Supper or What to Eat and How to Prepare it* (1897).

Cre-Fydd's Family Fare. The Young Housewife's Daily Assistant of all matters relating to Cookery and Housekeeping. New edition, revised. London: Simpkin, Marshall, and Co., 1871. First edition 1864.

NICH. CULPEPPER, Gent. Student in Physic and Astrology. *The English Physician Enlarged. With Three Hundred and Sixty-Nine Medicines, made of English Herbs, that were not in any impression until this. Being an Astrologo-Physical Discourse of the Vulgar Herbs of this Nation, containing a complete Method*

TWENTIETH CENTURY
COOK BOOK

CONTAINING

ALL THE LATEST APPROVED RECIPES IN EVERY DEPARTMENT OF COOKING, INSTRUCTIONS FOR SELECTING MEATS AND CARVING, DESCRIPTIONS OF THE BEST KITCHEN UTENSILS, ETC.

INCLUDING

HYGIENIC AND SCIENTIFIC COOKING

RULES FOR DINNER GIVING, USE OF THE CHAFING DISH; MENU CARDS FOR ALL SPECIAL OCCASIONS, COOKING FOR INVALIDS, VALUABLE HINTS FOR ECONOMICAL HOUSEKEEPING, ETC.

THE WHOLE FORMING

A STANDARD AUTHORITY ON THE CULINARY ART

BY

MAUD C. COOKE

Author of "Social Etiquette" for Etc.

Superbly Embellished with Engravings in Colors and Phototype Illustrations

CHICAGO ILL.
A. B. KUHLMAN & CO.,
CAXTON BUILDING.

of Physic, whereby a Man may preserve his Body in Health, or cure himself, being Sick, for Three-pence charge, with such Things only as grow in England, they being most fit for English Bodies . . . Gainsborough: Printed by and for Henry Mozley, 1653. Reprinted 1813.

Cups and Their Customs. Second edition. London: John Van Voorst, Paternoster Row, 1869.

[E. S. DALLAS.] *Kettner's Book Of The Table.* First published 1877. Republished by Centaur Press, Ltd., 1968, with a Preface by Derek Hudson.

[THOMAS DAWSON.] *The Second part of the good Huswives Jewell. Where is to be found most apt and readiest wayes to distill many wholsome and sweet waters. In which likewise is shewed the best maner in preserving of divers sorts of Fruits, & making of Sirrops. With divers conceits in Cookerie with the Booke of Carving.* At London: Printed by E. Allde for Edward White, dwelling at the little North doore of Paules Church at the signe of the Gun, 1597.

MRS. [HARRIET] DE SALIS. *The Housewife's Referee. A Treatise on Culinary and Household Subjects.* London: Hutchinson & Co., 1898.

MRS. [HARRIET A.] DE SALIS. *National Viands À La Mode.* London: Longmans, Green, and Co., 1895.

SIR KENELME DIGBY KT. *The Closet Of the Eminently Learned Sir Kenelme Digby Kt. Opened: Whereby is Discovered Several ways for making of Metheglin, Sider, Cherry-Wine, &c. Together with Excellent Directions for Cookery: As Also for Preserving, Conserving, Candying, &c. Published by his Son's Consent.* London: Printed by E. C. & A. C. for H. Brome, at the West-End of St. Pauls, 1671.

SUSANNA W. DODDS, A.M., M.D. *Health in the Household; or, Hygienic Cookery.* New York: Fowler & Wells Co., 1888.

DR. [JOHN] DORAN. *Table Traits, With Something On Them.* London: Richard Bentley, New Burlington Street; Oliver & Boyd, Edinburgh; Hodges & Smith, Dublin; And to be had of all Booksellers, and at the Railway Stations, 1854.

ALICE MORSE EARLE. *Customs and Fashions in Old*

THE
ENGLISH PHYSICIAN
ENLARGED
WITH THREE HUNDRED AND SIXTY-NINE
MEDICINES,
MADE OF
ENGLISH HERBS,
THAT WERE NOT IN ANY IMPRESSION UNTIL THIS.

BEING

An Astrologo-Physical Discourse of the Vulgar Herbs of this Nation, containing a complete Method of Physic, whereby a Man may preserve his Body in Health, or cure himself, being Sick, for Three-pence charge, with such Things only as grow in England, they being most fit for English Bodies.

Herein is also shewed,

1. The Way of making Plaisters, Ointments, Oils, Poultices, Syrups, Decoctions, Juleps, or Waters of all Sorts of Physical Herbs, that you may have them ready for your use at all times of the Year. 2. What Planet governeth every Herb or Tree (used in Physic) that groweth in England. 3. The Time of gathering all Herbs, both Vulgarly and Astrologically. 4. The Way of drying and keeping the Herbs all the Year. 5. The Way of keeping their Juice ready for Use at all Times. 6. The Way of making and keeping all kinds of useful Compounds made of Herbs. 7. The Way of mixing Medicines according to the Cause and Mixture of the Disease, and Part of the Body afflicted.

BY NICH. CULPEPPER, GENT.
STUDENT IN PHYSIC AND ASTROLOGY.

GAINSBOROUGH:
PRINTED BY AND FOR HENRY MOZLEY.

1813.

New England. New York: Charles Scribner's Sons, 1893.

LINA ECKENSTEIN. *Comparative Studies in Nursery Rhymes*. London: Duckworth & Co., 1906. Reprinted 1911.

Epulario, Or, The Italian Banquet: Wherein is shewed the maner how to dresse and prepare all kind of Flesh, Foules or Fishes. As also how to make Sauces, Tartes, Pies, &c. After the maner of all Countries. With an addition of many other profitable and necessary things. Translated out of Italian into English. London: Printed by A. J. for William Barley, and are to bee sold at his shop in Gratious street, neere Leaden-hall, 1598.

J. E. [JOHN EVELYN] S.R.S. Author of the Kalendarium. *Acetaria. A Discourse of Sallets*. London: Printed for B. Tooke at the Middle-Temple Gate in Fleetstreet, 1699.

EMMA P. EWING, Superintendent of the Chautauqua School of Cookery, formerly Professor of Domestic Economy in the Iowa State Agricultural College, and of Household Science in Purdue University, Indiana. *The Art of Cookery. A Manual for Homes and Schools.* Meadville, Pa.: Flood and Vincent, The Chautauqua-Century Press, 1896.

The Family Friend. London: Houlston and Stoneman, 65, Paternoster Row, 1850 (vol. 2), 1851 (vol. 3), 1851 (vol. 4).

JOHN FARLEY, Formerly Principal Cook at The London Tavern. *The London Art of Cookery, and Domestic Housekeepers' Complete Assistant, Uniting the Principles of Elegance, Taste, and Economy; and adapted to the use of servants, and families of every description.* Twelfth edition. London: Printed for Scatcherd and Letterman, Ave-Maria Lane, 1811.

FANNIE MERRITT FARMER. *The Boston Cooking-School Cook Book.* Boston: Little, Brown, and Company, 1896.

ALESSANDRO FILIPPINI of Delmonico's. *The Table: How to buy food, how to cook it, and how to serve it.* Revised edition, with supplements. New York: Charles L. Webster & Company; Baltimore: Hopper, McGaw & Co., 1891, 1895. First edition 1889.

ALLESANDRO FILIPPINI

266

[MRS. ABBY FISHER, Late of Mobile, Ala.] *What Mrs. Fisher Knows About Old Southern Cooking, Soups, Pickles, Preserves, Etc.* Diploma Awarded At Sacramento State Fair, 1879. San Francisco: Women's Co-operative Printing Office, 1881.

The Forme of Cury (The Art of Cookery). Compiled by the master cooks and advisors to King Richard the Second of England, after the conquest, in order to teach "a man for to make commune pottages and commune meetis for howshold, as they shold be made, craftly and holsomly." [c. 1390.]

This manuscript was included in a book by The Reverend Richard Warner, of Sway, near Lymington, Hants., which was entitled: "Antiquitates Culinariae; or Curious Tracts relating to the Culinary affairs of the Old English." London: Printed for R. Blamire, Strand, 1791.

CHARLES ELMÉ FRANCATELLI, pupil of the celebrated Careme, seven years chef de cuisine to the Reform Club, and late maître-d'hôtel and chief cook to Her Majesty the Queen. *The Cook's Guide, and Housekeeper's & Butler's Assistant: A practical treatise on English and foreign cookery in all its branches; containing plain instructions for pickling and preserving vegetables, fruits, game, &c.; The Curing of Hams' and Bacon; The Art of Confectionary and Ice-making, and the arrangement of desserts. With valuable directions for the preparation of proper diet for invalids; also for a variety of wine-cups and epicurean salads; American drinks, and summer beverages.* London: Richard Bentley & Son, New Burlington Street, Publishers in Ordinary to Her Majesty the Queen. 1884. First edition, 1861.

S. ANNIE FROST. *Our New Cook Book and Household Receipts. Carefully Selected and indexed.* Philadelphia: American Publishing Company, 1883.

THEODORE FRANCIS GARRETT, ed. *The Encyclopædia of Practical Cookery: A Complete Dictionary of all pertaining to the Art of Cookery and Table Service.* Three volumes. London: L. Upcott Gill, 1892-4.

[MRS. FANNY LEMIRA GILLETTE.] *Mrs. Gillette's Cook Book. Fifty Years of Practical Housekeeping.* New York, Akron, Chicago: The Werner Company, 1899.

CHARLES ELMÉ FRANCATELLI

Mrs. F. L. Gillette

Very sincerely yours,
Marion Harland

MRS. F. L. GILLETTE and HUGO ZIEMANN, Steward of the White House. *The White-House Cook-Book. Cooking, Toilet and Household Recipes, Menus, Dinner-Giving, Table Etiquette, Care of the Sick, Health Suggestions, Facts Worth Knowing, Etc., Etc. The Whole Comprising A Comprehensive Cyclopedia of Information for the Home.* Chicago: The Werner Company, 1894. First edition 1887.

BY A LADY [HANNAH GLASSE]. *The Art of Cookery, Made Plain and Easy; Which far exceeds any Thing of the Kind ever yet published . . .* Second edition. London: Printed for the Author, and sold at Mrs. Wharton's Toy-Shop, the Bluecoat-Boy, near the Royal-Exchange; at Mrs. Ashburn's China-Shop, the Corner of Fleet-Ditch; at Mrs. Condall's Toy-Shop, the King's Head and Parrot, in Holborn; at Mr. Underwood's Toy-Shop, near St. James's-Gate; and at most Market-Towns in England, 1747.

Godey's Lady's Book and Magazine. Edited by Mrs. Sarah J. Hale, and Louis A. Godey. Vol. LXXXIX. From July to December, 1874. Philadelphia: Published by Louis A. Godey. N. E. Cor. Sixth and Chestnut Sts.

MAY PERRIN GOFF, ed. *The Household (of the Detroit Free Press). A Cyclopædia of practical hints for modern homes. Containing new ideas upon aquariums, ferneries, birds, cabinets, children's amusements, fancy work, plants and flowers, home decoration, house furnishing, housekeeping, health, knitting and crochet, painting, music, useful and ornamental needlework, laundry, toilet, and hundreds of minor home subjects. With a full and complete treatise on cookery.* Third edition. Detroit: The Detroit Free Press Co., 1881.

SYLVESTER GRAHAM. *A Treatise On Bread, and Bread-Making.* Boston: Light & Stearns, 1837. Reprinted by Lee Foundation for Nutritional Research, Milwaukee, n.d.

The Grocer's Companion and Merchant's Hand-Book. Containing a comprehensive account of the growth, manufacture and qualities of every article sold by grocers. Also, tables of weights and measures, and information of a general nature of value to grocers and country merchants. Boston: New England Grocer Office, 10 Broad Street. Benjamin Johnson, Publisher, 1883.

The Guide To Service. The Cook. London: Charles Knight and Co., Ludgate Street, 1842.

FREDERICK W. HACKWOOD. *Good Cheer. The Romance of Food and Feasting.* London: Adelphi Terrace, T. Fisher Unwin, 1911.

SARAH JOSEPHA HALE. *The Ladies' New Book of Cookery . . .* Third edition. New York: H. Long & Brother, 1852.

Mrs. Hale was editor of *Godey's Lady's Book* and the author of ''Mary Had a Little Lamb.''

FLORENCE HOWE HALL. *Social Customs.* Boston: Estes and Lauriat, 1887.

MARION HARLAND, pseudonym of Mrs. Terhune (Mary Virginia Hawes). *Common Sense In The Household: A Manual of Practical Housewifery.* New York: Scribner, Armstrong & Co., 1877.

HARLEIAN MS. 279 (c. 1430). Edited by Thomas Austin and included in his work: *Two Fifteenth-Century Cookery-Books.* London: The Early English Text Society, 1888.

HARLEIAN MS. 4016 (c. 1450). Edited by Thomas Austin and included in his work: *Two Fifteenth-Century Cookery-Books.* London: The Early English Text Society, 1888.

W. CAREW HAZLITT. *Faiths and Folklore. A Dictionary of National Beliefs, Superstitions and Popular Customs, Past and Current, with their Classical and Foreign Analogues, Described and Illustrated. Forming a New Edition of ''The Popular Antiquities of Great Britain'' By Brand and Ellis, largely extended, corrected, brought down to the present time, and now first alphabetically arranged.* Two volumes. London: Reeves & Turner; New York: Charles Scribner's Sons, 1905. Reprinted by Benjamin Blom, Inc., 1965.

MRS. MARY F. HENDERSON. *Practical Cooking and Dinner Giving. A Treatise Containing Practical Instructions in Cooking; In the Combination and Serving of Dishes; and in the Fashionable Modes of Entertain-*

W. A. JARRIN

ing at Breakfast, Lunch, and Dinner. New York: Harper & Brothers, Publishers, 1895. First edition 1876.

MRS. MARY HOLLAND, Professed Cook. *The Complete Economical Cook, and Frugal Housewife; An entirely new system of Domestic Cookery . . .* Fourteenth edition. London: Printed for T. Tegg & Son, Cheapside, 1837.

WILLIAM HONE. *The Every-Day Book; or, Everlasting Calendar of Popular Amusements, Sports, Pastimes, Ceremonies, Manners, Customs, and Events, Incident to each of the Three Hundred and Sixty-Five Days, in Past and Present Times; Forming a Complete History of the Year, Months, & Seasons, and a Perpetual Key To The Almanack; Including Accounts of the Weather, Rules for Health and Conduct, Remarkable and Important Anecdotes, Fact, and Notices, in Chronology, Antiquities, Topography, Biography, Natural History, Art, Science, and General Literature; Derived from the Most Authentic Sources, and Valuable Original Communications, With Poetical Elucidations, For Daily Use and Diversion.* Two volumes. London: Published for William Hone, by Hunt and Clarke, Covent-Garden, 1826 (vol. I), 1827 (vol. II). Republished Ward, Lock & Co., 1888 (vol. I), 1889 (vol. II).

Hood's Practical Cook's Book for the Average Household. Lowell, Mass.: C. I. Hood & Co., 1897.

MARGARET HUNTINGTON HOOKER. *Yᵉ Gentlewoman's Housewifery containing Scarce, Curious, and Valuable Receipts for making ready all sorts of Viands. A repository of useful knowledge adapted to meet the wants of good wives and tender mothers. Also sundry salutory remedies of sovereign and approved efficacy and choice secrets on the improvement of female beauty. Compiled from old and reliable sources.* New York: Dodd, Mead and Company, 1896.

The Housekeeper Cook Book. Minneapolis: The Housekeeper Publishing Company, 1894.

The Housewife. A Practical Magazine Concerning Everything In And About The Home. Volume X. London: Offices of ''The Christian Million,'' 20 and 22, St. Bride Street, E.C., 1895.

MRS. HUMPHRY ("Madge" of "Truth"). *Cookery Up-To-Date.* London: Chapman & Hall, Ltd., 1896.

W. A. JARRIN, Confectioner. *The Italian Confectioner; Or, Complete Economy of Desserts, According to the Most Modern and Approved Practice.* Routledge, Warne, and Routledge, London, Farringdon Street, and New York, 56, Walker Street, 1861. First edition 1820.

The Jewish Manual; or Practical Information in Jewish and Modern Cookery. Edited By A Lady. London: T. & W. Boone, 29 New Bond Street, 1846.

MARY JEWRY, compiler and editor. *Warne's Model Cookery with Complete Instructions in Household Management.* London: Frederick Warne & Co., 1893.

JOHN JOSSELYN, Gent. *New-Englands Rarities Discovered: In Birds, Beasts, Fishes, Serpents, and Plants of that Country. Together with The Physical and Chyrurgical Remedies wherewith the Natives constantly use to Cure their Distempers, Wounds, and Sores. Also A perfect Description of an Indian Squa, in all her Bravery; with a Poem not improperly conferr'd upon her. Lastly A Chronological Table of the most remarkable Passages in that Country amongst the English.* London: Printed for G. Widdowes at the Green Dragon in St. Pauls Church-yard, 1672. Facsimile edition: W. Junk, Berlin, 1926.

The Kansas Home Cook-Book. Consisting of recipes contributed by ladies of Leavenworth and other cities and towns. Published by the Board of Managers for the benefit of the Home for the Friendless. Leavenworth, Kans.: Crew & Bro., Booksellers and Publishers, 1879.

BY SEVERAL HANDS [MARY KETTILBY]. *A Collection Of above Three Hundred Receipts in Cookery, Physick, and Surgery; For the Use of all Good Wives, Tender Mothers, and Careful Nurses.* Fifth edition. London: Printed for the Executrix of Mary Kettilby; and sold by W. Parker, at the King's Head in St. Paul's Church-yard, 1734.

E. KIDDER [Edw. Kidder, Pastry-maker]. *E. Kidder's Receipts of Pastry and Cookery, For the Use of his Scholars. Who teaches at his School in Queen Street near St. Thomas Apostles. On Mondays, Tuesdays &*

Y^e Gentlewoman's Housewifery

CONTAINING

Scarce, Curious, and Valuable Receipts For making ready all sorts of Viands A REPOSITORY of USEFUL KNOWLEDGE Adapted to meet the wants of GOOD WIVES AND TENDER MOTHERS

ALSO

Sundry Salutory Remedies of Sovereign and Approved Efficacy And Choice Secrets on the Improvement of Female Beauty

COMPILED FROM OLD AND RELIABLE SOURCES

By MARGARET HUNTINGTON HOOKER

At the Publishing House of Dodd, Mead and Company, New York MDCCCXCVI

WARNE'S MODEL COOKERY

WITH

Complete Instructions in Household Management,

AND RECEIPTS FOR

COMPILED AND EDITED BY MARY JEWRY.

With Original Illustrations, printed in colours.

LONDON FREDERICK WARNE & CO AND NEW YORK 1893

[All rights reserved]

E. KIDDER

DR. WILLIAM KITCHINER

Wednesdays, In the Afternoon. Also On Thursdays, Fridays & Saturdays, In the Afternoon, at his School next to Furnivals Inn in Holborn. Ladies may be taught at their own Houses [c. 1730].

[DR. WILLIAM KITCHINER.] *The Cook's Oracle; Containing Receipts For Plain Cookery . . . The Quantity of each Article is Accurately stated by Weight and Measure; The Whole Being The Result of Actual Experiments Instituted in The Kitchen of a Physician.* Fifth edition. London: Printed for A. Constable & Co. Edinburgh; and Hurst, Robinson, & Co. Cheapside, 1823.

SEBASTIAN KNEIPP, Secret Chamberlain of the Pope, Parish Priest of Wörishofen (Bavaria). *Hints and Advices for The Healthy and the Sick on A Simple and Rational Mode of Life and A Natural Method of Cure.* Translated from the 23d German edition. The Only Authorized and Original Edition. Popular Edition For America. Kempten (Bavaria): Jos. Koesel, Publisher, 1897.

MAJOR L. . . . . *The Pytchley book of Refined Cookery and Bills of Fare.* London: Chapman and Hall, 1889.

LADIES' AID SOCIETY, Fort street M. E. [Methodist Episcopal] Church. *Los Angeles Cookery.* Los Angeles: Mirror Printing and Binding House, 1881.

LADIES OF CALIFORNIA. *California Recipe Book.* San Francisco: Cubery & Company, Book and Job Printers, No. 536 Market Street, opp. Second, 1873.

Compiled by Ladies of Toronto and Chief Cities and Towns in Canada. *The Home Cook Book.* Toronto: Rose Publishing Company, 1889. First edition 1877.

CHARLES LAMB. *Essays of Elia.* 1823. In the collection "Essays of Elia and Eliana" by Charles Lamb, with a memoir by Barry Cornwall, vol. I., London, 1892.

BY A BOSTON HOUSEKEEPER [MRS. N. K. M. LEE]. *The Cook's Own Book, and Housekeeper's Register: Comprehending all Valuable Receipts for cooking Meat, Fish, and Fowl; and composing every kind of Soup, Gravy, Pastry, Preserves, Essences, &c. that have been published or invented during the last twenty years . . . To which is added, Miss Leslie's*

Seventy-Five Receipts for Pastry, Cakes, and Sweet-meats. Alphabetically Arranged, and Blank Pages Inserted for Family Memorandums. Boston: Munroe & Frances; New York: Charles S. Francis; Philadelphia: Carey, Lea, and Blanchard, and Grigg and Elliot, 1835.

MISS [ELIZA] LESLIE. *Miss Leslie's New Cookery Book.* Philadelphia: T. B. Peterson and Brothers, 1857.

Mrs. D. A. LINCOLN of the Boston Cooking School. *Mrs. Lincoln's Boston Cook Book. What to do and what not to do in cooking.* Boston: Roberts Brothers, 1891. First edition 1883.

WILLIAM LITHGOW. *The Totall Discourse, Of the rare Adventures, and painefull Peregrinations of long nineteene yeares Travailes from Scotland, to the most famous Kingdomes in Europe, Asia, and Africa . . . Wherein is contayned an exact Relation of the Lawes, Religions, Policies and Governments of all their Princes, Potentates and People. Together with the grievous Tortures he suffered by the Inquisition of Malaga in Spaine: His miraculous Discovery and Delivery. And of his last and late returns from the Northern Isles, and other places adjacent.* Imprinted at London by J. Okes, 1640.

G. M. [GERVASE MARKHAM]. *Countrey Contentments, or The English Huswife. Containing the inward and outward Vertues which ought to be in a compleate Woman. As her skill in Physicke, Surgerie, Extraction of Oyles, Banqueting-stuffe, Ordering of great Feasts, Preserving of all sorts of Wines, Conceited Secrets, Distillations, Perfumes, ordering of Wooll, Hempe, Flax, making Cloth, Dying, the knowledge of Dayries, office of Malting, Oats, their excellent uses in a Family, Brewing, Baking, and all other things belonging to an Houshold. A Worke generally approved, and now much augmented, purged and made most profitable and necessarie for all men, and Dedicated to the Honour of the Noble House of Exceter, and the generall good of this Kingdome.* Printed at London by J. B. for R. Jackson, and are to be sold at his shop neere Fleet-streete Conduit, 1623.

———. *The English House-wife. Containing The in-*

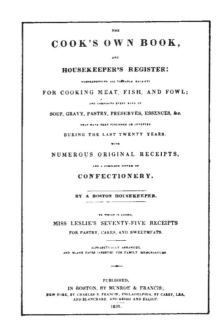

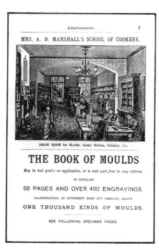

ward and outward Vertues which ought to be in a
compleate Woman . . . A Worke generally approved,
and now the fourth time much augmented, purged
and made most profitable and necessary for all men,
and the generall good of this Kingdome. London:
Printed by Nicholas Okes for John Harison, and are
to be sold at his shop at the signe of the golden Uni-
corne in Pater-noster-row, 1631.

[AGNES B. MARSHALL.] *Mrs. A. B. Marshall's Cookery Book*. London: Simpkin, Marshall, Hamilton,
Kent, & Co., Ltd.; Marshall's School of Cookery, n.d.
[c. 1888].

ROBERT MAY. *The Accomplisht Cook, or the Art and
Mystery of Cookery. Wherein the whole ART is
revealed in a more easie and perfect Method, than
hath been publist in any language. Expert and
ready Ways for the Dressing of all Sorts of Flesh,
Fowl, and Fish, with variety of Sauces proper for
each of them; and how to raise all manner of Pastes;
the best Directions for all sorts of Kickshaws, also
the Terms of Carving and Sewing. An exact account
of all Dishes for all Seasons of the Year, with other
A-la-mode Curiosities. The Fourth Edition . . . Approved by the fifty five Years Experience and Industry of Robert May, in his Attendance on several
Persons of great Honour.* London: Printed for
Obadiah Blagrave at the Bear in St. Pauls Church-
Yard, near the Little North-Door, 1678.

MRS. C. F. MORITZ and MISS ADÈLE KAHN. *The Twentieth Century Cook Book*. New York: G. W. Dilling-
ham Co., 1898.

JOHN MURRELL, Professor thereof. *A Delightfull daily
exercise for Ladies and Gentlewomen Whereby is set
foorth the secrete misteries of the purest preservings
in Glasses and other Confrictionaries, as making of
Breads, Pastes, Preserves, Suckets, Marmalates, Tart-
stuffes, rough Candies, with many other things never
before in Print.* London, 1621.

My Favorite Receipt. Seventh edition. New York: Royal
Baking Powder Co., 1895. First edition 1880.

*Natura Exenterata: or Nature Unbowelled By the most
Exquisite Anatomizers of Her. Wherein are con-*

tained, Her choicest Secrets digested into Receipts, fitted for the Cure of all sorts of Infirmities, whether Internal or External, Acute or Chronical, that are Incident to the Body of Man. Collected and preserved by several Persons of Quality and great Experience in the Art of Medicine, whose names are prefixed to the Book. London: Printed for, and are to be sold by H. Twiford at his shop in Vine Court Middle Temple, G. Bedell at the Middel Temple Gate Fleet-street, and N. Ekins at the Gun neer the West-end of S. Pauls Church, 1655.

A Noble Boke Off Cookry ffor a Prynce Houssolde or Eny Other Estately Houssolde [c. 1467]. Edited by Mrs. Alexander Napier. London: Elliot Stock, 1882.

This book of fifteenth-century cookery was "Reprinted Verbatim From A Rare MS. In The Holkham Collection."

Madame Le Normand, *Fortune-Teller To The Emperor Napoleon. The Unerring Fortune-Teller: Containing the Celebrated Oracle of Human Destiny, or Book of Fate: Being An Accurate Interpreter of the Mystical Signs and Heavenly Bodies; Also embracing the French, Italian, and English methods of telling fortunes with cards, and a new and entertaining process of fortune-telling with dice. Also containing seventy-nine good and bad omens, with their interpretations, one hundred and eighty-seven weather omens, and Napoleon's Oraculum.* New York: Dick and Fitzgerald, Publishers, 1866.

Iona and Peter Opie. *The Oxford Dictionary of Nursery Rhymes.* Oxford: The Clarendon Press, 1966.

Oscar Tschirky, Maître D'Hôtel, the Waldorf. *The Cook Book by "Oscar" of the Waldorf.* Chicago: The Werner Company, 1896.

Mrs. Frances E. Owens. *Mrs. Owens' Cook Book and useful hints for the Household.* Chicago: Household Helps Publication Society, 1882. First edition 1881.

Maria Parloa, Founder of the original Cooking-School in Boston; Principal of the School of Cookery in New York. *Miss Parloa's Kitchen Companion. A guide for all who would be good housekeepers.* Boston: Dana Estes and Company, 1887.

A. G. PAYNE, B.A. *Cassell's Vegetarian Cookery. A Manual of Cheap and Wholesome Diet.* London, Paris & Melbourne: Cassell & Company, Ltd., 1891.

[THOMAS PAYNELL]. *The Civilitie of Childehode, with the discipline and institucion of Children, distributed in small and compendious Chapiters, and translated oute of French into Englysh, by Thomas Paynell.* Anno. Do. 1560.

[HUGH PLATT]. *Delightes for Ladies, to adorne their Persons, Tables, closets and distillatories. With Beauties, banquets, perfumes and waters. Reade, practise, and censure.* London: Printed by Peter Short, 1603.

HUGH PLATTE, of Lincolnes Inne, Gentleman. *The Jewell House of Art and Nature. Conteining divers rare and profitable Inventions, together with sundry new experimentes in the Art of Husbandry, Distillation, and Moulding. Faithfully and familiarly set downe, according to the Authors owne experience, by Hugh Platte, of Lincolnes Inne Gentleman.* London: Printed by Peter Short, dwelling on Breadstreat hill, at the signe of the Star, and are to be solde in Paules Churchyard, 1594.

Written by H. P. [HUGH PLATT] Esq. uppon thoccasion of this present Dearth. *Sundrie new and Artificiall remedies against Famine.* Printed by P. S. dwelling on Breadstreet hill, at the signe of the Starre, 1596.

A Proper newe Booke of Cokerye, declaryne what maner of meates be beste in season, for al times in the yere, and how they ought to be dressed, and served at the table, bothe for fleshe dayes, and fyshe dayes. With a newe addition, verye necessary for all them that delyghteth in Cokerye [c. 1548–72].

Edited by Catherine Frances Frere, with Notes, Introduction and Glossary; together with Some Account of Domestic Life, Cookery and Feasts in Tudor Days, and of the first owners of the Book, Matthew Parker, Archbishop of Canterbury, and Margaret Parker his Wife. Reprinted at Cambridge: W. Heffer & Sons Ltd., 1913.

MRS. E[LIZABETH] PUTNAM. *Mrs. Putnam's Receipt Book, and Young Housekeeper's Assistant.* New

York: Sheldon and Company, 498 & 500 Broadway, 1858, 1867 (both parts collected in one book, 1870).

ELIZABETH RAFFALD. *The Experienced English House-Keeper, For the Use and Ease of Ladies, House-Keepers, Cooks, &c. Wrote purely from Practice, and dedicated to the Hon. Lady Elizabeth Warburton, Whom the Author lately served as House-Keeper: Consisting of near Eight Hundred Original Receipts most of which never appeared in Print* . . . Sixth edition. Dublin: Printed by J. Williams, No. 21, Skinner-Row, 1778.

CHARLES RANHOFFER, Chef of Delmonicos'. *The Epicurean. A Complete Treatise of analytical and practical studies on the culinary art including table and Wine Service, How to Prepare and Cook Dishes, an Index for Marketing, a Great Variety of Bills of Fare for Breakfasts, Luncheons, Dinners, Suppers, Ambigus, Buffets, etc., and a Selection of Interesting Bills of Fare of Delmonico's, from 1862 to 1894, making a Franco-American Culinary Encyclopedia.* New York: Charles Ranhoffer, Publisher, 1894. Reprinted New York: Dover Publications, Inc., 1971.

Recipes For The Million. A Handy Book for the Household. London: T. Fisher Unwin, Paternoster Square [c. 1897].

[*The Regiment of Health, or A Direction for the Life of Man.*] *Regimen Sanitatis Salerni. The Schoole of Salernes most learned and juditious Directorie, or Methodicall Instructions, for the guide and governing the health of Man. Dedicated, and sent by them, to the High and Mighty King of England, and published (by consent of Learned and skilfull Physitions) for the good and benefite of all in generall. Perused, and corrected from many great and grosse imperfections, committed in former Impressions: With the Comment, and all the Latine verses reduced into English, and ordered in their apt and due places.* London: Imprinted by Barnard Alsop, and are to be sold by John Burnes, at his shop in Hosier Lane, 1617.

WILLIAM RHIND, Member of The Royal College of Surgeons; of The Royal Medical Society, Edin. *A History Of The Vegetable Kingdom: Embracing the*

frontispiece
RANHOFER'S THE EPICUREAN

Physiology, Classification, and Culture of Plants, with their various uses to man and the lower animals; and their application in the Arts, Manufactures, and Domestic Economy. Glasgow: Blackie & Son, Queen Street [c. 1842].

MARY RONALD. *The Century Cook Book. This book contains directions for cooking in its various branches, from the simplest forms to high-class dishes and ornamental pieces; a group of New England dishes furnished by Susan Coolidge; and a few receipts of distinctively Southern dishes. It gives also the etiquette of dinner entertainments—how to serve dinners—table decorations, and many items relative to household affairs.* New York: The Century Co., 1895.

MRS. S. T. RORER, Principal of the Philadelphia Cooking School. *How to cook vegetables.* Philadelphia: W. Atlee Burpee & Co., Seed Growers, 1892.

SARAH TYSON RORER. *Mrs. Rorer's New Cook Book. A Manual of Housekeeping.* Philadelphia: Arnold and Company, 1898. Reprinted by The Ladies' Home Journal Cook Book Club, 1970.

GILES ROSE, one of the Master Cooks in His Majesties Kitchen. *A perfect School of Instructions For The Officers of the Mouth: Shewing The Whole Art of A Master of the Houshold, A Master Carver, A Master Butler, A Master Confectioner, A Master Cook, A Master Pastryman. Being a Work of singular Use for Ladies and Gentlewomen, and all Persons whatsoever that are desirous to be acquainted with the most Excellent Arts of Carving, Cookery, Pastry, Preserving, and Laying a Cloth for Grand Entertainments. The like never before extant in any language. Adorned with Pictures curiously Ingraven, displaying the whole Arts.* London: Printed for R. Bentley and M. Magnes, in Russel-street in Covent-Garden, 1682.

MRS. RUNDELL. *Domestic Cookery, For The Use of Private Families.* London: Milner and Sowerby, Paternoster Row, [c. 1850].

[MARIA ELIZA RUNDELL.] *The Experienced American Housekeeper, or Domestic Cookery: Formed on Principles of Economy for the use of Private Families.*

New-York: Published by N. C. Nafis, 278 Pearl & 98 Catharine St. [1836].

By A Lady [Maria Eliza Rundell]. *A New System of Domestic Cookery, Formed upon Principles of Economy, and adapted to the use of Private Families.* Boston: William Andrews, No. 1, Cornhill, 1807.

Lady Harriet St. Clair (Late Countess Münster). *Dainty Dishes.* London: John Hogg, 1884. First published 1866.

J. H. [Dr. William Salmon]. *The Family-Dictionary; or, Houshold Companion: Wherein are Alphabetically laid down Exact Rules and Choice Physical Receipts for The Preservation of Health, Prevention of Sickness, and Curing the several Diseases, Distempers, and Grievances, incident to Men, Women, and Children* . . . London: Printed for H. Rhodes, at the Star, the Corner of Bride-lane, in Fleetstreet, 1695.

Mrs. D. S. Sears. *The Practical Cook. A Collection of Tested Recipes. Compiled for the Benefit of the Presbyterian Church of Omaha.* Omaha, Neb.: Omaha Republican Steam Print, 1878.

Amelia Simmons, An American Orphan. *American Cookery, Or The Art of Dressing Viands, Fish, Poultry, and Vegetables, and the best modes of making Pastes, Puffs, Pies, Tarts, Puddings, Custards and Preserves, and all kinds of Cakes, from the Imperial Plumb to plain Cake. Adapted to this country, and all grades of life.* Published according to Act of Congress. Hartford: Printed for the Author, by Hudson & Goodwin, 1796. Reprinted with an Essay by Mary Tolford Wilson, by New York Oxford University Press, 1958.

André L. Simon. *The Star Chamber Dinner Accounts being some hitherto unpublished Accounts of Dinners provided for the Lords of the Privy Council in the Star Chamber, Westminster, during the reigns of Queen Elizabeth I and King James I of England with a Foreword and Commentary.* London: George Rainbird for The Wine and Food Society, 1959.

Smiley's Cook Book and Universal Household Guide. A Comprehensive Collection of Recipes and Useful In-

frontispiece
SOYER'S MODERN HOUSEWIFE

ALEXIS SOYER

formation Pertaining to Every Department of House-keeping. Chicago: Smiley Publishing Company, 1896.

E. SMITH. *The Compleat Housewife: Or, Accomplish'd Gentlewoman's Companion: Being a Collection of upwards of Six Hundred of the most approved Receipts in Cookery, Pastry, Confectionary, Preserving, Pickles, Cakes, Creams, Jellies, Made Wines, Cordials. With Copper Plates curiously engraven for the regular Disposition of Placing the various Dishes and Courses. And Also Bills of Fare for every Month in the Year. To which is added, A Collection of above Three Hundred Family Receipts of Medicines; viz. Drinks, Syrups, Salves, Ointments, and various other Things of sovereign and approved Efficacy in most Distempers, Pains, Aches, Wounds, Sores, &c. never before made publick; fit either for private Families, or such publick-spirited Gentlewomen as would be beneficent to their poor Neighbours.* Ninth edition. London: Printed for J. and J. Pemberton, at the Golden Buck, against St. Dunstan's Church in Fleet-street, 1739.

[JOHN SMITH OF MALTON.] *The Principles and Practice of Vegetarian Cookery. Founded on Chemical Analysis, and Embracing the Most Approved Methods of the Art.* London: Simpkin, Marshall, and Co., 1860.

MARY STUART SMITH. *Virginia Cookery-Book.* New York: Harper & Brothers, 1885.

ALEXIS SOYER (Reform Club). *The Modern Housewife or Ménagère.* London: Simpkin, Marshall, & Co., 1851.

EDWARD SPENCER ["NATHANIEL GUBBINS"]. *The Flowing Bowl. A Treatise on Drinks of all kinds and of all periods, interspersed with sundry anecdotes and reminiscences.* London: Grant Richards, 1898. Reprinted 1903.

Swedish-English Cookbook. Svensk-Amerikansk Kokbok. Fullständigaste. Chicago: The Engberg-Holmberg Publishing Co., 1897.

KATHERINE ELWES THOMAS. *The Real Personages of Mother Goose.* New York: Lothrop, Lee & Shepard Co., 1930.

J. L. W. THUDICHUM, M.D., F.R.C.P. Lond. *Cookery,*

Its Art and Practice. The History, Science, and Practical Import of the Art of Cookery with A Dictionary of Culinary Terms. London: Frederick Warne & Co., [c. 1895].

TABITHA TICKLETOOTH [CHARLES SELBY]. *The Dinner Question: or, How to dine well and economically. Combining The Rudiments of Cookery with Useful Hints on Dinner Giving and Serving, and other Household words of Advice: Garnished with Anecdotes of Eminent Cooks and Epicures, As Well As Wise Saws In Gastronomy From The Great Masters.* London, Farmingdon Street, and New York, 56, Walker Street: Routledge, Warne and Routledge, 1860.

T. P. J. P. R. C. N. B. and Several Other Approved Cooks of *London* and *Westminster. The Compleat Cook: Or The Whole Art of Cookery. Describing The Best and Newest Ways of Ordering and Dressing all sorts of Flesh, Fish, and Fowl, whether boiled, baked, stewed, roasted, broiled, frigacied, fryed, souc'd, marrinated, or pickled; with their proper Sauces and Garnishes. Together with all manner of the most Approved Soops and Potages used, either in England or France.* London: Printed, and Sold by G. Conyers at the Golden Ring in Little-Britain, over against Bartholomew's-Close-Gate, 1694.

R[USSEL] T[HACHER] TRALL, M.D. *The New Hydropathic Cook-Book; with Recipes for Cooking on Hygienic Principles: Containing also a philosophical exposition of the relations of food to health; the chemical elements and proximate constitution of alimentary principles; the nutritive properties of all kinds of aliments; the relative value of vegetable and animal substances; the selection and preservation of dietetic materials, etc., etc.* New York: Samuel R. Wells, No. 389 Broadway, 1869.

JOHN TIMBS, F.S.A. Author of Curiosities of London, and Editor of The Year-Book of Facts. *Things Not Generally Known.* London: David Bogue, Fleet Street, 1856.

THOMAS TUSSER. *A Hundreth good pointes of Husbandry, lately maried unto a Hundreth good poynts*

TABITHA TICKLETOOTH

281

frontispiece
WALTON'S COMPLEAT ANGLER

of Huswifery: newly corrected and amplified with dyvers proper lessons for Housholders, as by the table at the latter ende, more plainly may appeare: Set foorth by Thomas Tusser Gentle man, servant to the right honorable Lorde Pages of Beudesert. In oedibus Richardi Tottylli. Cum privilegio. Anno 1570.

MARION CABELL TYREE, ed. *Housekeeping In Old Virginia. Containing contributions from two hundred and fifty of Virginia's noted housewives, distinguished for their skill in the culinary art and other branches of domestic economy.* Louisville, Ky.: John P. Morton and Company, 1879. Reprinted by Favorite Recipes Press, Inc., 1965.

LOUIS EUSTACHE UDE, ci-devant cook to Louis XVI, and The Earl of Sefton; Late Steward to The United Service Club; To His Late Royal Highness The Duke of York; and now Maitre D'Hotel at Crockford's Club, St. James's Street. *The French Cook, A System of Fashionable and Economical Cookery, adapted to the use of English Families.* Tenth edition. London: John Ebers and Co., 27, Old Bond Street, 1829.

WILLIAM VERRAL, Master of the White-Hart Inn in Lewes, Sussex. *A Complete System of Cookery. In which is set forth, A Variety of genuine Receipts, collected from several Years Experience under the celebrated Mr. de St. Clouet, sometime since Cook to his Grace the Duke of Newcastle.* London: Printed for the Author, and sold by him; As also by Edward Verral Bookseller, in Lewes: And by John Rivington in St. Paul's Church-yard, London, 1759.

Thomas Gray (1716–71), the poet, made culinary annotations to his personal copy.

This book, with Thomas Gray's notes and an introduction by R. L. Mégroz, was republished in 1948 by Sylvan Press, Ltd., under the title "The Cook's Paradise."

WILLIAM S. WALSH. *Curiosities of Popular Customs and of Rites, Ceremonies, Observances, and Miscellaneous Antiquities.* Philadelphia and London: J. B. Lippincott Company, 1897. Reprinted in 1909.

IZAAK WALTON. *The Compleat Angler; or, Contemplative Man's Recreation, Being A Discourse On Rivers, Fishponds, Fish, and Fishing.* London: Henry

Washbourne, Salisbury Square, Fleet Street, 1653. Reprinted 1842.

THE REVEREND RICHARD WARNER. *Antiquitates Culinariae* (see *The Forme of Cury*).

MRS. A. L. WEBSTER. Alike Experienced In The Vicissitudes Of Life And In Housewifery Whom Admonitory Years Now Invite To A More Retired And Less Active Life, Cheered By Affectionate Remembrances of Patron-Friends. *The Improved Housewife, or Book of Receipts.* Twentieth edition, revised. Hartford: Ira Webster, 1854.

THE "ONLY WILLIAM" [WILLIAM SCHMIDT]. *The Flowing Bowl. When and what to drink. Full instructions how to prepare, mix and serve beverages.* New York: Charles L. Webster & Co., 1892.

W. MATTIEU WILLIAMS. *The Chemistry of Cookery.* New York: D. Appleton and Company, 1885.

WILLIAM WOOD. *New Englands Prospect. A true, lively, and experimentall description of that part of America, commonly called New England: discovering the state of that Countrie, both as it stands to our new-come English Planters; and to the old Native Inhabitants. Laying downe that which may both enrich the knowledge of the mind-travelling Reader, or benefit the future Voyager.* Printed at London by Tho. Cotes for John Bellamie, and are to be sold at his shop, at the three Golden Lyons in Corne-hill, neere the Royall Exchange, 1634.

HANNAH WOOLLEY. *The Gentlewomans Companion; Or, A Guide To The Female Sex: Containing Directions of Behavior, in all Places, Companies, Relations, and Conditions, from their Childhood down to Old Age: Viz. As, Children to Parents. Scholars to Governours. Single to Servants. Virgins to Suitors. Married to Husbands. Huswifes to the House. Mistresses to Servants. Mothers to Children. Widows to the World. Prudent to all. With Letters and Discourses upon all Occasions. Whereunto is added, A Guide for Cook-maids, Dairy-maids, Chamber-maids, and all others that go to Service. The whole being an exact Rule for the Female Sex in General.* London. Printed by A. Maxwell for Dorman Newmans at the Kings-Arms in the Poultry, 1673.

frontispiece
MRS. WEBSTER'S IMPROVED HOUSEWIFE

Remember those children whose parents be poor,
which hunger, yet dare not to crave at thy door.

Thomas Tusser, *A Hundreth Good Pointes of Husbandry*, 1570

GLOSSARY–INDEX

R

S